Podcast Solutions

The Complete Guide to Audio and Video Podcasting

Second Edition

Michael W. Geoghegan and Dan Klass

friendsof

DESIGNER TO DESIGNER™

an Apress® company

Podcast Solutions: The Complete Guide to Audio and Video Podcasting, Second Edition

ISBN-13 (pbk): 978-1-59059-905-1

ISBN-10 (pbk): 1-59059-905-5

Printed and bound in the United States of America 9 8 7 6 5 4 3 2 1

Distributed to the book trade worldwide by Springer-Verlag New York, Inc., 233 Spring Street, 6th Floor, New York, NY 10013. Phone 1-800-SPRINGER, fax 201-348-4505, e-mail orders-ny@springer-sbm.com, or visit www.springeronline.com.

For information on translations, please contact Apress directly at 2855 Telegraph Avenue, Suite 600, Berkeley, CA 94705. Phone 510-549-5930, fax 510-549-5939, e-mail info@apress.com, or visit www.apress.com.

The information in this book is distributed on an "as is" basis, without warranty. Although every precaution has been taken in the preparation of this work, neither the author(s) nor Apress shall have any liability to any person or entity with respect to any loss or damage caused or alleged to be caused directly or indirectly by the information contained in this work.

The source code for this book is freely available to readers at www.friendsofed.com in the Downloads section.

Credits

Lead Editors Chris Mills and Tony Campbell	**Associate Production Director** Kari Brooks-Copony
Technical Reviewer Paul Figgiani	**Production Editor** Laura Esterman
Editorial Board Steve Anglin, Ewan Buckingham, Tony Campbell, Gary Cornell, Jonathan Gennick, Jason Gilmore, Kevin Goff, Jonathan Hassell, Matthew Moodie, Joseph Ottinger, Jeffrey Pepper, Ben Renow-Clarke, Dominic Shakeshaft, Matt Wade, Tom Welsh	**Compositor** Dina Quan **Artist** April Milne **Proofreader** Martha Whitt
Project Manager Denise Santoro Lincoln	**Indexer** Broccoli Information Management
Copy Editor Kim Wimpsett	**Interior and Cover Designer** Kurt Krames
Manufacturing Director Tom Debolski	

*To my wife, Stefanie, and our two sons, Nicholas and William.
Thank you for all your support and patience.
—Michael W. Geoghegan*

*To Melissa, Hudson, and Tallu, for all your patience and love.
Thanks for the smooches. Well, except for Hudson, who
won't smooch me, because he's way too cool for that.
Hudson, thanks for the firm handshake.
—Dan Klass*

CONTENTS AT A GLANCE

CONTENTS

ABOUT THE AUTHORS

 Michael W. Geoghegan is a consultant, author, and entrepreneur widely regarded as one of pioneers of podcasting. His first podcast production, "Reel Reviews—Films Worth Watching" (www.reelreviewsradio.com), was the Internet's first film review, discussion, and commentary podcast. With the success of "Reel Reviews," and building on his enthusiasm for podcasting, Michael began helping others get involved in podcasting through his production company, Willnick Productions, Inc. He went on to create "Grape Radio" (http://graperadio.com), a top-rated podcast about wine that won Podcast of the Year in 2006 and was nominated for a coveted James Beard Foundation Award in 2007.

Michael is the first podcaster to have ever been contracted by a Fortune 100 company (The Walt Disney Company) to both host and produce a podcast. The Official Disneyland Resort Podcasts (www.disneyland.com/podcast) represented a watershed event in podcasting as large, established media players began to recognize the value of this emerging communications medium.

Michael recently completed the sale of podcast production technology developed by his current company, GigaVox Media, and continues to focus his entrepreneurial activities on podcasting. Michael speaks frequently on podcasting's impact on new media and its corporate applications. He has been featured as a podcasting expert for dozens of media outlets including the *New York Times*, *USA Today*, CNN, NPR, and *Wired* magazine.

Michael lives in Newport Beach, California, with his wife and two young sons.

Dan Klass has been involved in the Internet and interactive entertainment fields for almost 20 years (yes, there was interactive entertainment 20 years ago!), including working on interactive video toys for ViewMaster/Ideal and developing online "stand-up comedy" performances. Recently he was the creator/writer/producer/star of NewsPop, an animated series for a joint Internet venture between Steven Spielberg's DreamWorks SKG and Ron Howard's Imagine Entertainment.

Dan is currently devoting most of his time to podcasting. He produces and hosts two original audio podcasts: "Old Wave Radio: New 80's Music" (www.new80smusic.com), a retro-80's music show, and the much acclaimed "The Bitterest Pill" (www.thebitterestpill.com), a comedy/talk show that revolves around his musings as a stay-at-home dad on the outskirts of the entertainment industry. "The Bitterest Pill," arguably one of the most popular entertainment podcasts to date, has been featured on NBC, NPR, and Fox News, and in the *New York Times* and the *Christian Science Monitor*. Most recently, Dan launched "Animal Rescue Force Friends!" (www.arff.tv), a children's puppet show that he developed with his eight-year-old son, Hudson, through his production company, JacketMedia.com.

Dan lives in Los Angeles with his wife, two kids, and several Macs.

ABOUT THE TECHNICAL REVIEWER

Paul Figgiani worked on the floor of the New York Stock Exchange for 21 years and left in 2004 in order to pursue freelance media production. He now produces content for the Conversations Network and provides new-media production and consulting services for private clients.

ACKNOWLEDGMENTS

This book would not have been possible without the help of countless people whom we have been fortunate enough to meet through podcasting. Special thanks to Adam Curry; Doug Kaye ("IT Conversations"); Paul Figgiani ("The Point"); Dawn and Drew ("The Dawn and Drew Show"); Brian Ibbott ("Coverville"); Dave Slusher ("The Evil Genius Chronicles"); Michael Butler ("Rock and Roll Geek Show"); Craig Patchett (The Godcast Network); Chris McIntyre (Podcast Alley); Gary Leland (PodcastPickle.com); Brian Clark, Jay Selman, and Eric Anderson ("Grape Radio"); all the great bands of "Old Wave Radio: New 80's Music; Ray Slakinski; August Trometer; Jennifer Sanchez; Sam Levin; Tim Bourquin (Podcast and New Media Expo); Emile Bourquin ("Podcast Brothers"); Eric Rice (EricRice.com); K. Todd Storch ("Business Thoughts"); Greg Cangialosi ("The Trend Junkie"); Duncan Wardle; Mike Hyland and the incredible team at Disneyland Parks and Resorts, including Jason Burns, Lynda Miller, David Kooi, and Joe Popp; Jason Neidle (photographer extraordinaire); Darren Nemeth (Giant Squid Audio Labs); The Association of Music Podcasting; Chris McDonald; Forum E; Mike Spataro; Bob Goyetche ("Mostly Tunes"), Tim Schwieger, and the entire team at Broadcast Supply Worldwide (BSW); Griffin Technology; Israel Hyman ("Izzy Video"), Craig Syverson (Grunt Media); Tim Coyne ("The Hollywood Podcast"); Brian Hogg ("dotBoom"); Seth and Nathan Anderson ("Hear Me Now Brother"); Lance Anderson ("Verge of the Fringe"); Chris Hampel and everyone at Big Fantastic; Tim Street ("French Maid TV"); everyone at Apple Computers; and Rode and Marantz.

To all you whom we've forgotten and are reading this section only to look for your names, we tried to work you in but the editors cut you out . . .

INTRODUCTION

Welcome to *Podcast Solutions: The Complete Guide to Podcasting, Second Edition*. We had a simple goal in mind while we wrote this book: to give you a straightforward overview of podcasting and share the information necessary to get you up and running with a quality podcast. Within the pages of this book, you'll find everything you need to know to get started in podcasting. We'll cover the history of podcasting, how to download podcasts, and, most important, how to produce and distribute your own podcast.

We're not geeks, and this isn't a geek book. There's no way to detail step-by-step instructions for every piece of software that conceivably exists for podcasting, and we're not going to try to impress you with an exhaustive (and therefore exhausting) list of every website that has anything to do with podcasting (that's what Google is for). Things are moving so quickly in podcasting that it seems every day brings a new product or service announcement. If we covered them all, you'd never make it to the end of the book, and you'd never begin doing the one thing we really want to help you do: start making your own podcasts. Instead, we've used our combined experience to carefully select and detail the software, hardware, and services we feel stand out and deserve mention for helping people get started in podcasting.

While we're at it, we don't think you're a "dummy." Podcasting isn't for dummies. There's too much involved in the production and promotion of a successful podcast for it to be that easy. However, we've worked hard to provide simple explanations for processes that can be somewhat confusing at first, and we've tried to ensure that even a total beginner will be able to use and understand the information we present.

It's an exciting time in podcasting, and we're glad you've chosen our book to help guide you on your way to producing a podcast you'll be proud of. Let's get started.

Layout conventions

To keep this book as clear and easy to follow as possible, the following conventions are used throughout.

- Important words or concepts are highlighted on the first appearance in **bold** type.
- Menu commands are written in the form Menu ➤ Submenu ➤ Submenu.

- When we want to call attention to something or have a personal experience to share, we've highlighted it like this:

> *We are about to talk briefly about computer code. We would like to take this opportunity to make something very clear before we proceed: you do not now—nor will you ever—need to fully understand or be able to write code to listen to or produce your own podcasts. We promise.*

Chapter 1

PODCASTING 101

Podcasting is one of the most exciting and wonderfully disruptive technologies to emerge in recent history.

Podcasting is exciting because anybody can get involved, express themselves, exchange ideas, or pitch their products. Whatever interests people have, there is a place for them in podcasting.

Podcasting is disruptive because, like any worthwhile new technology, podcasting breaks all the rules. Can you make a podcast about retro kitchen appliances? Sure. Can it be a minute long? Of course. Can it be an hour long? If you'd like. Can it be in slang? Uh-huh.

Podcasting puts the power to communicate into the hands of *individuals*. Thousands of people are already involved, each as unique as their podcast. There is no working within "The System." In fact, there is no system. You don't need a fancy studio or an FCC license. You need only a microphone or a video camera, a computer, and something to share with the rest of the world. Yes, you read that correctly: *the world*.

A stage has been erected on which the "common man" (or woman, for that matter) can stand tall and be heard: the Internet. The price of admission is some basic equipment and a desire to communicate—that's all. Podcasters, with their first podcasts, can reach a more geographically diverse audience than a radio station with the most powerful AM/FM transmitter in the world. All with no transmitters, no satellites, no regulations. Audience members located in the United States, New Zealand, Japan,

1

India, France, and many other countries are common for popular podcasts. The whole world really *is* paying attention. Access to such a huge potential audience was a privilege once reserved only for large corporations and governments, but podcasting has changed everything. The individual has been empowered and given an equal voice—this means you.

> *This revolution will not be televised; it will be podcast.*

There's one thing we'd better clear up right from the start: *you do not need an iPod to listen to or watch podcasts, make podcasts, or learn about podcasts*. It's true. Thousands of people are creating and enjoying podcasts without ever having touched an iPod or any other piece of Apple hardware or software. Yes, the word "podcasting" does borrow a little interest from the "pod" in iPod, but that's where the connection ends. No one group or company controls any aspect of podcasting, from the hardware and software used to create podcasts to the hardware and software used to listen to podcasts. It's anybody's game.

What grew out of an experiment between a former MTV VJ and a computer programmer quickly became a form of media distribution that would grow and spread faster than perhaps any other new media development in recent history. First, it was the technical folks podcasting—the early adopters who were more interested in the fact that it actually worked than anything else. Soon, more people came to the party. Less "techie" folks embraced the opportunity and got involved. A married couple started podcasting out of a old farmhouse in Milwaukee, the bass player of a San Francisco rock band started spinning tunes and talking about his life at home between gigs, and a young father in Denver started a show made up exclusively of cover songs. By mid-2005, it seemed everybody, from radio stations to sci-fi television shows and from religious evangelicals to caustic drag queens, was getting into podcasting.

Sound like fun? Let's get started and on our way to getting you, dear reader, set up and producing your own podcast. We'll save the gory technical details for a bit later (but not too much later). In this chapter, we'll focus on the following topics:

- The history of podcasting so far
- What exactly podcasting is and why it has become so popular
- A brief overview of how podcasting works, to help you get your bearings

A brief history of podcasting

In 1877, Thomas Edison made the first sound recording on what was to be known as the phonograph. It wasn't until 1887 that the first commercially available gramophone was made available. OK, maybe we should jump ahead a little bit . . .

We want our MP3

Former MTV VJ and interactive media developer Adam Curry had been trying to find ways to use the Internet to broadcast video and audio streams for years. Curry surmised that with the coming abundance of broadband, there must be a better way to use that pipeline to transmit content to the

1

masses. His theory, which he coined "The Last Yard," was that since a broadband connection is "always on," people could have huge files downloading at night as they slept or in the background while they worked, and they could then be notified when the file download was complete. Instead of users feeling like they are sitting and waiting for hours for something to download, they simply click a button and *voilà*! The file is there.

In 2000, Curry met with respected programmer Dave Winer, who was instrumental in developing several computer and Internet applications as well as being the creator of **Really Simple Syndication (RSS)**. RSS is the means by which news stories and weblogs (aka blogs) are syndicated throughout the web. Together, Curry and Winer theorized that there must be a way to use RSS to deliver not only headlines but audio or video files as well. As a result of their discussions, Winer created the <enclosure> tag within his RSS specification, enabling applications to fetch files off the Internet by simply following the URL within the code pointing to that file.

Audioblogs

Enter **audioblogs**. The first audioblog may have been posted as early as August 2001 by a Canadian blogger living in San Francisco named Jish. (Podcasting is largely seen as an evolution of blogging, which uses a similar means to distribute text entries to readers.) Over the next two years, audioblogging started to pick up some steam as people began posting audio posts and various recordings on their sites. Many started to use Winer's <enclosure> tag. In October 2003, at the annual blogger conference known as BloggerCon, a blogger named Harold Gilchrist headed a session on the emergence of audioblogging, including demonstrations of some applications for downloading the associated enclosures (audio files).

During the same period, Christopher Lydon, a popular radio host, was posting audio interviews with an associated RSS feed that Winer helped him set up. (An **RSS feed** is simply a page of code, in this case pointing to the MP3 file—but more on that later.) Now that there was some audio content appearing, Curry went to work. He wanted a way to get Lydon's interviews to not only automatically download to his computer but also go a step further and sync to his iPod. Curry knew he needed an application that would check several RSS feeds, one at a time, for the <enclosure> tag and, when it found a new enclosure (MP3), download it automatically and move it onto his iPod. Unfortunately for Curry, he was not a computer programmer, and he had a hard time convincing any computer programmers to write the application for him. Soon he found himself learning to program in AppleScript so that he could hack away and carve out the first version of his **iPodder**. In Curry's words, the first version of iPodder "really sucked, because I'm not a developer. Observing open source projects led me to believe that releasing my code would attract other developers who might consider fixing and/or contributing to my work."

Source code

Curry soon realized that for programmers to have the best chance at truly testing the system, they would need a real-world testing situation. While others, including Dave Winer, Harold Gilchrist, and Christopher Lydon, had been occasionally publishing audio content using the <enclosure> tag, Curry decided to help move the development process along by launching the first show produced on a consistent basis. "Daily Source Code" (whose name was carefully chosen to attract tech-heads) enabled developers to accurately test the software outside of a lab setting. With the launch of Curry's show in August 2004, what would eventually be called "podcasting" was born. Of course at the time, there was no agreed-upon name for syndicated audio content using RSS, so most people just called it "audioblogging."

"If you build it, they will come," as the saying goes. Curry did, and they did. Soon developers and pro-grammers from around the world were tinkering with the program, adding to it, fixing it, and testing it. Some developers even decided to create their own versions of Curry's program.

Curry's "Daily Source Code" served as the bar that anyone could reach for. Through his easy charm and years of radio experience, Curry created a show of such casual professionalism and sincere enthu-siasm that he naturally became a Pied Piper of sorts for anyone who ever dreamt of getting behind a microphone. Soon he was not the only one producing a show. Before you knew it, the revolution was well under way.

The revolution has a name

Other early adopters included Dave Slusher, with his show "Evil Genius Chronicles," and Doug Kaye, who had already been producing "IT Conversations" with RSS syndication of his audio content for a lit-tle more than a year. Throughout early September 2004, things really started to move, but still with-out an agreed-upon name. Earlier, in February 2004, Ben Hammersley wrote an article about audioblogs and online radio in which he speculated about possible names for what people were doing, "podcasting" being among those names. Yet, barely recognized, the word would disappear for roughly seven months. In the interim, some people who liked the term registered domains, including Dannie Gregoire, who had independently created the name and registered podcaster.net. Then it happened: a confluence of ideas and little bit of luck.

Dave Slusher of "Evil Genius Chronicles" wrote on September 18, 2004, "I've been noticing something downloading audioblog posts with the user agent of 'podcaster.' There is an URL in there that points to podcaster.net, but there isn't anything yet. I wonder what this is? I do like this as a term for what it is when you are creating things to distribute via the iPod platform . . . 'Podcasting!' Right on."

Shortly thereafter, the term "podcasting" gained traction and became associated with the movement that was already under way. Throughout the following months, more and more people, led by the pio-neers such as Adam Curry, Dave Winer, and Dave Slusher, picked up the microphone and got involved. New shows were created and released at a breakneck pace. Directories and groups of podcasters were formed. Just a year after Gilchrist's session on audioblogs, the BloggerCon held in November 2004 included a session led by Curry dedicated to podcasting that was attended by an overflow crowd. This was an opportunity for many of the early pioneers to sit in the same room and talk face to face. By now it was too late to turn back; the word "podcasting" had taken hold. (Michael was fortunate enough to attend that BloggerCon session and says it was one of the magic moments in an emerging movement. You can listen to the audio from this historic session at www.itconversations.com/shows/detail275.html.)

By 2005, podcasting was becoming more and more mainstream (for an underground movement). In the spring, Apple launched iTunes 4.9, the first version of its popular music player/store that inte-grated podcasts directly into the software. Subscribing to, transferring, and listening to podcasts was almost effortless. The floodgates to a mass audience had been opened.

Podcasting has continued to grow, and much of its "history" is still being written. In fact, we hope someone reading this book will soon deserve a place in this text the next time it is updated. As we press on, let's not lose sight of one thing: podcasting is not simply a new way to distribute audio and video programs; it's a form of expression, of interaction, of community building. Through the unique dialogue that is a podcast, communities of enthusiasts are built, tools are created, and products are sold. Podcasting is a vibrant and exciting new world—one that we have only just begun to explore.

So, the question probably on your mind right now is, "What exactly *is* podcasting?" We'll answer that next.

What exactly is a podcast, and why is it so darned great?

Simply put, a **podcast** is audio or video content available on the Internet that can be automatically delivered to your computer or portable media player. Strip away all the upcoming potential confusion of feeds, aggregators, subscriptions, and so on, and what's left? Audio and video via subscription.

So, what's the big deal? We've had "Internet radio" on the web for more than a decade. RealAudio, QuickTime, and Windows Media have all promised in their own way to revolutionize the way we enjoy "media." Yet the revolution never happened with these products. All of these formats offer audio and/or video playback on demand via the web, but none has taken hold the way podcasting has. Why? Because there is nothing "sexy" about sitting at your desk waiting for a media file to buffer—that is not much of a revolution. Many web surfers, tired of waiting for the content to finally sputter to life, ended up turning the radio or television back on and getting on with their lives.

Why is podcasting different? How is it that *this* promise of audio and video over the web is so superior to its predecessors? Why are thousands—millions, perhaps—of people every day enjoying the fruits of the podcasting revolution? The sections that follow answer these questions by examining the main advantages of podcasting in some detail. To summarize quickly, podcasting is *automatic*, it's *easy to control* by the consumer, it's *portable*, and it's *always available*.

Automatic

Podcasts can be downloaded, automatically, onto your computer. Once you know which shows you like, you don't have to go looking for them—they come to you. Like a digital video recorder (DVR) recording your favorite shows by subscription, you have the benefit of being able to subscribe to your favorite podcasts via an RSS feed (which we'll explain later). Once you've found a podcast you'd like to listen to or watch regularly, you can simply subscribe to the feed. Using simple software called a **podcast aggregator** or **podcatcher** (such as Apple's iTunes), each new show listed in the feed will download automatically into your computer or portable media player as it becomes available. No hunting around the Internet. No time wasted visiting several websites to check out your favorite shows. The podcasts simply come to you.

So that there's no confusion, we'd like to emphasize that subscribing to podcasts doesn't cost anything. When we talk about "subscriptions" and "subscribing" to a podcast, we're merely referring to setting up your system to receive the RSS feed and to automatically download any new shows that are posted (more on that soon). As of today, the overwhelming majority of podcasts are delivered free of charge. In fact, podcasts that cost money are a rarity, though they are starting to appear as people try to grasp the business models podcasting can support. (We discuss ways to make money with your podcast in Chapter 12.)

Easy to control

Podcasting puts the listener in control. Unlike e-mail distribution, where the sender decides who will get the files whether the recipients want them or not, podcasting lets the audience decide. Because you control your list of subscriptions, if you no longer want to receive a show, you just unsubscribe. The shows stop coming—it's that simple. No opt-out requirements or begging to be removed from a list. Also, you don't have to worry about keeping your identity secure, because much like listening to the radio, subscribing to podcasts is anonymous. No one will know you're out there unless you decide to tell them. Finally, you don't need to worry about spam or viruses. RSS essentially forms a "trusted channel," where you know the only content put into the feed is that which the publisher has decided to add. Again, if you ever decide you no longer want to receive what the publisher is including in the feed, simply unsubscribe. You're in complete control.

Portable

Podcasts are predominantly MPEG-1 Audio Layer-3 (MP3) audio files and video files encoded specifically for use on the web and in portable players. The MP3 file format has been instrumental in making audio on the Internet such a success. In fact, among many Internet users, MP3s are quickly replacing compact discs in the same way compact discs replaced audiocassettes and vinyl in the 1990s. While there is some loss of fidelity with MP3, if you use care when converting your source master into an MP3 that will be reduced in size yet continue to maintain sonic quality, the quality can still far exceed that of both AM and FM radio. Because of the relatively small file sizes of MP3s and Internet-compatible video files, they're perfect for downloading from the Internet and transferring to a portable media player. Or, if you like, you can burn MP3s as an audio CD to take anywhere and share with just about anyone. You are no longer trapped at your desk, chained to a stuttering stream from one of the popular media players. Podcasts provide clear, steady audio and video that you can take with you and enjoy whenever and wherever you like.

Always available

The fact that you can enjoy podcasts whenever you like is another important part of the growing success of podcasting. This aspect of podcasting has caused many people to compare it to DVRs such as TiVo. Podcasts are, in essence, radio and television on demand, time-shifted to fit into *your* schedule. You don't have to worry about missing your favorite show, because it will be there, on your hard drive or portable media device, whenever you want it. Podcasting frees you from the appointment-based consumption dictated by traditional media. Have a meeting during your favorite show? With radio and TV, you're out of luck. With podcasting, subscribe to that show, and it will be waiting on your portable media player, ready for you to play it when you like.

In a nutshell

The sound and image quality of podcast encoding, the ease of subscribing and downloading, and the portability of these files all make podcasting an important advance in the distribution and enjoyment of digital media. With each passing day, more and more podcasts are being created, produced, uploaded, and downloaded around the world. Shows on every imaginable topic are available, right now, for free. Amateurs, skilled hobbyists, and seasoned professionals are putting together new and beautifully produced content every day, and it is all there for the downloading. Communities are springing up around the most obscure topics, information is being exchanged, and theories are being discussed on every imaginable subject. If you have a hobby, an interest, or a curiosity about anything, chances are there is a podcast for you. If not, there soon will be—or perhaps *you* should start a podcast of your own. You'll soon find you aren't the only one looking for a podcast on Nepalese goat herding.

How it all works

Downloading podcasts via subscription is a simple process that requires only three elements: the podcast itself, the RSS feed, and a podcatcher (such as iTunes or Juice).

As we said before, the podcast itself is an audio or video file, ranging in size anywhere from 1MB to 200MB (roughly a megabyte per minute or two for most audio shows and much more for video shows, depending on the frame rate, size, and so on). That may sound like a lot to download, but now that broadband access (such as cable and DSL) is so widely available, it takes far less time to download a file than you might expect. If you are still using a standard dial-up modem, then you will really appreciate the benefits of podcasting. You can set your podcast aggregator to download the podcasts you desire overnight. No more endless waiting for files to download—your aggregator will do it while you sleep or when your computer is sitting idle. Now *that's* efficient!

> *We are about to talk briefly about computer code. We would like to take this opportunity to make something very clear before we proceed: you do not now—nor will you ever—need to fully understand or be able to write code to listen to or produce your own podcasts. We promise.*

The second element is the RSS feed, which is a simple bit of eXtensible Markup Language (XML) code stored on the web as a raw text file. The code includes vital information about the podcast, including when the last show was added to the list, its title, and a brief description of that edition. RSS is the same code used to supply the news feeds for My Yahoo!, Bloglines, and other online newsreaders with up-to-date headlines, articles, and comic strips. In the case of a podcast, along with the code tags for the title and last date of publication of the feed, is an <enclosure> tag. This is the bit of magic that makes it all possible. The <enclosure> tag contains information about the location, size, and type of file associated with the feed. The feed does not contain the file itself; rather, it stores the web address, as a URL, of where the podcast file is stored on the Internet. With this information, your podcatcher knows where to go to retrieve the associated file.

Here are some bits of sample RSS code to give you an idea of what an RSS feed looks like—confusing at first glance to the non-geek, to be sure. Eventually we will get into the feed in great detail, but not right now. For clarity, we've included only the pieces of code that might make sense at this point in the process. With a lot of the distracting (mind-boggling) code stripped away, it becomes clear exactly how simple Really Simple Syndication really is:

```
<title>Podcast Solutions Podcast</title>
    <link>http://www.podcastsolutions.com</link>
    <description>Everything you need to know about
podcasting.  Based on the best-selling book,
Podcast Solutions.</description>
<pubDate>Wed, 04 Apr 2007 20:26:38 -0700</pubDate>
```

```
<item>
   <title>#1: Welcome to The Podcast Solutions Podcast!</title>
   <description>
        This is the first edition of our new podcast, to serve as an
        ever-updating addition to our book, Podcast Solutions.  If
        you have any questions or comments, or you just want to
        say hello, please drop us a line.
   </description>
   <author> pill@podcastsolutions.com (Michael Geoghegan
   and Dan Klass)</author>
   <pubDate>Wed, 06 Apr 2005 20:26:38 -0700</pubDate>
<enclosure url=http://www.podcastsolutions.com/podcasts/PS05_04_05.mp3
              length="14830355" type="audio/mpeg"/>
   </item>
```

When you check your subscriptions (a matter of clicking a button), the podcatcher checks each feed for a new enclosure. If a new enclosure (podcast) has been added to any of the feeds you subscribe to, the new file is automatically downloaded. The aggregator simply checks RSS feed addresses for new files, and when it finds them, it downloads them (see Figure 1-1) and manages them based on your podcatcher settings. This process is, however, invisible to the subscriber. All you do is click a button and wait while the latest podcasts from your active list of subscriptions download.

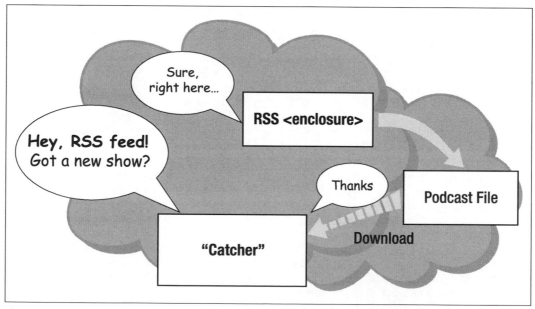

Figure 1-1. The podcatcher checks the feed for new enclosures, and, when it finds them, it downloads the files at the address in the feed.

Summary

As you can see, there's no hidden magic to podcasting. When you break it down, in fact, it's rather straightforward. As with most exciting creations, the ingredients were there all along—it just took some people willing to experiment to pull all the pieces together. Since we know you are anxious to get started, this chapter marks the end of the general podcasting overview. From here on out, it's nothing but details, examples, and explanations.

We've worked hard in this book to walk the line between leaving nothing out and bombarding you with too much information. Any less and we'd feel like we might be leaving out that tiny bit of information that makes it all click for you. There are as many ways to produce podcasts as there are podcasters. This book was written with the hope of giving people the information they need to enjoy podcasting on their own terms. There is no right way, there is no wrong way—there is only *your* way. Our sincerest hope is that within the pages of this book is the way that works for you.

Next, we're going to bring you up to speed on how to set up your podcast client and start receiving and enjoying some of the great shows that are available.

Chapter 2

WATCHING AND LISTENING TO PODCASTS

You may be getting anxious to get started on your podcast, but before you take a stab at creating one of your own, it's a good idea to first spend some time *listening and watching*. One of the best aspects of learning to podcast is sampling a variety of the available programs. Not only is this fun, but it's a great opportunity to get "plugged into" the podcast community—to *really* find out what is available and what void may be left to fill. Your experience exploring podcasts will help tremendously when it comes time to create your own show. By checking out an assortment of podcasts, you'll get a sense of what you like and dislike. You'll also start to form some ideas about how you want to do your show. As with most anything else, you can learn a lot from the people who are currently producing podcasts. Above all else, you'll have fun.

Soon we'll get into the mechanisms involved in getting podcasts to download effortlessly. Getting set up for this may involve using some new software and becoming familiar with a few new terms. If you're anxious to get a taste and aren't sure you want to plow through a podcast directory or set up software, check out a couple of the podcasts we've included in Appendix B of the book. We've provided a nice cross section of our favorites, categorized for easy sorting. Enjoy a few, and then let's get you set up.

Finding and "auditioning" podcasts

Before enjoying podcasts in the comfort of your own car, headset, stereo system, or whatever, you'll (obviously) need to *find* some podcasts. Finding podcasts is relatively easy, thanks to the tightly knit podcasting community and the ingenious web technologies that help keep information about active podcasts accurate and up to date. This is a wonderful time of exploration, as you dig deep into the podcasting treasure trove. You may even find that you're drawn to podcasts you never thought you'd be interested in. So, take your time, enjoy the journey, and do plenty of auditioning.

Once again, *you don't need an iPod*. All you need to enjoy podcasts are the following:

- A computer with an Internet connection
- A web browser or "podcatcher"
- Headphones or speakers

Depending on your tastes and the type of programming you're looking for, discovering a podcast that you think is a gem may take you all of ten seconds, or it may take several days. You never know. Some people just check out a top-ten list and have more than enough to keep them entertained and informed for weeks. Others have to dig. Finding the right podcasts for you may be like finding a needle in a haystack. Luckily, most of the podcasting haystacks are well explored and meticulously mapped. The best way to get to the needle is to dive right in and start going through the hay.

You can approach auditioning podcasts in several ways:

- Listen to samples/shows at a podcast directory
- Go to podcast websites to read about or listen to/watch a few episodes
- Seek recommendations from podcasters

Directories

Podcast directories are an indispensable tool for finding new podcasts. Most are well categorized and easily searchable, so finding podcasts of the type and tone you're looking for is pretty straightforward. The directories are usually web based, but each of the stand-alone podcatchers have built-in directories to make searching and subscribing a one-stop affair.

iTunes

Before the release of Apple iTunes 4.9, a few more steps were involved in finding, downloading, and getting podcasts into iTunes if you so desired. But no longer. Since the release of version 4.9, iTunes provides all of the functionality of finding, subscribing, and downloading podcasts within the program itself.

You can search for podcasts by name, host, or genre (comedy, politics, film and television, and so on), and you can listen to shows right from the directory by simply clicking the name of the podcast. Each podcast is represented within the iTunes Store (Figure 2-1) in much the same way an album from one of your favorite artists is. To subscribe to a given podcast, simply click the Subscribe button.

Needless to say, when iTunes 4.9 was released, it sent a shockwave of excitement through the podcasting community. Apple's wholehearted embrace of podcasts was a clear signal that podcasting was going mainstream.

Figure 2-1. The Apple iTunes Store's Podcasts section

PodcastPickle.com

Don't let the little green mascot fool you; PodcastPickle.com is a powerhouse (Figure 2-2). Named one of the Coolest Sites of 2006 by *Time* magazine, Gary Leland's Pickle is chock-full of active forums, contests, podcasts (12,000+), podcasting and podcaster merchandise, Top 100 lists, and more. In December 2005, Leland (aka P. Dilly) set out to give Podcast Alley a run for its money as the community's town square, and many have speculated that the Pickle has won that land grab.

Figure 2-2. "The Pickle"

Podcast Alley

Another notable web directory of podcasts is PodShow's Podcast Alley (www.podcastalley.com). The Alley is still a valuable resource when looking for shows, after having been (until iTunes 4.9) the premiere podcast directory. Not only does it include a robust listing of podcasts, but the site features a monthly ranking of podcasts based on votes, interviews with prominent podcasters, and several podcast forums ranging in topic from listening to podcasts, creating podcasts, equipment recommendations, and more. Podcast Alley's Top 10 and Top 50 listings have become a first stop for many people looking for something new to listen to or watch.

Other directories

Find a directory you like, and start clicking names and subjects that you find intriguing. It doesn't cost you anything but a few moments of time. You never know what you might find. Here are some other directories worth checking out:

- Podcast.net
- PodcastingNews.com

- indiePodder.org
- Podfeed.net

Most directory sites make it easy to audition entire podcasts straight from the directory listing. The podcast directory game is serious business. Each site strives to find that unique feature that'll keep people coming back. Several have their own audio players built in that will load the entire back catalog of a podcast and stream it for you right there. Each directory is going to give you most of the info you need on a podcast: the name, titles of past shows, feed info, links to their website, and even ratings.

Listen at the site

An ideal way to get to know a podcast quickly, aside from listening to a couple shows, is to visit the show's website. With few exceptions, all podcasts have their own site that will give you an immediate take on who the podcasters are and what they're all about. Photos, blog posts, and descriptions of each installment of the podcast are going to provide you with insights into the program, where it has been, and where it's headed. Also, you can easily check out several of a site's podcasts by simply clicking links on the site. The podcast MP3 will open in your browser or media player, and away you go.

Seek recommendations from podcasters/other podcasts

Want to find great podcasts? Then go to the great podcasters. Well, at least go to podcasters you like. Who better to steer you toward material that you might like than the very podcasters you already enjoy? These may be out-and-out recommendations, they may be mentions, or they may just be promos played on the show. Every podcaster who has been around for any length of time has developed their own list of favorite podcasts. Podcasters love to talk about other podcasts almost as much as they like to talk about themselves, so you'll never have to wait long to get an opinion on who's doing what.

Listen to find out who your favorite podcaster is listening to, is friendly with, or is talking up. (If you don't have a favorite yet, check out "Reel Reviews—Films Worth Watching" and "The Bitterest Pill." Those two guys seem to be know-it-alls, but they should be able to suggest something decent.) You will be drawn to podcasters you think you have something in common with, whether it's a sense of humor or a distaste for the Emmy Awards. The podcasters you feel simpatico with are a good source for providing leads to other podcasts that might appeal to you. See where we're going with this? If a podcaster whose show you really enjoy is constantly referring to another podcast, *check out that podcast.*

Podroll

See whether your favorite podcast's web page has a **podroll**, a list of podcasts they enjoy and recommend. Podcasters support each other by linking to each other's websites. This can be of huge benefit to you in your search for something to listen to or watch. You can usually find the links along the side of the podcast site (Figure 2-3) or on a separate links page. Or, if you like a show, find out whether it is part of a network or a regional associate and see what shows they're associated with. Great minds think alike (or at least like minds think alike), so see who your favorites are surrounding themselves with.

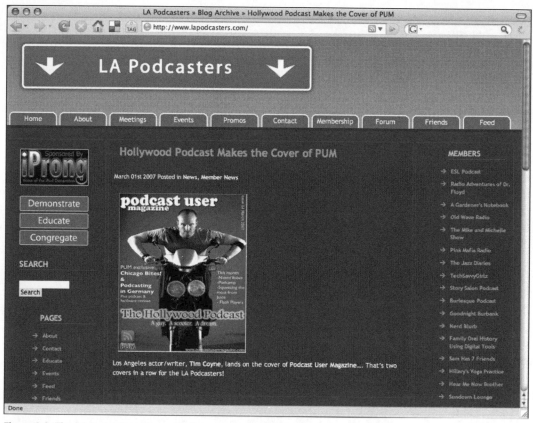

Figure 2-3. The LA Podcasters blog, with its extensive podroll/member list (far right)

Promos

Everybody needs to promote their show; newer shows are constantly sending promos to or calling into more established shows in hopes of tapping into a bigger audience. Very often you'll hear a caller to a listener line, cracking wise on a recent topic. You'll also notice that the caller always seems to mention a podcast URL. *They are plugging their podcast.* Now, if the caller is funny/informative/inspirational/whatever-you're-looking-for, take note of their URL. Maybe you'll end up listening to their show as well (or, instead). This is a great way to audition podcasts without even trying. Just keep your ears open and a pen handy (unless you're really good at remembering URLs), and you're golden.

By sifting through category listings and browsing through rankings and website recommendations, you're going to soon amass a list of podcasts you'll want to audition. You'll probably even find a couple you're not sure you can live without. You might even find yourself wondering, "Hey, I wonder when they're gonna upload the next show?" Well, well, well, you may already be hooked.

Podcatching

Whether it's the titles that pique your interest ("The Rock and Roll Geek Show," "Verge of the Fringe") or the subject matter ("The Mysteries and Myths of Nepalese Goat Herding"—OK, we made that one up), you'll soon realize it's time to get set up to receive podcasts automatically. Now, this is where it gets good. Please, stick with us. This is where we start talking a little (and just a little) about computer code and things you should know about but won't be tested on. Ever. We just want to make sure you have a basic understanding of how the whole thing works before we get too involved. It'll make setting up your podcast that much easier when you do.

The podcast client

While you can easily find and listen to podcasts with just a web browser, what you'll really want to do is have the podcasts automatically come to you. Instead of going from web page to web page clicking links, you will soon click just one button and, boom, there they are. Well, there they are after they download.

Early in the development of podcasting, people began calling the software used to receive podcasts **podcatchers**. It was a fun way to personify the two sides of the equation: the show creator would "cast" the show, and the listener would "catch" it. Of course, in computer geek-speak, these podcatchers are **podcast clients** or **podcast aggregators**, software designed to make finding and subscribing to podcasts simple. Best of all, they help manage the flow of podcasts from the Internet to your computer and ultimately onto your portable media player.

Are they difficult to use? No. Are they tricky to set up? Not really. Do we promise to never call them "aggregators" again? You betcha.

Lots of choices . . .

You can choose from plenty of podcatchers, regardless of what platform you're using and what budget you're working with. They all serve the same basic function: looking for and downloading new podcasts. How they handle finding, downloading, and saving the shows to your hard drive varies slightly from one to another, but the examples we give will most likely hold true for all the others. Each has a simple approach to subscribing to and managing feeds, as well as monitoring the progress of downloads. Most are also supported by robust online forums to help troubleshoot any problems you may have in running or configuring the software. Don't worry; help is always a couple of mouse clicks away, but you won't need it, trust us.

As we talked about before, iPodder was the first podcast client, its creation being, if not the official birth of podcasting, at least the beginning of labor. Shortly thereafter, teams of people started developing podcatchers based on the original iPodder concept.

iPodder Lemon (now called Juice and available for Windows/Mac OS X/Linux) and iPodderX (Mac OS X) emerged quickly in the early days of podcasting as the dominant catchers. Others were close behind, most notably Doppler (Windows), jPodder (Windows/Linux), and Nimiq (Windows). Since the release of iTunes 4.9, with podcatching features built right in, downloading and transferring podcasts to an iPod has never been easier. At this point in podcasting history, podcast clients are already made for Windows, Macintosh, Linux, Pocket PC, smartphones, and even Palm devices. Can a wireless unit with a catcher built into your car be far off?

In addition to stand-alone podcast clients, many RSS aggregators or newsreaders now offer automated podcast downloading too (NetNews Wire, NewsMac Pro, NewsFire, FeedDemon). Since podcasting is simply a component of RSS with the <enclosure> tag added (see Chapter 1), soon all RSS newsreaders will most likely support automated podcast downloading.

Time to subscribe

Now that you have found some podcasts you enjoy, it's time to automate the process of receiving new shows. This is accomplished by **subscribing** to the podcast. Remember, subscribing doesn't cost anything. No little prepaid postcards in the mail, no monthly bills. It simply means you're subscribing to the RSS feed and setting up your podcatcher to download new shows to your computer. The process is simple. As mentioned earlier, most podcast clients have a built-in directory, so if you know the name of the show, it's easy to add the feed to your subscription list.

Whether it's done manually or automatically, you subscribe to a podcast by adding the web address of the RSS feed into the catcher. That's it. You'll either click a button, cut and paste a URL, or hit the Add button, and you're done.

Subscribe with iTunes

Subscribing with Apple's iTunes couldn't be easier. It is so easy, in fact, that iTunes is the podcatcher of choice for the vast majority of podcast users. For this reason, we'll focus on iTunes when it comes to subscribing.

Search the iTunes podcast directory, click one of the many podcast icons in the front of the Podcasts section, and read through the shows in one of the category listings. Eventually, something is bound to tickle your fancy. When you find a show you'd like to receive automatically, simply click the Subscribe button on the podcast's iTunes page (Figure 2-4), and the latest show automatically begins downloading.

Figure 2-4. A podcast's page in iTunes

Then, each new podcast that is released will be downloaded automatically when you click your Refresh button (Figure 2-5, lower right). To "unsubscribe," highlight the podcast in your iTunes podcast area, and click the Unsubscribe button (lower left).

Figure 2-5. The Unsubscribe (left) and Refresh (right) buttons in iTunes

That's all there is to it. Now, if you stop listening to a podcast you've subscribed to in iTunes, it will stop downloading new episodes until you tell it to resume your subscription.

Summary

To truly appreciate a podcast, you should listen to it "your way." With a podcast, you're not bound to your desk or your car radio. People enjoy podcasts everywhere and anywhere. So, download a couple of shows and transfer them to your portable media player, burn them to a CD or DVD, or do whatever it takes to experience it *where you want, when you want*. You'll find there is something incredibly empowering about having information and entertainment come to you, instead of having to go to it. The commute will feel that much shorter. Your time on the treadmill will change completely. You'll actually wish your dentist would keep you waiting a little longer so you can enjoy the end of a really great story. We didn't make that up. Someone actually wished that wish while catching up on her podcasts. Do you dare even get involved?

Chapter 3

PODCASTING HOW-TO

So, it's finally time to do it yourself. You've checked out a few shows, gotten yourself all worked up, and now it's time to fire up that equipment and start a podcast. Right? Well, not quite.

You could just jump right in and hit Record, "blah, blah, blah," and then upload and hope for the best. Frankly, for some people, that might be the best approach. However, we want you to slow down, plan ahead, and set yourself up to really enjoy the experience, not just the first time, but every time. We want your podcast to be the best it can be. More important, we don't want you to have to make some of the mistakes the so-called pioneers had to suffer through to get everyone to this point.

For most of the rest of this book, we're going to be talking in detail about the different aspects of making a podcast. So, we thought it would be best to give you a quick overview of the entire process before we start so that when we get to the details, you'll already feel like you're in familiar territory.

Keep in mind that although this book deals with audio and video podcasts, much of the information is specifically about audio podcasts. And, conversely, although this book may seem very audio-specific, we highly recommend reading the entire book, including the audio and video chapters, regardless of the type of podcast you're planning to do. All sections have valuable information that may appear completely irrelevant to your situation but could actually contain that tiny bit of insight that makes it all come together for you.

In simple terms, making a podcast consists of creating an audio or video file and then going through a few extra steps to get it out to the world. That's it. If at any time you feel like we're throwing too much at you, just remember your new mantra: "It's just a file I'm gonna upload; it's just a file I'm gonna upload . . . "

Here's what we'll be covering in the next set of chapters. Each chapter will include generalized information that will apply to most any situation and then will present more specific examples of how those techniques are applied with specific pieces of software or hardware. We'll cover these topics:

- Developing your podcast conceptually
- Doing show prep
- Recording
- Editing and mastering
- Encoding for distribution
- Uploading
- Updating your feed

Depending on how much experience you've had with recording and editing digital audio and video or uploading files to the Internet, you may think this is an awful lot to go through. It's not. Besides, we're here to help guide you through the process. As you tackle each step along the way, you may experience that unsettling feeling you get when you do something for the first time—"Am I doing this correctly?" you may hear yourself say. Just remember, it's your first time only once. The steps we outline in this book are straightforward, and the book will always be here for you to reference. This may seem like a lot now, but after creating a couple of podcasts, the process will become as familiar as backing down your own driveway.

Developing your podcast

They love to use that term in Hollywood: **development**. They'll say, "We're developing a sitcom about a former superhero who's now a stay-at-home dad." What that means is they're "making up" a sitcom, working it out, and planning for its full gestation over several seasons. That's what you're going to do with your podcast. We'll help you make sure you know what you want it to be about, how you want it to look and sound, and how you want it to "feel." We'll talk about creating a format for your show so that each unique edition feels like it's part of the series of shows. Most important, we'll look at how you want your podcast to grow over time and where you'd like to take it in the future.

Doing show prep

Show preparation (**prep**) is different from development. Show prep is getting ready before each episode so that you can record your podcast. You may need to get some sound effects ready, cue up a voicemail recording to play, or do some research and get some facts straight about real estate investments in Guam. Show prep is also about setting up your studio and checking to make sure everything is working properly, that you have enough hard disk space to record to, and that you can properly monitor your recording through headphones.

Video folks think of this as **preproduction**, the point in the production process when you know what you want to shoot but haven't started yet. It's the time when you make lists and gather props, actors, locations, equipment, and such, all to make sure you are ready to roll tape.

Setting up your studio and recording

For audio podcasters, we'll cover selecting a studio setup that's right for you and configuring that setup to work best while you're recording. We'll talk about the different types of microphones that podcasters use and why some mics may be better for you than others. We'll talk about the craft of proper mic technique and the art of "talking to one person at a time." "What does that mean?" you ask. Keep reading.

Recording and saving your podcast with good recording levels is essential. We'll talk about some of the industry standards you can easily adhere to in your home studio, making your podcast sound as professional as possible.

For video, we'll give you the inside scoop on how some of the top video podcasters are shooting and encoding their shows. We'll talk about camera choices, microphone choices, and available editing suites.

Editing/mastering

Another classic Hollywood expression is, "Don't worry, we'll fix it in post!" *Post* being postproduction, that is. In the case of podcasting, **postproduction** means editing, mixing, and mastering the raw files into the show you want to podcast and doing any kind of processing to the file you need to get the type of quality you're looking for your show. There are plenty of software plug-ins, filters, and hardware processes you can use to help make your tiny home setup sound like the biggest FM station in town, or your little home video shoot look like an "indie."

Encoding for distribution

This is where you take your new work of art and compress it down to a fraction of its original size. The compression process can mean the difference between a slight loss in sound and picture quality and turning your masterpiece into a potential form of torture. We'll discuss *podcast standards* for encoding, and we'll suggest a few different approaches to encoding that'll keep your workflow flowing.

Uploading

You actually have several ways to upload your podcast to the Internet. We'll talk about various methods of getting your podcast online and help determine which works best for you. Whether you end up using an FTP client (a simple mechanism that allows easy and secure upload of files to the Internet) or upload through the website of your service provider, we'll get you uploaded and online.

Updating your feed

You guessed it! You will soon have one of those fancy RSS feeds we keep mentioning. We know, all this talk of feeds can get a bit old, especially when you're not sure you've ever even used a feed. Not to worry. Whether you update the code by hand (a simple matter of cutting and pasting), use a stand-alone RSS application (easy, easy, easy), or use the RSS functions of your blog (effortless and automatic), we'll get your feed updated and your podcast downloadable without a hitch.

Summary

Prep, record, edit, master, encode, upload, update. Pretty straightforward. Remember, if you ever have a question about what something means, there's an exhaustive glossary in the back of this book that'll give you the meaning of anything we mention. Well, let's not put things off any longer. It's time to unearth that hidden podcast and get it out into the light. Shall we begin?

Chapter 4

PLANNING YOUR PODCAST

So you want to do a podcast, huh? Well, we're not going to stop you. In fact, we'll help! But, before you begin, we advise taking a hard look at why you want to podcast.

Your motivation to podcast is going to be what keeps you committed to producing your show. When you are clear on your motivation, you will be free to let your enthusiasm for your show and the subject matter shine through. Ultimately, it is your enthusiasm that will "sell" your show. Most podcasters are producing podcasts because they are genuinely enthusiastic about their subject. Whatever the topic is, they love it—passion for their show is spilling out of them, and they will spend much of their free time and disposable income to get the enthusiasm out of their bodies and into your podcatcher. If you have no enthusiasm for your planned show—no true love of it—don't start. It will be too much work to manufacture the energy to do a show week after week, and trust us, the audience can spot a phony from a gigabyte away.

We know that's not you—you're excited and enthusiastic, right? Then let's get to it. In this chapter, we'll take a look at the following topics:

- **Developing your podcast**: Who, what, how often, and how long
- **Formatting and structuring your podcast**: The freedom of confinement, working clean, and defamation

- **Using music legally in your podcast**: The Recording Industry Association of America (RIAA), indie artists, and the benefits of Creative Commons
- **Incorporating other elements into your podcast**: Voicemail messages and live phone calls from listeners, segments from other podcasts, and other elements

Developing your podcast

Somewhat ironically, there are likely hundreds of pages on the Internet—no, probably thousands—dealing with the topic of producing and distributing podcasts: what mics to use, what mixer is preferable, what directories to get listed in, and so on. However, there is almost no information available about how to create and develop a concept for a podcast. No information on how to make it the best, most effective podcast it can be.

It could be a matter of ego; everyone likes to think they can pull that kind of stuff off without assistance. Perhaps people are in such a hurry to get their podcast online that they want to just hit the Record button and hope for the best. There was a time in the not-so-distant past when, as a podcaster, you could afford to stumble around a bit before you really "found" your show. Nowadays, there are too many shows, too much attention, and too much at stake to jump into the pool without at least first thinking about how to swim. You may have an idea for a show you've been dying to do. If so, do it the honor of letting it gestate and form fully before you release it into the world.

As you plan your podcast, to ensure its success and longevity, you need to take some time and really consider the following questions:

- Who are you, and why should we subscribe?
- How will you and your audience benefit from focusing on a specific topic?
- How long a podcast should you try to put together, and how often can you do it and keep it interesting?

Who are you, and why should we subscribe?

When people talk about podcasts and what they like about them, there is a single concept that comes up over and over. It's more than the lack of commercials and more than the wide array of subject matter. One element of a good podcast seems to be universal, whether it is a religious podcast, a comedy podcast, or a music podcast: connection.

> *A fact of human nature is that people would rather listen to something they connect with that is poorly produced than something that looks and sounds like a million bucks and is, to them, a complete bore.*

Honest connection with other human beings seems to be the linchpin in a successful podcast. Not that you have to tell your deepest and darkest secrets, admit your fascination with Ricky Martin, or give out your ATM pin number. You just have to be honest about who you are, what the podcast is all about, and what your intentions are. If you start doing a podcast about movies, but you aren't really *that* big a movie fan, your podcast will wither on the vine. If your heart isn't in it, your tiny audience will soon smell a rat. Also, if you're trying to sell your audience a book, a diet plan, or a set of steak knives, don't try to fool them into thinking they're listening to anything other than a sales pitch. Podcast listeners are smart, savvy people who easily spot a fraud. If you're honest with them, they'll connect with you and your show. If you don't break that connection by betraying their trust, they'll stay connected to your show for the long run. It's essential to choose a topic that fascinates, inspires, and excites you, and it will fascinate, inspire, and excite others.

Respect your audience. You're asking them to find, subscribe, download, transfer, and listen to/watch your show. That requires some effort on their part. In return, give them an honest presentation. You have the privilege of whispering in their ears, following them from their homes to their jobs and schools, and accompanying them on their daily walk, and they want someone they can trust to join them on these journeys. You'll create a relationship in which you present them with thoughts and ideas, and they watch, listen, respond, and interact. Of the utmost importance is to decide what exactly your podcast will be about. What is it you're trying to accomplish with your podcast? Are you hoping to expose listeners to great undiscovered musical talent from your hometown? Perfect. Are you trying to create a support group for people who must maintain a low-carb diet for health reasons? Great. Do you just want to sit on the floor in your underwear taking about Dungeons & Dragons? Well, hey, who are we to judge?

> Listeners = Community

When audience members subscribe to your podcast, you and they are entering into an agreement of sorts. They agree to download your podcast on a regular basis, in the belief that you will be podcasting on a consistent basis on the topic and in the manner they've come to expect from you. This is an important point; you need to do your best to uphold your part of this bargain.

Also, the audience agrees to download the kind of podcast they heard the first couple of times they listened. They expect that each podcast in the "series" will be new and yet similar to the previous shows, much like watching a new episode of their favorite TV show. So, if you've been doing a simple, tight cooking show and then you suddenly go off on a rant on your views of privatizing public schools, you're violating the trust you've established with your audience. To avoid doing this, it is imperative that you be very clear about what podcast you're producing so you can continue to produce the show your audience expects. This isn't to say that you can't do a show on whatever happens to be on your mind—you just need to let listeners know that is what your show is about. Essentially, you need to manage the expectations of those who subscribe.

Narrowcasting: The benefits of a well-defined concept

You may be thinking, "A Dungeons & Dragons podcast? Are these guys serious?" Sure. D&D, badminton, chewing rocks, whatever subject you like. This is the age of **narrowcasting**, or making programs available that may appeal only to a small percentage of a total potential audience. But, for those the program appeals to, that appeal is immeasurable.

We hate to be the ones to break it to you, but you are not completely unique. Sure, you're unique in that technical, "every snowflake is different" kind of way. But as far as humans go, you're not completely singular. Other people have the same interests and hobbies you have. It may seem like you're all alone in your curiosities, depending on just how curious they are, but plenty of fellow *whatevers* are out there. If there's a podcast that you think you'd like to subscribe to, then that is the one for you to produce.

Not everyone is going to be interested in a podcast about playing badminton. Actually, it might happen that very few people are. But, to those few people who are interested in that kind of show, it might be to them the greatest show ever made in the history of electronic media. Where else are badminton fanatics going to get information and entertainment revolving around the game they love? Certainly not radio. Not television. Yet a podcast about badminton, or any other narrowly defined subject, is more than just a show: it is potentially the center of a community. A well-defined podcast is going to get immediate interest from people who share the same interest. As the podcast grows, so does the audience base. Soon the audience and the podcasters are all sharing stories, tips, and information about that subject matter. Before you know it, a podcast you thought only a handful of people would enjoy is indispensable to an entire community.

Determining your podcast's length and frequency

The length of your podcast and how frequently you make a new one available can have a major effect on your podcast's appeal, especially if you don't know what you're getting yourself into.

Show length and the law of diminishing returns

For new audio podcasters, once they get over the initial growing pains of the first show or two, many think they could talk on and on for hours. But a longer show is not *necessarily* a better show for audio or video. Trial and error has shown that between 15 and 30 minutes is about the optimum length for a solid audio podcast, and anywhere from 1 minute to perhaps 7 is ideal for video. If you are going to err, err on the side of brevity. A shorter podcast has a higher likelihood of being enjoyed regularly, as compared to a longer one ("Sam Has Seven Friends" is a riveting 90 seconds daily). Also, by making a show that is too long, you are weakening "the brand." People's attention will wander during an hour-long show unless it is rock solid. And, if it is rock solid, break it into two separate podcasts. You'll reduce the chances of losing the audience while building anticipation for the next installment. Odds are that if you're recording for an hour, you could stand to cut it down. You won't regret it.

You're never locked into a set length for your podcast. Just because your first one is 25 minutes, that doesn't mean you have to make every one 25 minutes, especially if you don't have 25 minutes' worth of content. The length of each show is up to you and should be determined by the amount of material you have for that podcast. Remember, this isn't "old media."

Show frequency and the law of diminishing returns

Doing a daily show sounds exciting at first. You sit down at the mic every day, pontificate for 25 minutes, and you're golden. Heck, you're doing your listeners a favor by giving them something to listen to every day. The downside, of course, is that you don't have much to say every day (unless you're "Keith and the Girl"). Or, if you do have something to say every day, your listeners probably don't have time to listen that often (unless you're "Keith and the Girl"). Now, that being said, there are several great daily podcasts, the most notable being Adam Curry's "Daily Source Code." But Adam Curry has decades of experience as a broadcaster, and he also has many in the podcasting community supplying him with information, promos, songs, and so forth, to fill his show. A "normal" podcast will not have this luxury. You would need to come up with new material every day that's fresh and tight enough to require its own show.

If you are doing a new podcast, you may need to edge another show off a subscription list to get downloaded on a regular basis. There are only so many hours in a day, and only so many of those can be devoted to podcasts. The best way to get new people to subscribe to your show is to not overwhelm them up front. Sometimes it is true that "less is more." Give listeners and viewers a tight, well-put-together taste and no more. An age-old, but still valid, cliché from the entertainment world applies here: "Always leave them wanting more." (Not less . . .)

> *Find a schedule that works for you. When I first started doing "Reel Reviews—Films Worth Watching" (*www.reelreviewsradio.com*), I established a pace of roughly two to three movie review podcasts per week. That was great in the beginning, but I soon realized that pace was too optimistic. In addition to watching the film (often more than once), listening to commentaries, reading, doing research, recording, editing, and posting, I found that I also had to spend time running the site, responding to e-mails, and taking care of other general podcaster responsibilities. All of that plus running a business and spending time with my family proved to be too much. I ended up finding a sweet spot at roughly one "Reel Review" podcast per week. Now I do not feel rushed, and I can devote the time necessary to produce a solid show. In the long run, I know that the show content benefits from the extra time, and ultimately that is only thing that matters. Remember, content is king.*
>
> *—Michael Geoghegan*

Formatting and structuring your podcast

One of the attractive aspects of doing a podcast is that there are no rules. The Federal Communications Commission (FCC) doesn't tell you what you can and cannot do. There is no programming director or group of shareholders to tell you what to say or what to play. As long as you don't infringe on anyone's copyright, you're set. You're your own podcaster, ready to take on the world however you see fit. To hell with the old way—you're going to reinvent the wheel and roll, baby!

In a lot of ways, before you can break the rules, you have to make the rules. We strongly suggest you create a format for your show, which will be the wheel on which you ride.

People in the radio industry actually use the analogy of a wheel or a clock to determine when to do things, what to play when, and so on, as shown in Figure 4-1. At the top of the hour (wheel), they play an upbeat new hit, then they play another song, and then at quarter past the hour they go to a commercial break. After the commercial break, they play another big hit, followed by an old favorite, and so on. The entire day is formatted by this wheel, with different songs, commercials, and promos being plugged in at the appropriate times.

4

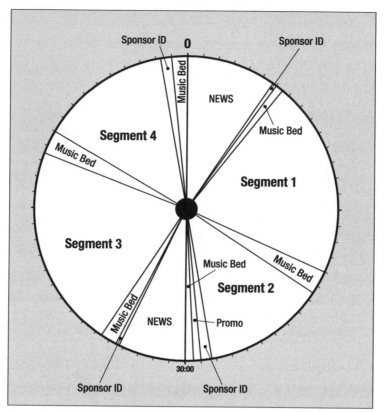

Figure 4-1. An example of a radio "clock," based on the format clock for NPR's "All Things Considered"

Since your podcast doesn't go on and on all day like a radio station, maybe it's best to see your podcast in a linear fashion, with a beginning, middle, and end. Every good book, every classic movie, and every song you've ever liked has had this beginning, middle, and end format. So should your podcast. Think about how you want to begin and end each program and how you should order the various segments in between. Audiences love structure. They especially love to see a tried-and-true structure applied in a new and surprising way. Why do people watch episode after episode of the same sitcom for years, sometimes decades? Because they love seeing the same characters butt heads in the same ways over new problems every week. The structure of the show never changes, but how that structure is lived in each episode is what is so fascinating.

This may sound a bit binding at first. It isn't. Advertising legend David Ogilvy was famous for saying "Give me the freedom of a tightly defined strategy" (or something to that effect). If you leave yourself too much freedom (no format), you will flounder around show after show, unsure of what to do next. Worse, you will quickly frustrate your audience. But, if you give yourself total freedom within a tight format, you will never stop thinking of ways to use that structure.

Here are a few examples of how you might format a 15–30 minute audio podcast. You'll soon see what we mean when we say there is freedom in constraint.

Example format for a talk show:

- Intro music
- Greetings and thanks
- Listener mail
- B topic (short)
- Listener voicemail message
- A topic (long)
- URL/phone number
- Outro music

Example format for a music show:

- Show ID
- Up-tempo song
- Slower song
- "Back sell" first songs, give URL/phone number
- Up-tempo song
- Requested song
- "Back sell" with album information, promote next show
- Last song

Example format for a technology show:

- Voicemail message
- Intro song
- Tech news and reviews
- B topic (short)
- Question from mail/voicemail
- Promote upcoming show
- Phone interview with expert guest on topic A (long)
- Outro music

These are just a few examples to give you an idea of what we mean by **format**. Do you have to do exactly the same thing every time? No, but your format will be there when you need it, like a security blanket. You can deviate from it as much as you like, change it, destroy it, and put it back together. If you start with a structured format in mind, you will never regret it. Remember, before you can break the rules, you need to know what the rules are.

A perfect example of a show with a good structured format is "The Dawn and Drew Show!" (www.dawnanddrew.com). While the show has a somewhat free-form feel, which Dawn and Drew acknowledge to anyone listening, it always ends with a segment of feedback from people who have called the show's comment line. You can always count on it. Because Dawn and Drew always include the caller feedback segment in their show, they end up receiving a lot of calls on the comment line. It is a great way to get listeners involved with and ultimately part of the show.

As you are developing the format for your audio show, keep in mind that your show is a podcast, not a radio broadcast. People who rely too heavily on radio as a model find themselves breaking up segments with musical segues and then reintroducing their guest or topic, as is always done in radio. They do this in radio because radio is live, so listeners don't necessarily hear every moment of the program. Podcast listeners are there from the beginning of the program to the end, so reintroducing guests or topics is not necessary. Actually, it is painfully annoying.

With video podcasts, you have even more freedom to play with structure. Your show could be a video blog, a news show, sketch comedy, a how-to, a documentary, a mockumentary . . . it could look like a sitcom or a feature film. Decide what it is (and what it isn't), and put together a consistent structure for the program. Consider a flashy opening sequence (see "DotBoom" and "Digg") or a memorable musical signature ("Ask a Ninja," "Mr. Diety"). Take what you think works from television and film, and run with it, leaving the rest behind.

Start strong, finish big

You don't have to be brilliant from the first word to the last in your podcast. Actually, you don't ever have to be brilliant. What you should be, to stack the deck in your own favor, is strong out of the gate. Start strong, and they will keep listening. The best comedian in the world will lose an audience immediately if he flounders in the first moments on stage. The audience members start shifting their feet, stirring their drinks, and checking their watches to see how long this clown has to go before he gets off stage. They're stuck in the club and have to either wait the guy out or leave. As a podcaster, you don't have the luxury of a captive audience. While a live comic has a chance to get the audience back on his side, if you lose your audience in the first moments of your podcast, they are gone with the press of a button. Off to another program they go, perhaps never to return. Your audience has thousands of podcasts to choose from. Make them feel like they're in good hands right away.

Lead with your strength. Be upbeat and get into it. Dragging your feet and waiting to get up to speed is risky business with several thousand other podcasts waiting in the wings. Make sure the opening of your show reflects the tone and pace of the program. If you have a trademark opening that works, stick with it. The theme song of your show, a familiar sound effect, and a catchphrase all can help kick-start each podcast and help build that initial momentum.

Even more important than starting strong is finishing big. The old showbiz adage of "Save the best for last" holds true for podcasts. Save some of your strongest material for the end. If you leave people with a message that really resonates with them, that is what they will remember. They will forgive all the missteps and missed cues, all the bad jokes and awkward transitions, if you leave them with your best stuff. This goes for comedy, information, sales . . . you name it: finish big.

As a side note, consider putting longer segments toward the end of the show. If you start with one long segment and you then do several shorter segments, the podcast will seem top-heavy and unsteady. People are used to what they're used to. "But podcasting is about breaking the rules?!" you may scream. Yes, it is. It's about breaking the rules of content and the rules of business. It's about re-examining the way broadcasting has failed, and it's about making podcasting better. It is not, however, about fighting human nature. Humans inherently, for whatever reason, have come to expect certain story structures. Don't fight it. Embrace it and use it to your advantage.

Working "clean"

Podcasting means no FCC—only pure and unbridled free speech for as far as the ear can hear. *You're free to say exactly what you want, to show exactly what you want* (within the limits of the law, of course). But should you? Is using adult language the only way to achieve your desired effect? This is something you need to make a conscious decision about before you start.

There is and always will be an audience for adult material. There's a feeling of exclusivity, of freedom, when listening to something kind of dirty. Sure it's childish, but there's something thrilling about listening to something your parents wouldn't listen to—that you could never listen to at school or in the office but might excitedly whisper about to someone else in the halls. If your target audience is young adults, you may think using adult language is required. If you must, you must. But don't do it if it's not natural. Nothing sounds worse than awkward swearing.

If you decide not to swear, you need to stick to it (see the previous section for more about your audience's expectations). However, if you do decide to "work blue," just be aware that you're potentially alienating just as many listeners as you may be attracting. You'll certainly reduce the number of listeners who may want to listen to your show at work or when the kids are around. This may not sound like a big deal, but depending on your target audience, using adult language could deal a sizable blow to your potential audience base. If your show could be heard by people in an open area, don't go blue—it's not going to get played. The office is out. School is out. Carpool is out. Sure, listening to a podcast is an individual thing, done by many people wearing headphones. But not everyone wears headphones. If listeners don't feel comfortable listening to your podcast in public, your show won't be played in public. That means missed opportunities to reach new listeners. Oops. Is it that important?

> *I was a stand-up comedian for many years, performing in clubs and coffeehouses all over Los Angeles. And, frankly, I worked "blue." Swear, swear, swear. As far as I was concerned at the time, the swearing was not gratuitous. The bad words all fit in with the rhythm of the jokes, with my persona, with the venue. All my favorites had been masters of adult language: Lenny Bruce, Richard Pryor, Bill Hicks, Chris Rock . . .*
>
> *When I first heard about podcasting, I immediately realized it was the perfect way for me to get back into doing comedy without hanging around clubs until all hours of the night. Because it was podcasting, I could say anything I wanted to say. But I didn't. I was tempted. Frankly, I had to fight the urge to swear with all my might. Even now, there are many times I stumble around for a word to substitute for the swear word in my head.*
>
> *I made the decision not to swear because I was greedy. Greedy for listeners. I admit it, I didn't want to do anything to turn anyone away. So, I plowed ahead, "clean."*
>
> *I realized that most of my new material was about being a husband and a father and that many of my listeners would be family types, too, who would want to be able to listen to the show around the kids.*
>
> *It got frustrating. I felt like I was stifling myself. I talked about it on a podcast and quickly found out that the listeners didn't want me to swear. The content didn't require it. I soon realized that the material actually hadn't been suffering because of my working clean. I was talking about exactly what I wanted to but using innuendo and malapropisms instead of curse words. I have continued to keep the show as clean as I can ever since.*
>
> *I have never received an e-mail or a voicemail message from anyone saying they wished I would swear more. I have received countless messages saying how glad people are that I don't.*
>
> —*Dan Klass*

Your decision to use adult language or not should be dictated by the show you're trying to do. If it's a family show, a business show or an informational/educational show, adult language is going to hold you and your podcast back. Many podcasters attract listeners by labeling their shows "work safe" and/or "kid safe." That way, listeners know they won't be embarrassed (or worse) by listening to or watching the podcast in a public place.

Consider, too, if down the line you're going to try to attract sponsors or advertising. Do you need to limit yourself to the kinds of advertisers who will pay for an adult-themed show? Or is that exactly the market you'd be looking at? Let the future of the podcast dictate this.

And, lastly, consider iTunes. Exposure in the iTunes Music Store is arguably the best exposure for a podcast there is. Next time you check out the front page of their podcasting area and see all the big banners and staff picks, ask yourself the questions: "How many of these shows include adult content?" "What level of adult content is represented, and what level just plain isn't?" The impression you will get is that iTunes supports only those podcasts that are TV safe, or just barely beyond that. No "F-bombs," no nudity. Of course, there could be exceptions to this rule, but it is easy to generalize: anything too foul is not promoted by iTunes.

A few words about defamation and slander

We don't really know where else to put this in the book, but we thought we should throw in a fact or two about slander. **Slander** is the oral communication of false or malicious statements about or charges against someone that are injurious to that person's reputation, business, and so on. If you are new to broadcasting/podcasting, you may have never even considered the legalities of what you may and may not say. If you did say something slanderous about someone, it would not be difficult for the person's attorney to get hold of a copy of the slanderous podcast. Be careful! Podcasts are not a small discussion among trusted friends; they are publicly available content just like radio and TV, and some of the same rules will apply.

Generally speaking, there are three defenses to an accusation of slander:

- The statement is true. This is often referred to as an **absolute defense**, meaning if it is true, it can't be slander.
- It is a statement of opinion.
- The person referred to in the statement is a public figure, or it is "fair comment on a matter of public interest."

Of course, there are other defenses, and protecting yourself against accusations of slander is more complicated than just following a set of rules. Even though the preceding are defenses, you can still end up spending tens of thousands of dollars "defending" yourself. Please keep in mind that we are *not* lawyers—we are podcasters—so be sure to check with your lawyer before speaking out too frankly against someone.

Using music in podcasts

Welcome to the minefield. Including music in podcasts is the area of podcasting most fraught with danger, confusion, and potential liability.

Almost every podcast has music in it, whether it's in the form of entire songs or short, ten-second segues. The amount of music you'll use is something to consider up front, because using music in podcasts can legally be a tricky situation. We're living in an era of file-sharing paranoia on the part of major record labels and a "music should be free" mentality on the part of many Internet users. Let's be very clear up front: *music is not free*. Music costs money to produce, to promote, and to distribute. The writers of the songs spend a lot of time, and the record labels spend a lot of money, to get that music written, recorded, and out into the world. So, to protect that investment, they all closely control the use of that music and the rights to reproduce it. Everybody wants to get paid and protected, and rightfully so.

To cut to the chase, if you use music in a podcast without the express permission of the persons/entities that own that music, you are in violation of copyright.

It's true that most unknown, independent artists would be more than happy for a little podcast exposure, and very few would come looking to sue you over playing one of their songs. But just as you may not want people freely giving away your podcast to anyone who will take a copy, you can't assume that a recording artist (or any artist, for that matter) is OK with you using her work, even if she has songs available on the Internet for free download. The recording artist may want to reserve her "right to copy."

To distribute a musical work you did not create and do not own legally, you need to get permission from the writer of the song, the performer of the song, and the owner of the master recordings.

Composers' rights

The **composers' rights** of musical works are handled by any one of three rights organizations: the American Society of Composers, Authors, and Publishers (ASCAP, www.ascap.com); Broadcast Music, Inc. (BMI, www.bmi.com); and the Society of European Stage Authors and Composers (SESAC, www.sesac.com). These organizations track the use of a composer's works in radio, television, film, and other media, and they collect payments to the composer for such use.

On January 1, 2005, ASCAP introduced its "Non-Interactive Experimental License Agreement for Internet Sites & Services—Release 5.0" license, which is designed to handle the needs of webcasters and web developers using ASCAP music where the song segment is less than 60 seconds in length. Clearly, this does not apply directly to podcasters. Assuming that it's the closest license we have to go by as a guide and that BMI and SESAC have similar licenses, a podcaster would be required to pay an annual fee of US$300 for ASCAP, another $300 annually for BMI, and approximately $170 for SESAC, and that's only covering the written element of the song. (Actually, it's only covering the written element of the song if you're webcasting, which hasn't yet been defined to include podcasting.)

Performers' rights

So, assuming you've secured the composers' rights from ASCAP or BMI (assuming that you need to), you are cleared only to perform the song yourself or have someone perform it for you (on a webcast). If you are hoping to use an existing recording of a song, you still need to secure the **performers' rights**, which are controlled by the record labels. Two separate elements are required to license the performers' rights: the mechanical license and the master use license.

The **mechanical license** covers the right to reproduce a performance of a particular song on a song-by-song basis and is handled by the Harry Fox Agency. The Harry Fox Agency explains very clearly under what circumstances someone is required to obtain a mechanical license on its website (www.harryfox.com):

> "If you are manufacturing and distributing copies of a song which you did not write, and you have not already reached an agreement with the song's publisher, you need to obtain a mechanical license. This is required under U.S. Copyright Law, regardless of whether or not you are selling the copies that you made.

> "You do not need a mechanical license if you are recording and distributing a song you wrote yourself, or if the song is in the public domain. If you are not sure if the song you are looking to license is in the public domain, and therefore does not require license authority, we suggest you use the search on www.pdinfo.com."

The issuing and the costs surrounding a **master use license** are controlled completely and solely by the owner of the master recordings, which is usually the record label. The label will determine the licensing rate based on how popular the song or artist is, how current the work is, and, frankly, how much it thinks it can get for the license. Now, the label is under no obligation to issue anyone a license to use any song. If the label sees podcasting as a potential avenue of lost revenues, it simply will not grant you permission, or it will set the licensing fee so high as to make it impossible for you to license the work.

To keep the licensing fees for Internet use in check, SoundExchange (www.soundexchange.com) was created to act as the licensing entity for the record labels. According to SoundExchange, the group has "been designated by the U.S. Copyright Office to collect and distribute statutory royalties to sound recording copyright owners and featured and nonfeatured artists." Although SoundExchange has set a relatively low annual fee for Internet use of RIAA music, the wording of the licensing agreement is such that it *does not actually apply to podcasts* but rather (as is usually the case) applies to streaming media.

Using mash-ups and remixes

The mash-up trend is in full swing, with more mash-up DJs popping up every week and more radio stations playing mash-ups on a regular basis. A **mash-up** is a song created out of pieces of two or more songs, usually by overlaying the vocal track of one song seamlessly over the music track of another. A classic example is the infamous "Ray of Gob," put together by mash-up genius Mark Vidler (www.gohomeproductions.co.uk), which expertly combines bits of several songs by the Sex Pistols with Madonna's "Ray of Light." The song got worldwide attention and radio airplay (by none other than Steve Jones of the Sex Pistols), and Vidler got "legitimate" remix work with Madonna.

Mash-ups are incredible fun and a fascinating way to reexperience some of your favorite tunes. What mash-ups are not is **podsafe**. "Podsafe" is a term you'll hear quite a bit when talking about using music in podcasts. It means "music that is safe to include in your podcast, legally." Mash-ups are the opposite of podsafe. Just because you've heard mash-ups and remixes on other podcasts doesn't mean they're legal. If using one copyrighted song in your podcast is considered a copyright infringement, then distributing a mash-up would be violating the copyright of several songs at the same time! Just because a song is remixed, or mixed with another song, doesn't mean it suddenly falls into the public domain. Mash-ups are a legal nightmare, which is why you don't see many mash-up compilation CDs at your local record store. Radio stations can play them, because radio stations pay ASCAP, BMI, and so forth, for permission to broadcast. Remember, we're not in that game.

Using music legally

So, now that your mind has been boggled, you're most assuredly asking yourself, "So, how do I use RIAA music in my podcast?" The answer seems to be "Very carefully." To be frank, nobody is crystal clear about exactly how to go about getting approved music from major labels without opening themselves up to potential liability. There is no precedent at this time to indicate whether securing a mechanical license and a master use license would be enough. Rest assured that there are very few—if any—podcasters who have the financial resources required to fight the major record labels if one of the labels decided to make an example of them and sue them for copyright infringement.

Your best bet is to find music anywhere else but in your CD collection, unless of course your CD collection is made up only of independent artists who would be willing to grant you all rights to use their music . . .

Brian Ibbott produces and hosts "Coverville" (www.coverville.com), one of the most widely listened to independent music podcasts on the internet. On "Coverville," Ibbott plays, as you might imagine, nothing but cover songs, performed and recorded by major label and independent recording artists. He has made every effort to include the music that he wants to on his show legally. Here is what Brian has to say about ASCAP, BMI, and the state of the music podcast:

> *Podcast Solutions: How soon after starting did you realize you might need to get "legal" about it?*
>
> *Brian Ibbott: Oh, it was the first show. I knew that what I was doing probably wasn't that different from what Sean Fanning was doing with the whole Napster deal, even though, all right, I'm neatly packaging five, six songs into a nice little 30-minute MP3, but it's ending up as an MP3 on somebody else's desktop.*
>
> *Around the middle of October [2004], I started calling ASCAP and BMI and saying, "All right, here's what I'm doing, here's this thing called podcasting, what kind of license do I need for this? Is it something that is licensable?" And I spent about an hour on the phone with each of them. And they said, "All right, we'll just fit you into a web streaming license; that's close enough." They were really lax about it and said, "Webcasting license, close enough. Here's a bill for 250 bucks, go ahead and get started . . . "*
>
> *I kind of suspected that was only half of the equation. It was pretty much later in October when I did a little more research and found out about the whole mechanical rights side of it, with the RIAA, SoundExchange, and Harry Fox and all that.*
>
> *I've talked to the RIAA, I've talked to SoundExchange and Harry Fox, and they're all aware of podcasting, and they're all aware of what I'm doing, so it's certainly no secret. But, until there's a way, until there's a method for me to pay for the mechanical rights, I do as much contacting of the artists as I can, which is a lot easier with the smaller groups, and in the other cases I just play it and cross my fingers.*
>
> *Every quarter I put together a list (for ASCAP and BMI) of all the songs I've played, and I have to put down on what date, what show it appeared on, and who the performer was, and who the songwriter was. And they basically take the $280 or whatever it is that I pay for a license, divide it by the number of songs I play, and send out a check to each of those songwriters.*

"Fair use"

"But I'm just using about ten seconds of this song for my intro . . . " Doesn't matter.

Many people still believe in the myth of **fair use**—that if you use only a small portion of a song, or use it as part of a review, a news story, or a parody, that it is legally without liability. Guess what? That's just not the case. Perhaps it should be, but it isn't. Corporate owners of intellectual property are very protective these days (as you learned in the preceding section), and they are as inclined to control the use of small sections of their properties as they are the use of complete works.

Even if it is just a short snippet of music for the intro or closing of your show, it needs to be music that you have permission to use or that can be used freely without the need to pay royalties.

Public domain

Using music that is in the **public domain**, because of the copyright of that work expiring, is just as tricky a situation as using the work of a major label artist. The public domain status of a work is often difficult to establish, and that status can be challenged at any time. Under current laws, the character Mickey Mouse will soon enter into the public domain. Needless to say, the Walt Disney Company (and its corporate brethren) is spending millions of dollars to have the guidelines of the public domain changed, or at least muddied, to protect their invaluable icon (even though their greatest earlier films were based on works in the public domain). If you think you know a work is in the public domain and you use it, you may find out the hard way later on that you were quite mistaken. Is *It's a Wonderful Life* in the public domain? What about *Charade*? Can we use clips from either movie without getting permission from the stars' estates? If the movie is in the public domain, is the accompanying score (music)?

Especially as podcasting grows, the eyes and ears of the legal departments at all the major record labels, movie studios, and the like will be keeping close tabs on the shows flying around the Internet. Unless you are planning to use a sound that is widely accepted as being in the public domain (none spring to mind), be very cautious about including supposedly public domain music in your podcast.

Getting your hands on an original copy of a work in the public domain is usually quite a feat. If you simply go down to the music store and start buying discs of old music, you may still be violating copyright if you use those songs. If a public domain work has been extensively restored, the restored version of the work (the version you'd most likely find on Amazon) could be copyrighted. The underlying work is in the public domain, but not the version you just purchased. Be careful.

Creative Commons

Some music on the Internet is not necessarily copyrighted in the traditional sense, but is protected by what is quickly becoming a popular means of restricting some rights to intellectual property while allowing others: a Creative Commons license. The Creative Commons organization was founded in 2001 to create a simple, straightforward way for content creators to protect their works, while giving clear and concise information on how those works can be used and redistributed by others.

A Creative Commons license can be applied to work in any medium: sound recordings, videos, films, photographs, and written works. There are hundreds of hours of songs under Creative Commons license that you can freely use, as long as you adhere to the license guidelines of those works. These guidelines grant or restrict the right to build upon the work and sample the work, or indicate whether or not a work can be used for commercial purposes (see Figure 4-2). Most songs and podcasts are licensed under the "Attribution-NonCommercial-NoDerivs 3.0" license, which states that others are free "to copy, distribute, display, and perform the work" (podcast), as long as the creator is given credit for the work, the work is not used for commercial purposes (sold), and the work is not built upon.

> As a side note—and we are surely getting ahead of ourselves here—you might consider licensing your podcast under a Creative Commons license.

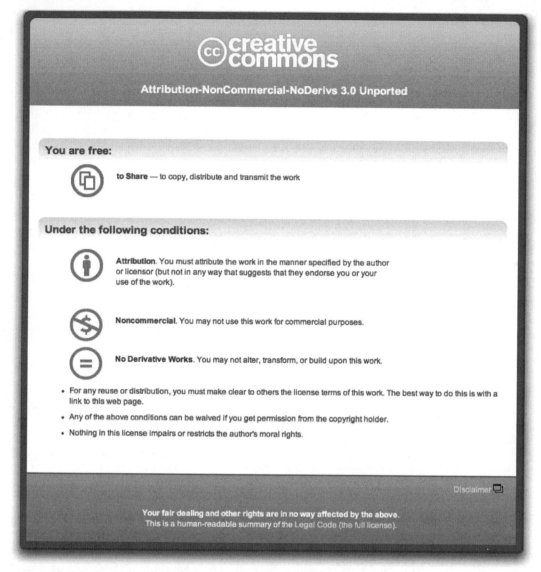

Figure 4-2. A Creative Commons "Attribution-NonCommercial-NoDerivs 3.0" license

The Creative Commons "Sampling License" allows you to use excerpts of a work, but not the entire piece. This is perfect for remixes and mash-ups, and it may also be a perfect license for a podcast. Other producers would be able to repurpose small sections of your program (which would be great promotion for you), but they couldn't legally use the whole thing.

Finding Creative Commons music and video is as simple as using the search tool built into the Creative Commons website (www.creativecommons.org) or Yahoo's Creative Commons Search (http://search.yahoo.com/cc). Also, Internet Archive (www.archive.org) is a valuable resource for finding Creative Commons (and reportedly public domain) works, either through independent artists or through **net labels** (that is, music labels that make their catalog available under Creative Commons license on the web).

Indie artists and easily licensed music

Luckily for podcasters, not all bands are signed to major labels, and not all music is as closely regulated and licensed as the music of major recording stars. Before most singers, songwriters, and bands become major recording stars, they are usually unknown recording artists. They pour their hearts and souls into their music, playing live and recording their songs in the hope that people will appreciate their work. They may not all want to be on a major label or be a famous face on MTV, but rest assured that most of them would like their music to be heard.

The Internet is full of websites promoting independent recording artists and their music, and most of these artists would be thrilled to have their music featured on a podcast. The one thing we can't stress enough is that by looking to independent recording artists, you are not compromising the sound of your podcast. Actually, upon beginning your search for music by independent artists, or **indies**, you will soon realize that the music being put out today by "unknown" bands is just as good as, if not better than, the stuff you're sick of hearing on the radio. In terms of production quality, sheer songwriting/singing talent, and musicianship, there is a nearly endless supply of music that is of major label quality.

Of course, as podcasting has experienced meteoric growth, so has a little social-networking website called MySpace. MySpace is not only a great place to find pictures of teenage girls taking photos of themselves sucking in their cheeks, it is also a great way to find independent music. Just follow the "Friends" trail. Find one band that you like, and then check out their "Top Eight Friends" list. Click one of the bands or fans there, and you'll undoubtedly find a band or two you'll like on that page. Check out *their* friends list, and keep going. There is an almost endless supply of music on MySpace, as long as you're willing to click around for it.

Now, even though making a song available for free download on a website would seem to constitute "tacit consent" to distribute, it is better to err on the side of caution. Dan has been sending out requests for permission to play music on his music podcast, "Old Wave Radio," and has, as of this writing, never been turned down. The artists want to be heard. Just get permission before you use their music.

Here is an extremely valuable chunk of legalese, created by Chris MacDonald for the Association of Music Podcasting (musicpodcasting.org), when securing permission to use an artist's music for AMP or one of his many IndieFeed channels (www.indiefeed.com). Adapt this text to your needs when approaching bands for your programs.

COPYRIGHT DISCLAIMER: In order to submit your works to the Association of Music Podcasting, either for sale or for promotion on an AMP Podcast, you must first agree with our copyright disclaimer:

1. I agree that all works I submit to AMP are my property, and that I own the rights to these works. I grant the Association of Music Podcasting permission to distribute my mechanical production of song or songs within a Podcast, for promotional purposes, and I indemnify and hold harmless AMP from any additional claim of interest related to these songs for this express purpose.

4

2. I agree that all submitted works contain no recordings, lyrics, copyrights, or other elements that are the copyright of any other artist, except under the limited provisions of the Creative Commons License Agreement http://www.creativecommons.org.

3. I agree that although I may have recording contracts with RIAA, ASCAP, BMI, or other recording industry entity, my contract states that I retain ownership of my works, and I am free to distribute, broadcast, or sell these works at my discretion, and waive any rights to royalties, fees, or payments related to Podcast play on AMP.

If you agree to the terms above, and electronically submit to us, or send us copies of your CD for Podcast play, online store sales, or both; this constitutes an agreement that you understand and agree with the terms above.

The right artists will be anxious to get exposure on podcasts. Be sure to protect them—and yourself— by getting specific and implicit permission up front. You'll never regret it.

Podsafe music sites

One of the easiest ways to begin looking for music to incorporate into your podcast is to look into websites specializing in independent music, such as IODA Promonet, GarageBand, the Podsafe Music Network, IndieHeaven, and Magnatunes. GarageBand and the Podsafe Music Network alone represent a community of thousands of independent artists and their work in dozens of genres. GarageBand offers a free "Webcasters/Podcasters License." You can search GarageBand by CD title, song title, band name, and genre to find the exact sound you want. By obtaining the free license, you are able to include any song you choose from the GarageBand catalog in your podcast at no charge. With the other sites, it is prudent to contact the artists directly to obtain permission to play their songs. The Podsafe Music Network (www.podsafemusicnetwork.com) offers several ways to search for and find music, and its ever-growing catalog even includes tracks by major recording artists, such as James Brown, Thomas Dolby, Deep Purple, and Rancid, and favorite newer acts such as Modest Mouse and Dashboard Confessional. Anyone can audition the tracks, but only registered podcasters have download permission at no charge.

Royalty-free music

Nothing is this world is free, even royalty-free music. Well, some of it may be free, but most of it you pay for, at least once. Still, beautifully produced royalty-free music can be found in just about any style you can imagine, and at any length, so finding something that suits your needs is a snap. The fees are reasonable (much more reasonable than being fined for copyright infringement), and each service offers differing licensing plans to suit your preference. Freeplay Music (www.freeplaymusic.com) charges a small annual fee per individual song, while Sounddogs (www.sounddogs.com) goes with the à la carte method, but it charges only a one-time usage fee and you're set.

Because each music service is so different, it's imperative that you read the service agreements carefully. Some services require annual renewal, while others don't. Some charges are based on listenership, while some involve flat, one-time fees. There are as many ways of going about it as there are services, so be careful and read the fine print.

Make it or buy it

After all this talk of music licensing, it may be refreshing to know that there's one way to use music that doesn't require any kind of license or fee: make the music yourself. Sure, you're not a musician. If you were a musician, you would have skipped this entire section on music rights. But, since this is the computer age, making music for your podcast may be as simple as sliding around some samples. Apple's GarageBand software (no relation to the GarageBand site mentioned earlier) or similar software for Windows makes creating music out of royalty-free loops easy for even the most tone-deaf wannabe producer.

Or, if that seems like too much time and effort, remember this: if you hire someone to record a music track for you, you own that track. You own it, you control it, and you can use it whenever and however you would like. Looking in your area for a small independent record producer may unearth the all-in-one writer/musician/producer you need to put the ideal theme song together. This kind of all-in-one arrangement can work for fast, cheap, and amazing results.

Voicemail messages and phone calls

We've said it before, and we'll say it many times over: one of the best aspects of podcasts is the interaction you have with listeners from around the world. A great way to incorporate this interaction into your show is to drop voicemail messages or incorporate "live" phone calls into your podcast.

Voicemail messages

You might be surprised to find out just how easy it is to include voicemail messages in your podcast. Several free and pay services are available that will give you a phone number where listeners can leave messages, and those messages can be sent to you via e-mail. The sound quality varies based on the service, but even the worst free service is better than nothing.

Perhaps the most widely used of the free services is K7 (www.k7.net). Although the sound quality is somewhat poor (especially if your listener is calling from a cell phone), the audio can be cleaned up nicely with noise reduction software such as BIAS's SoundSoap (www.bias-inc.com/products/soundsoap). Of course, now you're buying software to clean up free voice messages instead of paying for a service where the sound quality is better (and doesn't need to be cleaned up). Weighing the pros and cons is up to you. Some people would rather buy software and get the calls for free. Others don't want to bother with the software and would rather just pay for the service.

Before you commit to any service, be careful to read the entire service agreement. There can easily be hidden limits on calls and call lengths that can end up costing you more than you expect.

Phone calls

You may decide that playing prerecorded phone messages just isn't enough, and you want to take some "live" callers. Well, given the prerecorded nature of podcasting, unless you tell your listeners ahead of time exactly when you'll be recording, most of your "live" calls will be outbound. Recording phone conversations can be a tricky affair that requires extra software and/or hardware to make it happen. Sure, you can just "MacGyver" it and set up a microphone next to your speakerphone and hope for the best, but that isn't necessary. Like many other areas of podcasting, you can spend as little or as much as you'd like to get phone conversations into your podcast. From free Internet telephony technologies such as Skype to simple Radio Shack adapters ($20 to $30) to professional-grade digital hybrids costing hundreds or even thousands of dollars, there are plenty of ways to go about it. We'll delve deeply into the mechanics of the various options when we talk about equipment in Chapter 5.

Other elements

You may also need to plan playing sponsorship announcements and advertisements or segments of other people's podcasts during your show.

Sponsorships and advertisements

You'll need to plan ahead before including sponsorship announcements or advertisements in your podcast. We'll talk more about the specifics of these in Chapter 11, but for now make sure you know whether you're reading live announcements or playing a prerecorded element. Also, give thought to where in your podcast to play these announcements. Most podcasters tend to get them out of the way early on, so once the show starts, it can flow without interruption. Others like to play or read sponsorship announcements or ads during a transition in the middle of the show, once things have gotten off to a clean start. Really, any time is worthwhile, except at the end. If you leave the plug until the end of your podcast, your sponsor or advertiser may feel like you're burying their announcement where people can too easily stop listening.

Segments of other podcasts

You never know, you may want to play segments from other people's podcasts on your own, whether you're reviewing their show, recommending their show, or ridiculing their show. Regardless of your intentions, get permission from the other podcaster to use the segment. The other podcaster will most likely be flattered that you thought of him and could end up becoming a valuable friend and ally later on (more on this topic in Chapter 10).

Summary

Wow. If you've gone through all the development and planning we've talked about in this chapter, you're just about ready to roll. Get yourself together, find a theme song, get permission to use it, and sit down for your first show prep session. You've done well, Grasshopper. Congratulations.

But you're not ready to podcast just yet—you still have to get your gadgets together. If you're into looking at and buying electronic equipment in the least, the next chapter should be a lot of fun. If you are *not* into equipment, or you have an aversion to anything that plugs into a wall, don't fret; we have some suggestions and recommendations for professional-quality, inexpensive equipment that will get you set up and looking/sounding great with little to no stress.

Chapter 5

AUDIO PODCASTING TOOLS

It's time to do some soul searching and some serious shopping. It's time to put together your podcast studio. Now, as we said before, the price of entry is relatively low. You can record and prep your podcast with nothing more than a microphone and a handful of free software applications. On the other hand, you can very easily spend thousands of dollars on a "power podcaster" rig to ensure you have broadcast-quality sound.

When you first begin to consider all the possibilities—all the hardware and software options—it can be a bit overwhelming. Fear not. In this chapter, we'll discuss everything, from the different kinds of cables you may encounter to what type of microphone to use, and we'll give you insights into the various tools you'll need to record, edit, mix, and master your podcasts. We'll cover the following topics in depth:

- Microphones
- Pop filters
- Headphones
- Mixers
- Cables and connectors
- Balanced and unbalanced audio
- Computer connectors
- Hardware processors

- Audio interfaces and sound cards
- Phone patches and digital hybrids
- Digital recorders and mobile rigs
- Audio recording software

We'll also present "The podcast studio buyer's guide," which outlines our suggestions for complete hardware and software packages. These packages range from a very basic single microphone to an elaborate high-end recording setup. The Broadcast Supply Worldwide (BSW) was so impressed with our podcast studio suggestions that the company now carries these products at a great discount on its website at www.bswusa.com/podcastsolutions. Check out the BSW site for great savings. We've purchased a lot of equipment from BSW, and we're thrilled that the company has chosen to offer these packages to our readers.

The equipment required to podcast spans the gamut from simple to complex. As an interesting note, in fall 2004, Duke University equipped the entire incoming freshman class with a "podcasting kit" (whether the students knew it or not). Many read about the fact that the students all received Apple iPods, but what didn't receive quite as much attention was that they also received a Griffin iTalk, which allowed them to record on their iPods (see Figure 5-1). That is all it takes to turn an iPod into a voice recorder. Simple solutions like that, or the Personal Audio Recorder software for Palm, enable you to get some basic voice recording done. In fact, many of the Duke University students ended up using their new setups to record field notes for their classes.

Figure 5-1. The Griffin iTalk Pro plugs directly into any iPod with a dock connector to turn it into a CD-quality recording device.

Let's take a look at the equipment it takes to set up a quality podcast studio for you to record your new show.

Microphones

Many would argue—and rightfully so—that the microphone is the single most important piece of hardware in an audio toolbox. The weakest link in your audio chain is going to determine your recording's sound quality. That being the case, why start out with a weak link?

Before trying to determine which mic might be best for you, let's go over some microphone terminology so you have a better idea of what you're getting into.

Types of microphones

Microphones generally pick up sound waves and convert those waves into a form that can be used by electronic equipment in one of two ways.

Dynamic microphone

A **dynamic** microphone uses a wire coil and a magnet to create the audio signal. A diaphragm is attached to the coil, and as sound waves hit the diaphragm, they move the coil back and forth past the magnet. As you may remember from your junior high science class, a wire coil moving within a magnetic field generates an electrical current in the wire. This electrical current travels through the mic cable to the other equipment in the audio chain, where it may be saved as a recording or sent to a device, such as a loudspeaker or headphones, which can convert the electrical signal back into sound waves.

Dynamic mics are great general-purpose microphones, and because they have very few moving parts, they're rugged and durable. They generate their own current, so no external power source is needed.

Condenser microphone

A **condenser** (or **capacitor**) mic produces an audio signal when sound waves hitting the diaphragm cause two plates within a small capacitor to vibrate, creating variations in the voltage between the plates. When the plates are close together, a charge current occurs. When they are farther apart, a discharge current occurs. What does this mean? As with the dynamic mic, the variations in the electrical current can be reinterpreted as sound waves by the receiving electrical equipment.

A condenser mic needs a power source to work, since it requires voltage across the capacitor. The power is usually supplied by a small battery within the microphone or by external power known as **phantom power**.

> *Phantom power is a direct electrical current, usually between 12 and 48 volts, that supplies microphones and other equipment power through audio cables. Forty-eight-volt phantom power is the most common and is often supplied by mixers and mic preamps.*

Condenser mics are sensitive and very responsive, and they create a much stronger signal than dynamic mics. This makes them an ideal choice for studio work, where you may want to pick up subtle shades of vocal tones in speech. However, they are less durable than dynamic mics.

Pickup pattern

Just as mics vary in the ways they capture a sound wave mechanically, they also have differing **pickup patterns**. The pickup pattern establishes exactly from which directions the mic will and won't pick up sounds. In the sections that follow, we'll describe the pickup patterns mics fall into: omnidirectional, unidirectional, and bidirectional.

Omnidirectional

Omnidirectional mics pick up sound from all directions equally (see Figure 5-2). They are best suited for recording more than one or two people at a time with a single mic, but they will also pick up all the sounds around those people while they are talking. Also, they pick up too much extraneous sound for use in a studio (unless you want your audience to hear everything that's going on). Since you're capturing sound equally from all around, the resulting recording may be too unfocused for your use.

Unidirectional

As its name implies, a unidirectional mic will pick up a clear sound wave from only one direction. A unidirectional mic gives the best isolation of sound, since its pickup pattern is so finite. Unidirectional mics include the **cardioid** and **hypercardioid**.

Cardioid is a very scientific-sounding way of saying heart-shaped (see Figure 5-3). Sounds are picked up predominantly from the front, but with some pickup on the sides. This pattern is good for recording podcasts in the studio, since it is well suited for isolating the speaker's voice while still giving a little latitude in the pattern for side-to-side movement while speaking. For example, you can shift in your seat a little without affecting the level at which your voice is being recorded.

However, there are some drawbacks with cardioid mics. They tend to suffer from the **proximity effect**, in which the mic becomes more sensitive to low-frequency sounds as the sound source gets very close. If you're within a few inches of a cardioid mic, you may get excessive lows and "boominess." You may like that sound, but it's not natural or accurate. Also, because off-axis frequency response varies, if you use a cardioid as a handheld mic for a roving reporter–type interview, you'll get a distracting whooshing sound as you move the mic back and forth from person to person. That is why most reporters' handheld mics are omnidirectional.

Our general recommendation is to use a cardioid mic (unidirectional) in the studio and an omnidirectional mic for roving-reporter work. We'd like to emphasize that this is a "general" recommendation—there are exceptions to it, some of which we've noted in this chapter.

Hypercardioid is a more extreme version of the cardioid, with the sides of the pattern drawn in to form a narrow sweet spot (see Figure 5-4), making this pattern much more directional and rejecting almost all sound outside its pickup pattern. Hypercardioids are used in the movie business to record dialogue, and their typically long, thin design has earned them the moniker "shotgun mic."

Figure 5-2. This polar pattern is used to illustrate the directional properties of a microphone. The gray circle around the outside shows an omnidirectional pattern.

Figure 5-3. The heart-shaped pattern of a cardioid microphone

Figure 5-4. A hypercardioid pattern. Notice the narrowed sides and the extra area of pickup in the back of the mic.

Some of the top voice-over talents in the country use hypercardioids in their home studios. There is some debate about whether this is really the best way to go for podcasters, however, because a hypercardioid rejects so much sound that the recording can sound cold and unnatural. Only a very practiced voice artist can pull off using a shotgun mic to do voice-over work, because it requires that the artist never stray from that narrow pattern. We can't, in good faith, recommend going to a hypercardioid for your home studio. You'd just be begging for trouble.

Bidirectional

Although we haven't seen many of these, there are bidirectional mics with a double cardioid pattern that looks like a figure eight (see Figure 5-5). This might make a good mic for a two-person podcast, if the podcasters were dead-set against using separate mics.

Microphone recommendations

The microphone you buy will depend largely on your budget (as so many things in life do). The entry level for a decent mic starts at about US$100. As you might imagine, beyond that, the sky is the limit (Neumann sells a broadcast mic for around $4,000!). We can't recommend going overboard, but do keep in mind how important your mic is. In a way, your microphone is the first step in the portal to your listeners. Much like a bad camera lens can cloud or distort a photograph, a bad mic can ruin your audio.

Figure 5-5. A bidirectional pickup pattern

Please note that all prices listed in this chapter are approximate—though the prices were correct at the time of this writing, they are, of course, subject to change. All prices are in U.S. dollars.

Just starting out

Many podcasters have started out with a USB-type headset mic similar to those used for gaming or dictation. These can be found at most computer or office-supply stores. USB headset mics are generally **noise canceling**, meaning they actually subtract the sound hitting one diaphragm from the sound that hits another. (Many broadcast headset microphones are also of this type.) So, the only sound that gets through is sound that is louder to one diaphragm than the other. These can be particularly advantageous in noisy environments. Using headset or head-worn mics is also advantageous during interviews with guests with bad mic technique, since the distance between the mic and a person's mouth stays fairly constant. A $50 USB headset for a podcaster who is going to be outside a controlled (quiet) environment and who will be recording himself or herself directly to a laptop is a good solution. That said, if you find yourself getting addicted to podcasting, we suggest you invest in a quality mic that will last for the long haul.

In the sections that follow, we'll recommend some microphones in each of a few budget brackets.

The $100 zone

You should probably start looking for a mic in at least the $100 range. You'll likely be disappointed with the sound quality if you purchase a mic for less than $100. Dan used a $50 mic he had lying around his house for more than 40 podcasts, but he had to struggle to work within its limits (he could never touch it while he was recording, or it would make a horrible sound). Michael was smart enough to get a decent mic early on, and it shows in his sound quality.

Plenty of mics are available in this price range, and for someone just starting out, the mics we suggest here will serve you very well. Should you later decide you have a need for a "better" mic, you can then make the choice to upgrade.

We recommend the Audio Technica AT2020. It is a great-sounding **side address** (meaning you talk into the side instead of the top) electret cardioid condenser mic with a clean and bright sound, and it has many of the same features as its siblings in the AT30 and AT40 series.

Another great find, recommended to us by Paul Figgiani of Podcast Academy (http.podcastacademy. com), is the KEL Audio HM-1 (www.kelaudio.com). Available only from KEL, it is a small and rugged mic with a warm, round tone, and it's perfect for adding some character to thin or edgy sounds. Check out the KEL website to hear samples of various voices and instruments recorded with an HM-1.

One of the mics in this price range most commonly used among podcasters is the Marshall MXL-990, which retails for around $60 to $70. It's reasonable price, and the included carrying case and shock mount make it very attractive to budget-conscious podcasters. Strangely, the MXL-990 wasn't designed for vocal use, but it has somehow managed to catch on among podcasters anyway.

The mics just listed are all for studio use and require phantom power. If you are looking for a rugged handheld mic for on-the-go interviews, check out the Electrovoice 635A. It is a great omnidirectional dynamic mic that is also extremely durable. Another mic to take a look at for double-duty studio work and fieldwork is the Sennheiser E835.

The $200–$300 zone

In this price range, we recommend the big brothers of the Audio Technica AT2020: the AT3035 ($200) and the AT4040 ($300).

For out-in-the-field interview work, take a look at the Sennheiser MD46 ($180). (Yes, we know it is a cardioid mic and therefore contradicts our earlier recommendation of cardioids for the studio and omnidirectionals for the field, but trust us, this is the exception that proves the rule.)

For headset fans who want a professional-level combination of noise-canceling mic and headphones (think sportscaster and live event commentary), take a look at the Beyerdynamic DT290 ($240). When ordering, make sure to ask whether it has XLR and TRS connectors added for the mic and headset. The DT290 used with the handheld Sennheiser MD46 makes for a great live event interview and recording setup.

The $350–$400 zone

Without a doubt, the big boys of podcast recording (and broadcasting, for that matter) are the Electrovoice RE20 ($400) and the Shure SM7B ($350). These are both professional-level dynamic cardioid microphones used extensively in broadcast and recording studios around the United States. Both are known for their relative lack of proximity effect. Because they are dynamic mics, they require no phantom power. The downside is that they need to be used with powerful and extremely quiet mic preamps. Careful selection of equipment to complement these impressive mics will yield superior audio quality.

More than $400

If you're looking to spend more than $400 on a microphone, you're on your own. Frankly, if you're willing to put that kind of money into a mic to record audio that will be compressed to an MP3, you're crazier than we are. Let us know what you get and how it sounds.

Pop filters

You'll also need a **pop filter**, for when you're "popping your p's." A pop filter is a windscreen or foam filter that helps reduce popping noises created by breath or speech when a person says a plosive such as "p" or "b." A **plosive** is a consonant that is pronounced by completely closing the lips or air passage and then releasing air suddenly. Without a pop filter between you and your microphone, your listeners will feel like they're being barraged by popping explosions—not a relaxing listening experience. You can use the foam version that fits snugly over your mic or the screen version that is suspended between you and the mic. Either way, use one.

Headphones

Besides your mic, your headphones are the next most important piece of gear for your podcast studio. You can choose from a great many headphones. Make sure the ones you select are comfortable, because you'll wear them not only when you record but also when you edit. If you don't already have a set, take a look at the bargain-priced Sennheiser HD202 ($20) or the favorite among broadcasting professionals, the Sony MDR 7506 ($100). These headphones are the standard "clamshell" style and come highly recommended, and with them you'll be able to clearly hear what's going on during recording and editing.

Another option is "in-ear" monitors. These are small ear bud–style earphones that actually sit slightly into your ear canal, sealing it off for better sound reproduction. Popular options include the Etymotic ER4 ($299) and any number of options from Ultimate Ears. Although Ultimate Ears have different models at numerous price points, Michael has had good luck with his pair of triple.fi 10 pros ($399) (see Figure 5-6).

Figure 5-6. Ultimate Ears triple.fi 10 pro in ear–style headphones

You'll also find us reminding you at every opportunity to make sure you connect your headphones as far along in the audio chain as possible so you can hear the cumulative effect of all your audio gear.

For the truly audiophile sound obsessed, you can consider a headphone amplifier. As you might imagine, the folks who built your computer wanted to make sure you would get sound out of that headphone jack, but it is fair to say that it was not necessarily their priority that it was pristine audio—it just needed to work. By bypassing the internal headphone amplifier in your computer and using an outboard model, you can get superior sound resolution. The best part is, it makes your CD and DVDs sound better also. Take a look at the offerings from HeadRoom (www.headphone.com, Figure 5-7). Michael has been using both their portable and desktop units for years.

Figure 5-7. HeadRoom Total Bithead portable headphone amplifier

Mixers

Some podcasters, depending on their setup and the software they're using, opt to not use a mixer or any external audio sources such as CD players, MP3 players, and so forth. They record on to their computer as the computer plays any additional audio. We'll discuss later how that all works. However, unless you are using a USB microphone, we strongly suggest you use a mixer, particularly because it will allow you to use many of the microphones listed in the previous section.

For the most part, podcasters use mixers to combine (**mix**) the sounds from their microphones with other audio sources while they are recording. A mixer allows you to have independent control over each of these various inputs as you combine them in your audio chain. As an example, a mixer allows you to have two different mics set at different input volumes. This may be helpful, for example, with a husband and wife podcast, where the husband may naturally speak, well, louder. The mixer can be used to adjust for this. A mixer will give you multiple inputs, each with its own volume adjustments and, in some cases, equalization controls. Also, a good mixer will supply phantom power should you choose to use a condenser mic. Finally, many mics don't have enough output to drive a PC's mic input on their own—a mixer solves this problem. The bottom line is that you should use a mixer.

Using a mixer, you can play your intro music and adjust its level while you begin recording your voice, and then perhaps you can add in a recorded comment or another song as you record. Or you can use the mixer simply as an interface between your computer and your audio equipment.

Since you will most likely be recording on your computer, we need to note that many computers don't come with the perfect audio inputs needed for recording. That is why you need to be aware of how you will connect your mixer to your computer. Some of the mixers we recommend have connectors built right in, while others require a bit of outside assistance. Also, you need to make sure that your sound card enables you to record sound at top quality (16-bit/44kHz).

In addition, you'll need to give some thought to whether you want to use external dynamics processors such as compressors, limiters, and gates. We'll get into what each of these actually does in the next chapter, but for now just understand that dynamics processors help make your recording more even and polished-sounding. Some dynamics processing can be done with software plug-ins, but other processes are best handled during recording by hardware. If you want to use hardware processors (we know, it's a bit early to determine that now; hang in there), you'll need a mixer that has channel inserts. We'll talk more about channel inserts in the upcoming "Cables and connectors" section.

The main things to look for in a mixer are as follows:

- Quiet mic preamps (that raise the level of the mic signal)
- Enough microphone inputs for your needs
- Channel inserts (if you will use external processors)
- Phantom power (if you are using a condenser mic)

Recommended mixers

Now let's look at a few mixers we recommend for podcasting in the different price ranges.

5

Less than $100

The mixer known by many as the "podcaster's best friend" is the Behringer UB802, also known as the Eurorack 8. This is a basic mixer with two mic preamps and six total inputs. Best of all, you can find it for around $60.

Less than $200

A number of nice mixers are available in this price range. Take a look at the Yamaha MG10-2 ($129) or the Tapco Blend 6 ($149). Our personal favorite is the Alesis Multi Mix 8 USB ($199), which features four mic inputs, eight total channels, and EQ. Best of all, it provides a means of communicating with your computer via USB. We have heard good things about this mixer from many of the podcasters using it.

More than $200

In this price range, you're paying for the number of channels and the quality of components. Michael uses the Mackie Onyx 1220 (around $640). The Onyx series by Mackie is used by a number of podcasters who have taken the studio route (for example, "Reel Reviews," "Grape Radio," "IT Conversations," and "The Point Podcast"). They include boutique-quality preamps, Perkins EQ, and all kinds of nice features, including the ability to add a 24-bit/96kHz multichannel FireWire output card. Overall, it's a very nice unit.

Cables and connectors

Things may start to get a bit confusing if we don't talk for a moment about the different cables and connectors you will encounter as you are planning, purchasing, and setting up your podcast studio. You may not end up using each of the audio equipment connectors mentioned in the sections that follow, but it is good to know what they all are.

RCA connector

RCA connectors are the small, nonlocking mono connectors (see Figure 5-8) you've been using all your life on your stereo equipment to attach turntables, tape decks, and CD players to your amplifier or receiver. Red is for the right channel, white is for the left channel, and yellow is for video.

Figure 5-8. RCA connectors

1/4" phone jack

The "phone" in "phone jack" relates to *gramophone*, not *telephone*. These are the large, 1/4" connectors commonly associated with guitars and headphones (well, old-school headphones). Phone jacks are used for mono signals and stereo signals, as well as channel inserts to connect hardware boxes to mixers. At a glance, all phone jacks look the same, but they are not. Depending on the type of tip a phone jack has and the way that tip is wired, the phone jack will serve very different functions (see Figure 5-9):

- **Tip-sleeve (TS)**: This is a mono phone jack, where there is a connection on the tip of the jack and one on the sleeve. These are used for unbalanced audio.

- **Tip-ring-sleeve (TRS)**: This is a 1/4" plug with three connections (the tip, the ring, and the sleeve). It is used for balanced audio (see the section "Balanced and unbalanced audio" for more information). The same type of plug, with different wiring, is used for stereo headphones.

Figure 5-9. Two types of phone jacks: tip-sleeve (top) and tip-ring-sleeve (bottom)

Channel insert cable

This is a special Y-shaped cable (see Figure 5-10) used to connect effects processors such as compressors and gates to your mixer. Using a channel insert cable isn't the only way to connect these items, but it is by far the easiest.

A single TRS phone jack is connected to the mixer channel insert jack, offering three separate connections. The cable then connects to the effects processor after splitting into two TS phone jacks: one to input the signal and one to send it back to the mixer. In this way, the signal goes from the mixer through the effects processor and then back to the mixer, to be combined with other audio elements.

Figure 5-10. A channel insert cable sends a signal from the mixer to an effects processor and back.

1/8" mini plug

The most common 1/8" mini plug is a tiny version of a TRS phone jack. It's used for post-Walkman-era stereo headphones and other input/output devises. Mono (TS) versions also exist. It looks just like the TS plug shown in Figure 5-9, only smaller.

XLR connector

XLR connectors are the large, professional-grade connectors you'll see on pro and semi-pro audio gear (see Figure 5-11). They are locking connectors that can carry a balanced audio signal and phantom power. If you have a choice between using an XLR cable to connect your mic to a mixer and a 1/4" TRS phone jack, choose the XLR cable—it is more rugged, and it will produce a cleaner, stronger signal.

Figure 5-11. XLR connectors

XLR/phone combo jack

We're starting to see combo jacks on more and more audio equipment, especially the newer, smaller home studio computer interfaces. Small and versatile, these combination jacks work with either 1/4" plugs or XLR plugs.

Balanced and unbalanced audio

Balanced audio is a way of greatly reducing noise and interference from your cables, resulting in cleaner recordings. Long audio cables make wonderful antennae, and they pick up all sorts of stray signals floating around in the air: radio waves, radiation from computer monitors, and interference from electrical currents.

In an unbalanced cable, two wires are used to carry the signal. The one that carries the sound is the **hot line**, and the other is the **earth** or **ground line**. These cables are fine for short distances and consumer electronics. As soon as you get into longer cables and pro gear, preventing potential noise in the line becomes a concern. Also, because mic signals are at a much lower level, balanced audio is almost always necessary.

Balanced cables have three wires: two hot lines and one ground line. Using an XLR connector as an example, pins 2 and 3 carry the opposite sides of the signal. The audio is the difference or the voltage between the two hot lines. Let's call them, for example, ground A and B. The audio is A–B—that's what you get if you connect a voltmeter or any other device across the two wires. The ground is only for shielding; it carries no signal. Cut the ground, and you still get the audio. It shields noise because the A and B wires are twisted together, and if any noise or hum gets into one, it tends to get into both. So if you have noise on A and the same noise on B, the A–B (difference) between them tends toward zero.

Computer connectors

In the following sections, we'll take a look at the most common computer connectors used with audio gear.

USB

Universal Serial Bus (USB) was designed to replace the array of serial connectors and parallel ports and attach everything from mice to printers to your computer quickly and easily (see Figure 5-12). USB provides a serial bus standard, which makes the hot swapping of devices possible, without restarting the computer. USB connectors offer transfer rates well above what is needed to push audio into your computer; therefore, they have become a very common means of connecting PCs with mics, mixers, and audio interfaces.

Figure 5-12. USB connectors

FireWire/IEEE 1394

FireWire started as a way for Apple engineers to achieve high-speed transfers to and from their internal hard drives, while simplifying the cabling system. It was a great idea that didn't work out as the company had planned. Instead, Apple realized that its "FireWire" was much more useful for connecting to external drives and peripherals. Apple took its new technology to the Institute of Electrical and Electronics Engineers (IEEE), and in 1995 the official FireWire specifications were released as IEEE 1394. FireWire made possible transfers at speeds of roughly between 100 Mbps and 400Mbps. In 2003, Apple commercially introduced FireWire 800 (IEEE 1394b), which enables transfers of up to 800Mbps and in 2007 published specs for FireWire S800T, with updated port specs and hopes of leading toward a future combined FireWire/Ethernet port.

FireWire made it possible for Windows and Mac users to connect high-speed, high-load devices to their computers, and it essentially made the digital video revolution possible (Sony refers to its FireWire as **iLink**). FireWire (see Figure 5-13) is now used to connect PCs with video cameras, hard drives, scanners, webcams, and audio mixers. Yes, mixers. FireWire offers fast, clean, all-digital transfers of audio to your computer.

Figure 5-13. A six-pin FireWire connector (aka IEEE 1394 or iLink)

Audio interfaces and sound cards

Now that you know all about mixers and computer connectors, you need a way to get the audio from your mixer into your computer. Sometimes it's as easy as plugging the mixer directly into the computer, as with the Alesis mixer, which has a built-in USB connection. Usually, though, it's not quite that straightforward. While many computers come equipped with some sort of audio connection, a dedicated "quality" audio interface will probably serve you best in the long run. If your computer has USB inputs (and many do), a straightforward USB audio interface will do the trick nicely. If not, you may want to dive in and get a pro or "prosumer"-level sound card.

In the following sections, we'll start off by looking at the most basic interfaces, and then we'll move on to cover the more high-end solutions.

USB audio interfaces

A USB interface acts as a fairly simple bridge between your audio equipment and your computer. The audio equipment plugs in on one end of the interface, and the interface plugs into a USB port on your computer. It's that simple.

The most pared-down version of a USB interface is probably the popular Griffin iMic (www.griffintechnology.com, $40), which accepts 1/8" stereo inputs at either line or mic level. It also supports line-level outputs for connecting your iMic to speakers or another recording device. According to Griffin, using the iMic will give you sound superior to what you would get using a built-in sound card. We've used the iMic and found it to be a handy and reliable interface.

The Edirol UA-1EX Audio Interface (www.edirol.com, $100) offers component-quality sound to and from your computer. The Edirol uses RCA inputs for superior sound, and it includes optical output to transfer digital signals to digital recorders and a headphone jack for monitoring the sound going to the computer.

The M-Audio MobilePre (www.m-audio.com, $150) is a USB-powered preamp and audio interface with three kinds of audio inputs and outputs, including two microphone/instrument preamps for crisp 16-bit/48kHz sound. For his very first podcasts, Michael paired this unit with a Radio Shack 33-3001 Pro-Unidirectional Dynamic mic and got very acceptable results.

The Edirol UA25 ($250), while somewhat expensive, comes highly recommended. It has a pair of XLR/TRS combo jacks with phantom power, S/P DIF optical I/O ports, and MIDI IN/OUT ports, as well as a built-in analog limiter. We can't recommend the UA25 enough.

As a side note, if all you will ever need to do is simply record from one or two mics and you will do all your "mixing" (such as adding music) in postproduction, any of the units just mentioned (Edirol or M-Audio) will work perfectly and take the place of your mixer.

FireWire-capable audio interfaces are also available. They can be rather expensive, but you have some high-quality choices. If you're interested, check out the PreSonus FIREBOX ($400), the M-Audio FireWire 410 ($300), or the MOTU Traveler ($895).

Sound cards

Whereas the audio interface is an external bridge between the computer and the audio equipment, a sound card is installed directly into the body of the machine to extend the audio capabilities of your PC. (Keep in mind that, generally speaking, an external interface will be superior to an internal sound card.) The card includes digital-to-analog converters for audio outputs and analog-to-digital converters for audio inputs. The inputs/outputs are often mounted to the card itself and end up giving you convenient connectors right on the side or back of the computer. Other times, the card connects to an external hub that houses your inputs and outputs. Either way, the goal is to get crystal-clear sound into and out of a PC that originally couldn't accomplish these tasks on its own.

SoundBlaster (www.soundblaster.com) from Creative Technology (maker of the Zen Micro MP3 player) was the sound card that started it all back in 1989. The current incarnations offer not only better-than-CD-quality input/output, but even support home theater standards such as DTS-ES and Dolby Digital EX, as well as beloved THX certification, for the ultimate in home theater and gaming sound.

Phone patches and digital hybrids

To record phone calls, you need to find a way to patch the audio from those calls into your mixer. To do this, you can use either a simple and inexpensive phone patch or a rather expensive, but completely professional, digital hybrid.

Phone patch

A **phone patch** or **tap** is a simple bit of hardware that takes the sound from your phone line and sends it directly into the mixer. The signal is not processed in any way, so what you record is every sound going through the phone: the caller's voice and your own. While this is not ideal, it certainly works. Check out the Radio Shack Recorder Control ($26).

Digital hybrid

A **digital hybrid** is a rather expensive piece of professional hardware that strips out the host's voice, leaving the caller's voice in isolation. The hybrid is connected to your mixer so that you can use your microphone for your side of the conversation and record the caller's voice on a separate channel. While there is still some bleed-through, it can easily be cleaned up in postproduction. For our phone interviews for "Podcast Solutions" (www.podcastsolutions.com), we used a Telos One ($895). Telos (www.telos-systems.com) makes some of the best hybrids on the market. Another popular manufacturer of hybrids is JK Audio (www.jkaudio.com).

> *Here's a tip that applies to using hybrids as well as any time you have an interview with two main sources. Record each on a separate track or channel. For example, record your mic track on the left channel and the hybrid audio on the right channel. That way, you can tweak and adjust the channels separately prior to a final mixdown. This would be impossible if you recorded the two channels as a combined audio signal. By following this advice, you can repair all kinds of audio "sins" that would otherwise be impossible to fix. This is how all the "Podcast Solutions" (www.podcastsolutions.com) phone interviews were recorded.*

Double-ender

There is a way to get around having any hardware to break out the sound. If your callers are also set up to record themselves, you can try a technique referred to as a **double-ender**. (This method is perfect for recording other podcasters, since they are already set up to record.) Here's how it works: while you talk to your guest on the phone, you record your end of the conversation as you would any podcast by speaking into your microphone. Have your guest do the same from his end. When the call is finished, you and your guest will each have a pristine recording of your own side of the conversation. Now, simply edit the two "ends" together by laying one on top of the other and syncing them up. Voilà! It sounds like you had a live, in-studio guest, even though the other person could have actually been located miles and miles away during your conversation.

Of course, recording and mixing a double-ender every time you want to take a caller may end up being more trouble than it's worth, and not every caller will have the necessary equipment or skills to make the audio sound good.

Stand-alone digital recorders and mobile rigs

We've assumed up to this point that you're recording sound to your computer. Actually, that isn't necessarily the only solution. It's an incredibly practical one, because odds are good that you already own a computer and don't have any other means of recording digital audio, but a number of noncomputer options are worth investigating, particularly if you're planning to do some recording in the field (that is, on location). Lugging a laptop around to interview people at a political rally may not be the best approach, either for your podcast or for your equipment. We recommend looking into using a digital recorder for this sort of task.

Another reason to investigate a digital recorder is to avoid the likelihood of losing a podcast because of a computer crash or hard drive "hiccup." Most podcasters have lost at least one recording to a system failure. Now, this is not to say that digital recorders are foolproof, but since they're designed solely for the purpose of recording and playing sound, they're far less likely to die on you midshow. Let's face it, isn't it a bit much to expect one machine to record, edit, encode, and upload, *as well as* balance your checkbook, retouch your photos, play Tetris, and catalog your DVD collection?

The very small player/recorders that took podcasting by storm in the first couple of years were the iRiver 700 and 800 series. They were compact and easy to use, and they recorded to a proprietary high-quality MP3 format (to their internal memory) that you could easily convert to standard MP3, WAV, or AIFF format. Recording to MP3 is never the best way to go, but considering the size of the iRivers and their incredibly reasonable price, it may have been worth the sacrifice. (The closest thing on the market to iRiver at this writing is their T60 series. Frankly, we don't know anyone who uses one, so we can't honestly recommend them. We would hate to advise you get one and then find out that there are no audio/mic inputs.)

For those who don't want to skimp in *any* department, there is the Marantz PMD670 Professional Solid State Portable Recorder. Marantz has been a leading name in portable recording units for about as long as we can remember, and it is leading the field in professional digital recorders. The Marantz machines record WAV, BWF, MP3, and MP2 format files to inexpensive CompactFlash cards, with more than 40 assignable quality settings. These units have RCA input/output and XLR inputs, so you can connect professional microphones directly to the recorder—even condenser mics that require phantom power. The Marantz PMD670 is such a solid machine that we even recommend it as a tabletop unit for in-studio use.

The podcast studio buyer's guide

In this section, we'll outline several potential podcast rigs for you to check out and compare. For each item, we include information on its current "street price" (as opposed to the much higher manufacturer's suggested retail price, or MSRP), but each of these podcast studio setups is available as a discounted package from our friends at BSW (www.bswusa.com/podcastsolutions).

We'd like to point out up front that our gear suggestions come from hard-won experience. We've discovered (the hard way) that the most inexpensive gear usually gets replaced very quickly, causing you to spend more than if you had just bought the right piece of equipment up front. You can acquire most of these packages piecemeal over time as you build your podcast studio. First we'll showcase our picks for various studio setups, and then we'll present some options for podcasters on the go.

Just a mic

If you're just looking for a microphone that you can plug directly into your PC, there are plenty to choose from, from the relatively simple to mics that seem to be self-contained studios. We recommend the following:

- Samson C01U USB Studio Condenser Micropohone ($89)
- Sound Engineering sE 2200A Studio Condenser Mic ($299)

Just plug it in and go. This USB mic is immediately recognized by your PC or Mac and is ready to record.

Podcast starter

These are our recommendations for those just starting out:

- Audio Technica AT2020 Studio Cardioid Condenser Microphone ($100)
- Alesis MultiMix 8 USB Mixer ($150)

The AT2020 offers unsurpassed sound for the price. There is no need for an additional audio interface, since the Alesis MultiMix has a USB connection built in.

Podcast veteran

Here's what we recommend for experienced podcasters:

- Audio Technica AT3035 Cardioid Condenser Microphone ($200)
- Yamaha MG 8 Mixer ($150)
- Edirol UA-1EX ($100)
- dbx 266XL Dual Compressor/Gate ($150)

The AT3035 offers the clear tones you'd expect for Audio Technica at twice the price. The Yahama mixer is a great piece of equipment, with very quiet preamps and channel inserts to enable proper connection to the dbx 266, a wonderful entry-priced professional compressor/gate. The 266XL accepts "dual" inputs, so you can use it with two separate mic inputs. The mixer connects to your PC or Mac via the Edirol UA-1X.

Podcast professional

Now for the professionals out there:

- Electrovoice RE20 ($400) or the Shure SM7B ($350).
- Mackie Onyx 1220 12-Channel Mixer ($640).
- dbx 1066 Compressor/Gate/Limiter ($400).
- Add the portable system mentioned in the next section, or connect directly to an audio interface such as the Edirol UA-1EX ($100).

The Mackie Onyx mixer is strong enough and quiet enough to push these fantastic broadcast mics, and the dbx 1066 offers top-notch signal processing. This podcast studio will never disappoint and is perfect for the podcast entrepreneur (see Chapter 11) or businesses that want quality audio to use in their podcasts.

Portable podcast professional

This is the same gear that Michael used when Disneyland brought him in to host and produce the Disneyland 50th Anniversary celebration (see Figure 5-14):

- Marantz PMD670 ($699)
- Sennheiser MD46 Interview Microphone ($170)

The Sennheiser MD46 performs flawlessly in high-noise environments where many on-the-go interviews are recorded. The Marantz PMD670 allows for a total portable recording solution direct to CompactFlash. Take this setup home and connect to any of the previously mentioned packages, and you have a perfect dual-purpose digital recording solution.

Figure 5-14. Marantz PMD670 and Sennheiser MD46 mic
(Photo © 2005 Jason Niedle)

Ultramobile rig

Finally, for those looking to record unobtrusively, take a look at this nice portable setup (see Figure 5-15 for a photo of the mic):

- iRiver 899 ($179)
- Giant Squid Audio Lab Omnidirectional Lapel Microphone ($55)

Figure 5-15. Giant Squid Audio Lab Omnidirectional Lapel Microphone

The iRiver 899 and the Giant Squid Audio Lab mic (www.giant-squid-audio-lab.com) are so small no one will even notice that you're podcasting. Sometimes, that's a good thing. In addition to this setup being a superb stealth rig, you can get some great audio out of it. Thanks to our friend Geoffrey Kleinman from DVDtalk (www.dvdtalk.com) for this great recommendation. Geoff actually uses this same setup to record press event interviews of movie and DVD releases for his website. His whole mobile recording "studio" fits in his pocket.

Or, take a look at the Griffin iTalk Pro (Figure 5-1), which plugs directly into the iPod's dock connector and records in full "CD-quality" stereo with its built-in microphones. The iTalk Pro even has a line-level audio input so you can plug a powered Giant Squid mic or mixer directly into the iPod for even better sound.

Podcast studio setups

Figure 5-16 and Figure 5-17 show podcast studios employing some of the gear outlined in this section.

Figure 5-16. Michael's home podcast studio, which is set up in the corner of his home theater where he does his "Reel Reviews" (Photo © 2005 Jason Niedle)

Figure 5-17. The "Grape Radio" studio (Photo © 2005 Jason Niedle)

Stringing it all together

So, how does all this equipment fit together? It's pretty simple, actually. Audio signals flow like water, so we'll talk about the setup in terms of the direction that the sounds flow from your mouth to the recording device.

Here's how to set up a standard configuration:

1. Connect your microphone to the mixer's mic inputs, using XLR cables.

2. Connect external sound sources (CD player, iPod, keyboard, and so on) to the mixer's line in inputs using phone plugs. You may need to get adaptors/connectors to make this work (RCA to phone adapters, mini stereo to phone, and so on).

3. If you are using hardware compressor/gates, use special channel insert cables to connect your equipment to the channel insert jacks. The sound will flow from the mixer to the external boxes and then back into the mixer. See the mixer's documentation for full details.

4. Connect a cable from the phone jack of your "main out" to the audio interface plugged into your computer or recording device, whether that is an external USB interface (for example, iMic, Edirol, and so on), a stand-alone recorder (for example, Marantz PMD670), or a sound card with RCA inputs.

5. Monitor your sound using headphones plugged into the headphone jack on the mixer.

It is imperative that you monitor the sound through headphones plugged into the mixer, not the computer. Monitoring the sound from the computer headphone jack will feed that sound back to your ears a split second or two after the sound actually occurs. For instance, you will speak, and then a fraction of a second later, you will hear yourself speak in the headphones. This effect is called **latency**, and it's a killer. When you can hear yourself instantly in your headphones, you can monitor your mic position, your breathing sounds, and so forth. When there is latency, your brain is so busy trying to get your ears to catch up with your mouth that you end up slurring your words like a freshman at a keg party. You will inexplicably elongate all your vowels.

Monitoring through the computer's headphone output is very tempting, especially if you're adding live software effects to your voice that you want to hear in your headphones. Don't do it. Listen to yourself when you're finished recording. You'll sound sober.

Audio recording software

The audio recording and editing software you choose, as much as the hardware you choose, will determine the experience you have recording and editing your podcasts. And, to be clear, you're not just going to be recording—you're going to be recording, editing, processing, mixing, and mastering. It sounds like a lot, and it is. How in depth you want to get with each level of this process (and we'll get into all of it in the following chapters) will to some extent determine what software you use.

The amazing thing about recording to your computer is that it's all digital—1s and 0s. If we were still recording and mixing using analog equipment, there is no way a new podcaster could afford the equipment needed to get the kind of sound quality we can all get now through digital recording.

Now that the sounds are digitized, they can be viewed as a **waveform** (a graphic representation of the dynamics of a sound) and in turn can be cut, copied, and pasted just like graphics or text. We can rearrange the sounds, add echo, reduce noise, change stereo to mono, and increase volume, all without degrading the sound or losing data.

In the following sections, we'll look at several audio recording applications, each available at a different price and with a slightly different set of tools. Keep in mind that even the simplest, least expensive recording software will deliver great sound, as long as the sound going into the computer is good (digital crap in, digital crap out). The major differences between the packages relate to how many features are built in and how well the packages may (or may not) handle certain production and postproduction tasks. Not every package listed here does everything you'll need. By the same token, you'll hardly need all of the features of many of these more robust applications.

Sony Sound Forge

Sony Sound Forge for Windows (see Figure 5-18) is an audio powerhouse that can open and edit WMA, WMV, WAV, MOV, AVI, PCA AIF, and MP3 files, and it can record at up to 24-bit/32-bit 192kHz files.

Figure 5-18. Sony Sound Forge

Audio Hijack Pro

For the Mac OS X, you can easily set up Audio Hijack Pro (www.rogueamoeba.com/audiohijackpro; see Figure 5-19) to record the audio from one application (for example, iTunes) or from all applications currently running by using its Record System Audio setting. This feature has made it an invaluable tool for Mac users, especially those who want to record their voice, music, and live callers all at the same time. At the time of this writing, Audio Hijack Pro has no editing functions, but it does a great job handling plug-ins, so you can easily add dynamic processing as you record.

Figure 5-19. Audio Hijack Pro

BIAS Peak

BIAS Peak (www.bias-inc.com/products/peak) is an industry-standard stereo audio recording, editing, and processing application (see Figure 5-20) for the Macintosh OS. It is the ideal audio utility for podcasters, audio professionals, and enthusiasts. In addition to fast and powerful audio editing, Peak integrates a wide variety of effects and signal processing tools to create custom fades, adjust audio gain, repair digital audio spikes, add real room ambience, change pitch and duration independently, and more, all while offering additional real-time effects such as parametric EQ, compression/limiting, reverb, dozens of other special effects, and access to third-party VST and Audio Unit plug-ins or additional solutions from BIAS such as the highly acclaimed SoundSoap family of audio noise reduction and restoration tools.

Figure 5-20. BIAS Peak

Two-track vs. multitrack

Please remember that there is a big difference between two-track and multitrack software. As we have pointed out, some of the software we have mentioned is two-track only, which is great for recording two stereo tracks, editing, processing, noise reduction . . . all that stuff. But you can't mix in music and so forth. For that, you need multitrack software. The sections that follow provide a few suggestions for multitrack software.

Audacity

Audacity (http://audacity.sourceforge.net) is a free, open source recording and editing application that features multitrack capabilities (see Figure 5-21). This means you can record one track, stop, and then record or paste in another separate track over or under the first. Multitrack capabilities are useful for adding music and sound effects after your initial recording take. Since it is not financed and maintained by a commercial concern, Audacity seems very bare bones, but actually it does most everything you need, and considering the price, it is great. It can handle even professional VST plug-ins, with the use of Audacity VST Enabler (http://audacityteam.org/vst). You can't use plug-ins to process sound as you record with Audacity, but they can be used for mixing and mastering.

Figure 5-21. The Audacity workspace

> *As a side note—and this may seem a bit blunt—you get what you pay for. Many peo-*
> *ple we know (present company included) who use Audacity have lost at least one*
> *recording session to a crash of the application or system. That said, we still think*
> *Audacity is a great starter application, but we suggest always having a backup. When*
> *possible, record to a separate hard drive from the one running the operating system*
> *and applications. This will help avoid many problems, and this advice applies to all*
> *audio editing and recording software.*

Since Audacity is free and is available for Windows, Mac, and Linux, we'll use it for many of the tutorials and screenshots in upcoming chapters.

Adobe Audition

Adobe Audition (www.adobe.com/products/audition/main.html) is a full-featured professional-level
multitrack audio-editing application. It offers advanced mixing and editing as well as support for
effects processing. Many podcasters use the versatile and powerful Audition application as their sole
audio-editing software.

n-Track Studio

n-Track Studio (www.fasoft.com) is an affordable multitrack audio-editing application that has more than enough power for the professional podcaster. n-Track Studio allows you to record and play back an almost unlimited number of independent tracks, limited only by the speed of your computer. It also allows you to apply real-time effects to each track. Support is available for multichannel 16-bit and 24-bit sound cards with sampling frequencies up to 192kHz.

Apple GarageBand

This application is included in the iLife suite on all new Apple Macintosh computers. Before looking elsewhere, give GarageBand a try if you are a Mac user. It has a great, easy-to-understand user interface and is more than capable for all but the most demanding podcasters. It comes preloaded with "radio" stingers and sound effects and is capable of doing live "ducking" (automatically reducing the levels of background music while the host is speaking). Some of the most successful podcasts are produced using GarageBand. But, be aware—if you tell GarageBand that you are making a *podcast*, you will be able to output only an .m4a or MP3 file. Therefore, we highly recommend (and we'll get into this more later) saving a copy of each of your shows at the highest resolution possible, which is not possible in GarageBand unless you tell it you are recording a song. If you choose the Song option before you begin, you can output your project to a full, uncompressed CD-quality file.

Apple Soundtrack Pro

This is the perfect solution for multitrack recording and editing on the Mac (especially if you'll also be working in video). Soundtrack Pro is a powerful professional-level audio-editing application with multitrack support and repair and restoration capabilities. It includes more than 50 effects plug-ins as well as more than 5,000 sound effects and music loops. You can build your own intro and outro music and a full audio effect studio with this one application.

Übercaster

The creators of Übercaster (they're from Germany, can you tell?) have taken elements of GarageBand, CastBlaster, and traditional broadcasting and melded them into one of the most complete podcasting apps you're bound to find (sorry folks, Mac only), mixing "live recording" elements with true multitrack production. As you record, you are able to trigger music beds and sound effects (Figure 5-22), bring in live callers from Voice over IP (see the next section), and play audio from any application on your machine, while Übercaster records each separate element onto a difference track. Why is this important? Now you can edit each track independently of the others, sliding each element around (or deleting it from) the project as you see fit. Even though you've recorded live, every element of your project is completely malleable. You are even able to add extra elements by simple dragging them into the project, or you can revise elements by "punching in" (recording over a specific section only). When you're done, update your podcast info right in Übercaster and output to several audio formats at once.

Figure 5-22. Recording "Old Wave Radio: New 80's Music" using Übercaster

Voice over IP

We weren't sure where to put this section, so we're including it here. Many podcasters use software called **Voice over IP** (**VoIP**) to record phone calls placed over the Internet. With several software packages available for VoIP, you can essentially have endless Internet phone calls with people and record them for your podcast. While the quality is not quite up to the level we would like, the price is right—it's often free.

> Because with VoIP the voice signals of the callers are carried as packets of data over the Internet and audio takes up quite a large file size, you need a decent connection speed to run VoIP applications. We recommend at least 512 kbps, preferably 1Mbps.

The most popular service for podcasters is Skype (www.skype.com), which is available free of charge for multiple platforms. Using a free Skype account and some of the following software you can easily record local and international calls for use in your podcast.

Windows users should check out the free "Skype Certified" Pamela Recorder (www.pamela-systems.com), with Skype call, chat, and video recording built right in. In Skype, click Tools ➤ Do More.

For Windows Vista, there is also HotRecorder (www.hotrecorder.com; around $15 without ads, free with ads), Total Recorder (www.highcriteria.com; around $36 for the professional version), or Replay Radio (www.replay-video.com/replay-radio; around $50). For the Mac, try Ambrosia Software's WireTap Pro (www.ambrosiasw.com; $19). It takes almost no setup and has an idiot-proof one-button interface.

When you use software such as this, you are asking your computer to do a lot: run the operating system, the VoIP software, and the recording software, as well as all those background applications that keep your computer humming along. When possible, to avoid audio recording problems, we highly suggest using an external recorder. Your computer will thank you. Also, as you can imagine, doing so helps you avoid asking your interview subject to redo the interview because your overtaxed computer just froze and ate the recording.

Lastly, remember: it is illegal to record a phone conversation without the consent of all parties on the call. We therefore especially caution against recording someone without their consent and then podcasting it (with your name, URL, and so on, along with it). Just remember to take a moment and make sure everyone knows they're being recorded.

TalkShoe

TalkShoe (Figure 5-23) is sort of a website, sort of an application, and sort of a hosting and ad revenue service. TalkShoe is perfect (or at least is getting perfect) for podcasters who want to have listeners call in to their shows while they are "on the air." Listeners can listen, text chat, or "call in" over the phone or through their computer. The podcaster/host controls which listeners can be heard/recorded on the show through the TalkShoe client (Windows and Mac). It takes some getting used to trying to weed through the chat comments and toggle the callers on and off, but it is the closest thing to doing a live radio show we've seen yet in the world of podcasting. Membership is free for show hosts and listeners, and there is no charge for hosting your recordings on their server and no limit to the number of downloads per month. TalkShoe also offers cash incentives to hosts for using the services and participation in ad revenues.

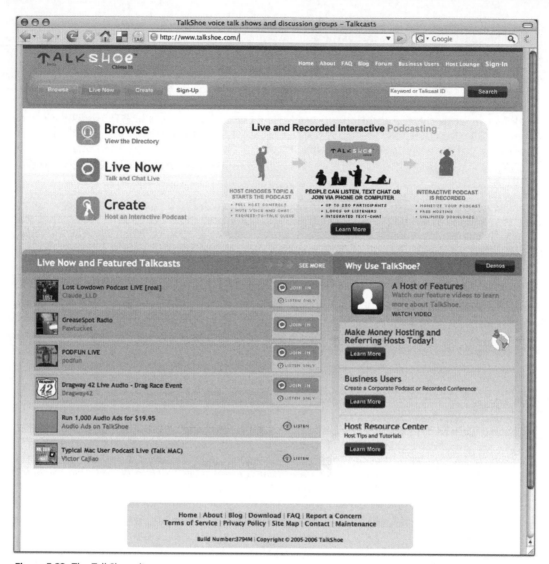

Figure 5-23. The TalkShoe site

Audio plug-ins

We talked briefly and vaguely about dynamics processors—compressors, limiters, gates, and so forth—in this chapter. Now, we know we haven't explained in detail what each of these does (we really get into it in the next chapter), but we do need to mention now that dynamics processing can be handled by stand-alone hardware (for example, dbx 266XL) or by software plug-ins.

Each of the recording applications we mentioned can handle processing using plug-ins, either in real time as you record or afterward when you apply them as you might apply a filter in Photoshop. Check each application's documentation to see exactly how it handles the plug-ins and where they need to be stored on your hard drive. Once the plug-ins are loaded properly, you have the software equivalent of thousands of dollars of audio hardware at your disposal.

If the application you end up using doesn't have many plug-ins preinstalled (for example, Audacity), you can download a great group of free mdaVST plug-ins from www.mda-vst.com (click VST Effects). Also check out Wave Arts at www.wavearts.com. If you ever need to clean up audio, the Master Restoration Suite has all the tools you need. It is a perfect tool to clean and polish your listener call-in line audio.

Summary

A tricky and sometimes nerve-racking part of the podcast setup process can be determining what the right tools are for you. The good news is that we've supplied you with some great starting points and lots of information to mull over. Keep reading the book, let your podcast develop, and then reread this chapter to make sure you're making the most informed decision possible. Many of the applications we've talk about offer downloadable demos, which are an invaluable way to try without buying. Worst-case scenario is to start out using Audacity until you feel the need to upgrade. You can't exactly sample the hardware we've discussed, but if you end up purchasing something that doesn't work out for you, you can always either return it or sell it on one of the many podcasting forums.

For more information on podcasting hardware and software, be sure to check out the Podcast Academy site (http://podcastacademy.com) moderated by Paul Figgiani. As well as having a superb podcasting forum, the Podcast Academy does an outstanding job of keeping up to date with all the developments in hardware and software, not only for use in podcasting, but for video and film production as well. It's well worth stopping by his site with any questions you might have on buying hardware, trying software, setting up equipment, and finding great deals.

Once you have at least your first studio set up, you'll be itching to record. Well, that's what Chapter 6 is all about—not just recording per se, but preparing to record, learning about all that processing we talked about earlier, and developing your voice talents like a pro. Take a deep breath, relax, and settle in. Up next, it's time to say "Hello."

5

Chapter 6

RECORDING AN AUDIO PODCAST

Now, here's where the fun stuff begins. It's time to slide on those headphones, clear your throat, and begin. But before you hit the Record button, let's first go over a few things about recording audio, using the microphone, and making sure your recording is clear with good "levels." The podcast you record today may still be getting hundreds (thousands?) of downloads in six months, so let's ensure you'll still be proud of the sound quality that far down the road. Still being proud of what you said is completely up to you.

If you are planning to do a video podcast, this chapter isn't a complete wash. Although most of this information is specific to recording an audio show, there is a fair amount of info to take away for video too (unless you are planning to do the first silent podcast). At the very least, read up on the next couple of sections, where we talk about the waveform and go over various and sundry audio terms. The idea is typically to get your video podcast to look as professional as possible, but it won't look professional if it doesn't *sound* professional.

Introducing the waveform

Figure 6-1 shows a **waveform**. Actually, it shows two waveforms. A waveform is a visual representation of a sound recording with the magnitude (loudness) of the sound being plotted vertically over time. The top waveform represents the sound recorded on the left stereo channel, and the bottom waveform represents the right

77

stereo channel. You'll notice that along the left side of the window are numbers decreasing from 1.0 to 0.5 to 0 and then increasing. When you look at a waveform, know that 0 is silence and 1.0 is "as loud as possible." Knowing this, you can begin to "read" a sound file. This will be helpful when you record, and it will be essential when it's time to edit your podcast.

> *This waveform measurement scale varies depending on your audio-editing software. In some editing software, the scale will be between -∞dB and 0dB, with 0dB indicating "as loud as possible." Another popular application uses the scale 0 to 100, with 100 representing the limit for peak audio. To avoid confusion, read the instructions that came with your chosen audio recording/editing software to understand the scale used.*

Figure 6-1. Sample waveforms, with a section of speaking, a section of silence, and a section of loud music

In the samples in Figure 6-1, the very beginning of the sound recording is of a person speaking. The dynamics of the voice create unique peaks and valleys in the form. The speech is followed by several seconds of silence, represented by the straight horizontal line at the 0 marker. After the silence is continuously loud rock music, with very little variation in the loudness of the track (it's all just plain loud).

Recording levels

Now, before we go any further, we would like to state that we aren't sound engineers, and if you share the following information with a *real* sound engineer, they'll think we're crazy. Audio engineers work within strict broadcast standards to which we, as podcasters, don't have to adhere. Now, that being said, we'll talk about broadcast standards and give you some insight into conforming to them enough so as not to limit your podcast's future. In the meantime, we're going to stick with what seems to be working for many podcasters.

To generalize, the goal of a good recording is to get relatively consistent levels of sound while allowing for an adequate amount of dynamic range and a total avoidance of **clipping**. This allows listeners to hear both the loud and soft portions of a recording without having to adjust the volume to compensate. Clipping occurs when you go above 1.0 on the scale in Figure 6-1. Once you exceed that limit, you are pushing too much sound into the recording software or device, and the recording will sound terrible. In fact, once you exceed this maximum limit, you will lose the audio portion at the top of the waveform (hence the term "clipping"). Once this digital sound information is lost, it cannot be retrieved. Remember, your final file will depend in large part on the quality of your original recording. The clipped parts will take on a sound not unlike scattering shards of glass on a concrete playground. Nothing sounds worse than a podcaster who continues to clip—it is downright irritating. Definitely not what you want.

If your recording levels are so high that you're experiencing clipping, you're losing sound that you'll never get back. That horrible glass-cracking noise won't go away. You can make it less loud, but that sound will be a permanent part of your recording. The only way to get rid of it is to cut it out (along with whatever you were saying or playing at the time).

It's better to record with your levels lower than you'd like than too high. If your recording levels are low, there are several ways to increase them to bring them up to your desired volume. However, there are compromises here as well. Keep in mind that as you increase the volume of the sound, you're increasing the volume of everything: speech, background noise, and hiss. Obviously, the best solution is to record with good, solid levels from the start. You need to find that balance of a high enough level to get a strong signal but without clipping. It's the Goldilocks approach: not too loud, not too soft—just right. Now you can see why sound engineers earn a good living.

To get more technical about it, you should monitor your sound levels not by looking at the waveform but by watching your meters during recording/playback (see Figure 6-2 later in this chapter) and listening through a pair of reliable headphones. Your headphones will tell you (obviously) what it actually sounds like, but your meters will give you a fairly precise reading of the amount of sound coming in or going out, measured in **decibels** or **dBs** (pronounced "dee bees") or, in the case of digital recording, in **dBfs** (digital full-scale). A professional sound engineer will tell you that your digital recording should maintain levels between –12dBfs and –6dBfs, with 0dBfs being the point at which the sound will degrade. Never go above 0dBfs, no matter what! In visual terms, you want your meters every now and then dipping into the red section; however, if they are always in the red, then you are recording too "hot."

Do a test recording, and check your levels as you go. When you've finished recording the test, see how the levels look on playback. If they're too high and you're clipping, adjust your input/output levels accordingly.

Remember, as we mentioned in Chapter 5, your headphones should be plugged into your audio chain as late in the process as possible. This way, you'll catch as many potential problems as possible while recording. And, you should *always* monitor your sound while you're recording. If you think you look too dorky with headphones on "in the field" (on location), use a pair of discreet ear buds. Just use *something*.

6

Important audio terms and concepts

Even with your levels at perfect output, at this point your recording will probably sound a bit thin. It's not because your voice is that much weaker than everybody else's; it's just that you aren't yet using as many of the tricks of the trade as the pros are in the form of **dynamics processors**. By processing your sound, you will make your thin, hollow recording sound like it's from a big-budget studio.

Before we go much further, let's go over some basic (and essential) audio-processing terms that will help in our discussion. As with all things audio, entire books have been written on each of these individual components and processes. We aren't aiming to give you a comprehensive education in dynamics processing but instead to give you a basic idea of what each component and process does so that you will have enough knowledge to know whether it applies to your situation.

Some of these terms will seem familiar, since we touched upon many of them briefly in the equipment chapter (Chapter 5), but now let's quickly discuss how each of these tools and techniques will affect the quality of your sound:

- **Dynamics**: This term refers to the variations in magnitude in a sound. If a sound has many variations in volume, it is said to have a wide **dynamic range**.

- **Loudness vs. voltage**: Loudness is not determined by the peak levels in the waveform—that is the voltage. If a waveform is very "fat," meaning that there is not much difference in volume between the highest peaks and the lowest, it is termed "loud." The quiet parts almost have the same magnitude as the loud parts. See the part of the waveform for rock music in Figure 6-1, for example. Although its voltage is lower than the spoken section, it is louder. Loudness equals "power."

- **Compression**: Compression takes the loudest parts of the audio (only) and reduces their magnitude, compressing the overall signal and thereby decreasing the dynamic range. When using a compressor, you specify the amount of compression to apply. Compression begins with a predetermined threshold and ratio. The threshold is the point at which compression engages. The ratio controls the amount of compression. Using a 3:1 ratio as an example, the input level will have to pass the threshold by 3dB for the subsequent output level to increase by 1dB. This can be very useful, particularly on the human voice. After compression has been applied, you can then increase the overall volume or magnitude of the track, making it "louder." Compressing your audio will start to give it that professional "broadcast" sound. When compression is done correctly, you end up with a pleasing average level for your entire audio file. Compression can be used during recording or in mastering.

- **Limiting**: Limiting is kind of like an extreme version of compression—it keeps the louder passages of your recording from exceeding a set level. Limiting is similar to compression, because it lowers the overall magnitude of the sound, but there is an appreciable difference in approach: limiting keeps the sound from exceeding a certain level, as opposed to compressing it to meet that level. Look at compression as pushing down against the louder portions and limiting as setting a barrier that cannot be moved. Limiting can be used during recording or in mastering.

- **Gain**: Gain is the fancy audio way of saying "volume." Most compressors/limiters will have a gain setting. Increasing the gain just means you are building in an increase of volume to the effect.

- **Expander**: An expander is the opposite of a compressor, and it's a useful tool for noise reduction. When the signal volume drops below a certain level, it's automatically reduced even further by the expander. This cleanly accentuates the quiet and alleviates background noise, room noise, and even breathing sounds. When the person being recorded stops talking, the expander smoothly reduces the input level and then increases it again when the speaking resumes. For example, think of someone who has her hand on the input volume dial. As the person speaking into the mic stops speaking, the person manning the dial turns it down even further so that background noise is not heard. When it becomes obvious the person is speaking again, the person manning the dial turns the dial back up again.

- **Gate**: A gate is a noise-reduction tool (it's often called a **noise gate**). Gates are the extreme version of expanders. Imagine a real gate swinging in the wind. When the wind blows enough, the gate opens. When the wind dies down, the gate closes, not yielding to the softer breeze. An audio "gate" works in the same way. When there is enough sound going into the system, the gate opens, allowing the sound to be recorded. When the sound level dips too low, the gate closes, not allowing unnecessary room hiss into the recording. This is another method for excluding background noise, such as general room noise, the sound of air conditioners, and so forth. Be careful: settings that are too extreme can create more problems than they solve.

- **Attack**: "Attack" is the term used for the amount of time an effect takes to engage once it's triggered. You'll see attack settings on your hardware and software compressors, limiters, expanders, and gates. Depending on the sound you are going for, you adjust the "attack" and "release" up and down. If the attack is too slow on your gate, for instance, the gate will clip the beginning off each spoken phrase. If it is too fast, the ends of words will be cut off. Not good. Finding the sweet spot on the gate's attack will keep the room hiss at bay and make the opening and closing of the gate undetectable to the listener.

- **De-esser**: This is a specific mode of compression that reduces the harsh tones of human speech in the sibilant frequencies by increasing the amount of compression of those frequencies. De-essers are used during recording, but they can also be applied during the mastering process.

- **Normalizer (or peak normalization)**: A normalizer is not actually a dynamics processor. A normalizer simply increases the volume of a track to its highest level or a percentage thereof before clipping occurs. Almost every piece of digital audio software has some kind of normalizing built in. Most sound engineers will tell you to never use it, but it is a very common postprocess for podcasters (see the earlier "Recording levels" section). Normalizing is done during the mixing and mastering stage.

- **RMS normalization**: This is a form of normalization that normalizes the apparent loudness of a sound (more on RMS normalization in Chapter 7). RMS normalization is also done during the mastering process.

- **Equalization (EQ)**: Equalization allows you to alter the overall emphasis of different frequency bands. As an example, you may want to reduce audio frequencies below 120Hz because they may add too much rumble to your spoken-word podcast. Alternatively, you may want to boost the frequency in the "presence" ranges to add sparkle or emphasis to your voice. Whole books have been written about EQ. Chapter 7 deals with this subject in more detail.

Once you have your studio set up and are about to record a few tests, get to know the different dynamics processors, and get a feel for what you like and how you'd like your voice to sound. Whether you apply the processors live as you record or in postproduction, giving the sound a going-over with a compressor/limiter will give your podcast a professional, big-budget feel.

> *Be aware that most dynamics processing is like salt: a little can improve some things, but a lot ruins everything.*

As an example, Figures 6-2 and 6-3 present a sample recording before and after compression, respectively.

Figure 6-2. A sample of a raw recording before processing

Figure 6-3. The same recording shown in Figure 6-2 after compression. Notice that the waveform is now much more consistent.

An important point is to develop your own recording standards. And listen. Listen to your recordings, listen to the recordings of others, and determine what it is you like and don't like about yours in comparison. Try not to overtweak your sound file. Each time you process the sound, you are distorting it and leaving behind artifacts (like the "jaggies" you get from overenlarging a digital photo) that you won't be able to get rid of.

When you experiment with different settings in your software, it is critical that you keep notes. Remember that compression will affect two files differently if the files were recorded at different levels. As such, you need to have a grasp on your settings going down the whole chain, from input to output. This way, if you ever need to change your setup for a different kind of recording or editing, you also have the guide to get everything back to your default standards. This may not seem terribly important right now, but trust us—nothing is worse than losing "your sound" and not knowing how to get it back. (For suggestions on basic settings, see Chapter 7.)

Recording yourself

OK, it's finally time to hit the mic. Phew! Now, let's be honest, recording yourself is half science and half art. Luckily, we've covered most of the science by now, so let's get to the really good stuff.

Experimenting with your microphone

"Hey, buddy, how do you get to Carnegie Hall?" "Practice."

Unless you've had some experience behind the mic, you owe it to yourself to spend a little time goofing around. Yes, goofing around. The world can wait for your first podcast until after you've had a little quality time with your mic and become good buddies. If you've done your homework, the microphone you're using is going to suit your needs for many, many podcasts to come. So why not take the time to get acquainted with it and learn how to best work with it?

We hope you've taken our advice and found yourself a unidirectional mic (we're assuming for the sake of this discussion that you're recording alone, in your new studio). If so, your microphone wasn't designed to record sound evenly from every direction. The great benefit to this is that it won't pick up unwanted sounds from all around your studio. This is particularly helpful if your studio is also a home-office/guestroom/laundry-sorting facility. Take another look at the pickup pattern of the mic, and make sure the mic (especially if it's a side-address model) is facing the right way and that you'll be talking into the right end/side.

As covered in the previous chapter, set up your equipment so that audio picked up by the mic is being routed to your headphones. Put your headphones on, clear your throat, and do a great, rock concert–style "Check, one, two . . . check." Didn't that feel good?

If you're set up properly, you hear your sound check in your headphones loud and clear, with no lag time (**latency**) between the time you spoke and the time you heard yourself in your headphones.

To find the optimum mic/mouth position to use when recording, sing yourself a little embarrassing nonsense song (OK, you can sing or say whatever you like) while slowly moving your head and mouth up and down and from side to side in front of the mic. It should immediately become evident at exactly what point in space the microphone is picking up your voice with the clearest sound. That is the place at which you need to speak into the mic; that is the sweet spot.

Adjust your mic, your chair, and/or your sitting position so that you naturally sit at the microphone in a position where your voice will hit that sweet spot when you're recording.

Developing voice technique

You don't have to speak loudly into the mic. If you find yourself yelling, perhaps you need to turn up the volume of your headphones. The converse is true, too: if you are speaking softly but it still seems to come through loudly, turn the cans down.

Relaxation is the key to good vocal technique. Relax your voice, not your body. You need to find a way to relax your voice but maintain good energy. This is why most voice-over artists record standing up. Doing so helps your energy, breathing, and blood flow.

> *I have done voice-over work for TV, radio, commercials, and movies. When you go into the recording booth, there is always a mic (of course), a music stand for your copy, and a pair of headphones. But there is never a chair.*
>
> —Dan Klass

Once you can relax and let your voice come from you naturally, you will hear an amazing improvement over your earlier recordings. "How do I relax?" you may ask. The answer is to spend time recording. The more time you spend recording, the less "new" it becomes. You'll get used to speaking into your mic's sweet spot and hearing your own voice played back to you in the headphones. In fact, you'll get used to the whole process.

We're used to hearing our own voices, but not as other people hear them. Other people hear only the sound that makes it from our mouth to their ears. What we hear of ourselves is a mix of what is coming out of our mouth and the sound of our voice as it resonates in our chest and throat. That's why a lot of people say they hate the sound of their own voice when it is recorded. It's because their voice sounds different from how they perceive it—they've never heard it isolated enough to get used to the sound.

Don't be afraid to talk with your chest. Some people talk with their throat. Some people talk through their sinuses. The voice-over guy who everyone says has such "great pipes" doesn't get the sound from his windpipe or his vocal cords. He gets it from his chest. Goof around with dragging your voice down into your chest and listen to the difference it makes. We're not suggesting that you should try to record yourself forcing your voice into your chest, but if you can relax enough, you will learn to allow your voice to resonate in your chest a little. It will give your voice a fuller, richer sound, effortlessly.

Talking to one person at a time

Part of your goal as a podcaster should be to speak clearly, convincingly, and (somewhat) professionally. You don't want to sound like a DJ from the 1950s, and you certainly don't want to sound like one of those overly enthusiastic guys who seem to always be pitching a new kitchen wonder on late-night infomercials. By contrast, you may not want to sound like an exhausted college kid from the local university FM station, either. Your goal should be to sound like yourself, or at least the polished, credible version of yourself you'd like to introduce to your audience.

You can spend thousands of dollars on voice-over classes if you'd like and invest hours of your free time going over advertising copy and public service announcements, hoping someday to learn the tricks to sounding natural behind the mic. Or we can just tell you the big voice-talent secret. It's up to you. Practice makes perfect, as we alluded to in the earlier Carnegie Hall line, but you need to make sure you are practicing the right way. There is one technique that, above all others, will help you sound simultaneously like a professional voice-talent and a real living and breathing human being:

Talk to one person at a time.

You do not want to try to talk to your entire audience at once, because you do not want to sound like you're giving a speech. Imagining yourself talking to a group will make you start to sound like a politician or one of those infomercial people (what's the difference?). People who talk to groups sound vague or fake. Their speech patterns become so rhythmic or so annoying that you can't bear to continue to listen. Most of their message is lost in the method. They are not truly connecting with anyone in the audience.

Speak as if you are speaking to one person. Talk to that person. Really talk. Don't think of what you're doing as podcasting or broadcasting or anything else. It is a conversation. It is a conversation where you are the only one talking, but it is still a conversation. The other side of the conversation comes to you in the form of e-mail, blog posts, and voicemail messages.

You want listeners to feel like you are talking directly to them, whispering directly into their ears. To really fine-tune this approach, here is another trick of the trade you can use that will help you create the specific tone you're looking for with your podcast:

Decide exactly who the one person you're talking to is.

The person you choose does not have to actually be listening. That isn't the point. The point is to give yourself a buddy, a listener, a point of reference. The person you choose to imagine you're talking to will affect the way you deliver every word. By focusing your attention on that person, you guarantee you'll never end up sounding like a political candidate.

Choose wisely. As an example, you may have one friend who, somehow, just makes you funny. Something about talking to him or her brings out the comedian in you. You are smarter, sharper, and quicker whenever the two of you talk. You've even thought to yourself, "Man, if we ever got together to do a podcast, it would be the greatest!" *That* is the person to talk to. If you think this sounds crazy, just humor us and give it a try. You'll see that instead of somewhat cautiously approaching the microphone, you are now not even thinking about the mic. You're thinking about how anxious you are to tell your "funny buddy" your latest story. He or she doesn't have to be in the room with you to be your podcast sidekick. Every show you do can be a show secretly recorded for the person who brings out the best in you.

Odds are good it's not your mother. It may not even be your significant other. The person you deliver the show to could be someone you hardly know, as long as there is something about talking to that person that turns you into the person you want to be in your podcast.

This technique is not by any means restricted to people doing entertainment podcasts. If you are doing an educational program or a sales program, this approach is a must. Who are you educating?

Is the person 19 years old or a middle-aged mother of two? New to the subject or experienced in the field? Choose someone to represent the student. Who exactly are you selling to? Imagine you are selling to a former or current customer—someone who seems to completely epitomize your target market. Don't choose an imaginary student or an imaginary sales prospect; choose real people.

Allowing yourself to make some mistakes

You don't have to be perfect. You don't even have to be good. Just do as your mom always told you and be yourself. Assume going into this, especially in the early stages, that you'll be editing your podcast before you send it off to the world. Remember, this isn't a broadcast—it's a podcast. You have complete control over what ends up in the final product. If you go into your first recording session knowing that you can take out any mistakes and edit down any incoherent ramblings, you'll be much more relaxed and much less likely to need to edit things. It sounds strange, but it's true.

In our research for this book, we realized something very telling: many well-established podcasters have taken their first podcast offline. The first show is gone—vanished. Podcaster after podcaster, no first episode to be found. Why? you may ask. Well, it's because the first one is often . . . well . . . bad. If it's not bad, it's at least not up to the podcaster's standards.

Let yourself make some mistakes. It is better to start and not do as well as you'd like than to not start at all. After completing the initial preparation recommended in this book, you can wait and wait until you feel like you're ready, or you can just jump in. The sooner you jump in and get started, the sooner you'll be past the first show.

This also goes for waiting until you're relaxed enough, prepared enough, rested enough. Don't wait to start because the house isn't clean, or you don't yet have the perfect microphone or the best story to tell. Just jump in and do it.

If you really hate it, don't upload it. There's no podcasting law that says if you recorded a podcast, you have to send it out into the world. Shelve it. Hide it away. Just don't throw it away. Someday you may have thousands of fans who would love to hear a recording of you back in the early days when you were just starting.

Recording a podcast

For our demonstration of the recording process, we'll use the Audacity audio editor and recorder (http://audacity.sourceforge.net). It's cross-platform (available for Windows, Mac, and Linux), it's easy to use, and it's free. Audacity is also a multitrack recorder, just like some of the higher-end recording packages. This gives you the option of either recording your music and sound effects "live" as you record your voice to one stereo track or mixing the music and sound effects in later by layering multiple tracks of sound, one on top of another. For our demonstration, we're going to record from a single source (the microphone). We discuss adding music and sound effects during podcast production in the next chapter.

Figure 6-4 shows Audacity's main recording window. Note the Pause, Stop, Play, and Record buttons at the top of the window. The playback and recording meters are at the top right of the window.

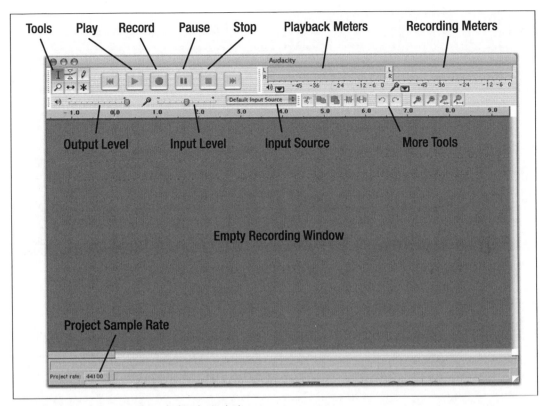

Figure 6-4. The main recording window in Audacity

> *If you aren't using Audacity, don't worry. All the concepts we're about to discuss are general enough that they should apply to almost any software you're using.*

Setting up the software

First you need to make sure the software knows how to get the sound and at what rate and in what format it should record and save the sound. To do so, follow these steps:

1. Launch Audacity, and create a new file.

2. Go to the Audacity Preferences window (see Figure 6-5), click the Audio I/O tab, and set the inputs to correspond to your recording setup.

87

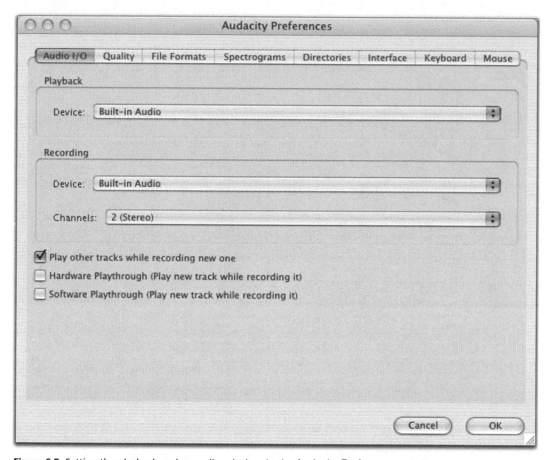

Figure 6-5. Setting the playback and recording devices in the Audacity Preferences window

3. Also in Audacity Preferences, click the Quality tab, set your default sample rate to 44100 Hz, and set your default sample format to 16-bit (see Figure 6-6). This will ensure that your recording is of "CD quality," without unnecessarily overtaxing your system. Depending on your recording software, you may have the option of recording in different formats (MP3, Apple Lossless, ACC, WMA, and so on). However, *we strongly recommend recording at 44.1kHz/16-bit*. It is truly the only way to go. Yes, the files are large, but you will thank yourself later when you decide to repurpose your podcast onto disc or broadcast it. Producing podcasts is hard work—do them the honor of full-quality recordings.

Record at 44.1kHz, and encode to MP3 at 44.1kHz or 22.050Hz, because many players can't handle other sample rates. Don't put your podcast at a disadvantage. All current editing software will be able to deal with 44.1kHz/16-bit audio. Some are restricted when editing at higher bit and sample rates. If you do decide to record at even higher bit or sample rates, check that your entire editing workflow can deal with those audio files.

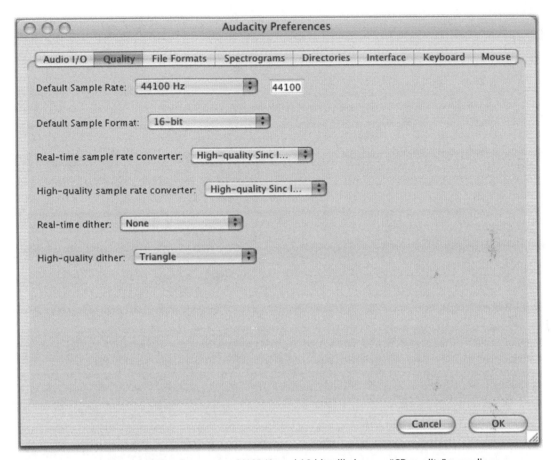

Figure 6-6. Setting your quality preferences to 44100 Hz and 16-bit will give you "CD-quality" recording.

4. There's one last thing you should set in the Audacity Preferences window. On the File Formats tab, select either WAV (if you are using Windows or a Mac) or AIFF (if you are using a Mac) as your desired file format, as shown in Figure 6-7.

5. Finally, click OK in the Audacity Preferences window to save any changes.

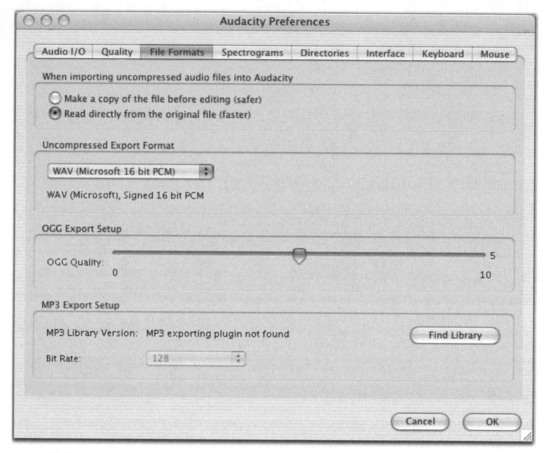

Figure 6-7. Choose your recording format: WAV (Windows and Mac) or AIFF (Mac).

Now you're ready to do a sample recording. One of the downsides of Audacity is that it won't give you readings on your recording meter unless you're actually recording. This makes it impossible to check your recording levels before you record. So, do a small sample recording to set levels, and then close out the recording without saving it. If you are using another recording application that does allow you to check levels without recording, always do so.

Your audio levels (as mentioned earlier) should normally fall between –12dBfs and –6dBfs on your meters. If you are going above –6dBfs, your signal is a bit too hot. If you are going all the way to 0, you need to turn down your mixer/preamp's output or stop talking so darned loud. If you go "into the red" (up to or past 0dBfs), you will get that horrible digital, glass-shattering sound. Not good.

Remember to leave yourself some **headroom**, or space between where your meters are hitting and 0dBfs. Give yourself at least 6dBfs to spare, or 12dBfs if yours is a low-noise audio chain. You can always pull the levels up later, but you'll never get rid of clipping.

> *Of course, if you are recording your podcast using a hardware solution such as a digital recorder, then your main focus will be on ensuring that you have your input levels set correctly. Be sure to refer to your device's instruction manual for complete recording setup instructions.*
>
> *An additional element to consider when using hardware to record a podcast is that you must be careful to ensure that you have not induced clipping anywhere in the recording chain. As an example, if you are using a freestanding compressor or mixing board, it is possible to induce clipping in one of those items prior to the sound ever reaching your recording device. This happened to me once. I had recorded everything with perfect levels on my digital recorder, but when I listened to the completed recording, I could hear the telltale sign of clipping. It was minor and only happened a few times in the recording, but it was there nonetheless. I racked my brain to figure out how this had happened and why I did not catch it when recording. The answer was rather straightforward: I was monitoring the audio from a point in the recording chain that was prior to the hardware that induced the clipping. The bottom line was that the output stage of my mixing board had clipped, and I failed to catch it because I was so focused on the levels on the final recording device. Lesson learned: make sure all the levels are correct throughout the recording chain.*
>
> *—Michael Geoghegan*

Remember: the dB scale we're talking about (dBfs) is for *software* monitoring and processing and is different from what is specified on an external mixer or processor. Knowing the difference now will save you headaches and confusion later.

Pushing buttons

The "buttons" on every piece of recording software we've ever seen (and we've seen a lot!) are designed to resemble the buttons on a conventional old-school tape recorder, as shown in Figure 6-8.

Figure 6-8. Three different control panels: BIAS Peak on top, Audacity in the middle, and GarageBand on the bottom. Notice that all the controls have a standardized appearance.

There are Play, Record, Pause, Rewind, Fast-Forward, and Stop buttons. (Oftentimes the Play button will serve double duty as the Pause button.) Your main focus right now is going to be the Record button. The Record button starts the magic. The Record button has all the muscle. The Record button isn't really your best friend, though. The button to keep by your side—the button that always has your back—is the Pause button.

If you get into trouble, pause. If you forget what you wanted to say, pause. If you stop, you've really stopped. You'll need to most likely reset the recording head (an analog tape term if we ever heard one) to the end of the recording and then start recording again from there. It's going to complicate things more than just pausing. If you pause, you've just paused. Nice and clean.

> *If you get into trouble, pause.*

Record, knowing you can edit later

Do yourself the favor of planning your recording session. Know ahead of time whether you're going to edit your podcast. If your podcast is supposed to be endearing and funny, you may want to leave in any gaffes and fumbles in the name of "character." However, if you're trying to do something a little more polished, you probably aren't going to want to let the rough edges show. If you know you'll be editing a little, record with that in mind. If you mess up, stop talking for a moment, back up your thoughts, and start again, clearly. When you go to edit, you will have given yourself a clean place to cut out the stumble (see Chapter 7 for more details). Actually, by pausing long enough, not only will you leave yourself a good edit point, but also the gap in the waveform will be easy to spot, making editing simpler. There is no reason to rush while you're recording. You'll have all the pieces of the podcast you need, and you can easily cut out the ones you don't.

Be sure to give yourself a little bit of silence at the beginning of the recording so you make sure that everything gets recorded. Even if you choose not to edit your podcast, you will most likely want to at least tidy up the ends so the podcast starts and ends quickly and cleanly.

Click the Record button. Talk. Play some music. Talk some more. Say good-bye and thank you. Click the Stop button.

Congratulations! You've recorded a podcast!

Yeah, it seemed like those instructions might have been longer, huh? Well, what more can we say about what to say? If you skipped the preceding chapters and came straight here, it's no wonder that seems like an awfully flippant way to describe the actual recording of a podcast. If you have read everything up until now, we are confident that you are well prepared to click, talk, and click.

If you forgot to say something (especially if it was the name of the podcast or your URL), start another file and record the omitted material. You will be able to easily cut it into the original recording. And if you decided to add your music and sound effects after the fact, don't worry. We're about to cover how to handle that in the next chapter. Just remember, this is not a broadcast—it is a podcast production.

Saving your podcast

Obviously, you'll need to save your recording. Since you'll be producing several podcasts, and your master recording isn't the only audio file you'll have to this particular edition, we recommend saving and organizing your podcast files with this in mind. How you do that is up to you. We suggest creating a Podcast directory (folder) on your hard drive and then making a separate subdirectory for each show. This will give you a specific place to save your master recording, as well as any edited versions or additional elements.

Summary

This has been quite a chapter, but you made it to the end. You've now configured your audio software to record at the highest quality necessary, set your audio in and out settings, and saved your first recordings. You even learned about the keys to presenting your podcast with connection and clarity. You've covered a lot of ground in a short amount of space, and yet, here you are: you've recorded your first podcast.

Don't worry about goofs. Don't worry about the part where you went off on a tangent. You'll fix all that when you edit the show in Chapter 7.

6

Chapter 7

ASSEMBLING SOUND

There are probably as many ways to handle the editing of audio as there are pod-casters. Some podcasters approach postproduction by simply hitting the Stop button on their recording device, while others labor for hours, fine-tuning their audio until it is perfect. (Of course, "perfect" is a completely subjective assessment.) Whether you're working on an audio or a video podcast, the approach you take toward edit-ing and processing the sound will depend, like so many other things, on you and your show. You may just want to record the show "live in studio" where whatever happens, happens. No editing, no assembly after the fact. Or you may want to assemble your podcast from various individual pieces, weaving the elements together in the editing process.

There are several schools of thought when it comes to producing audio podcasts. Some believe "less is more." Others believe "the more, the merrier." We believe "bet-ter is better." You don't want to spend your life editing and remixing your podcasts only to have them compressed to within a megabyte of their lives. But, you never know what even the immediate future holds, much less what you'll end up doing with your podcast later. This is why we want you to take the time to get your podcast sounding the best it can, before the big MP3 squeeze. This is something we are really committed to, and it's something we may stress a bit too much, but you'll thank us for it later.

And, let's face it, video is only half of a video production. The other half is the audio. Now, some of the stuff we're about to cover may not seem to apply to video podcasting, but the truth is it *does*. Nothing says "amateur hour" quite like bad audio in a video production. Low audio levels in dialogue scenes, inconsistent levels between scenes, and distracting ambient sounds all add up to a frustrating experience for the viewer. Keeping in mind that you can cut and process the sound of your video production separately from the audio will open up a world of possibilities when it comes time to make a passable shoot sound great.

In this chapter, we will discuss the following in great detail:

- Understanding the basics of digital audio editing
- Editing the podcast recording, including cutting on the silence before the sound, cleaning up the audio, and using a multitrack setup to add sound elements
- Examining dynamics processing
- Adjusting the volume of your podcast

Introduction to digital audio editing

Remember, podcasting isn't live. There is room for error while you're recording. You're not going out to your audience live, so you have complete control over what the audience will end up seeing and hearing. Coughs, "ums," mispronunciations, and mindless tangents can be removed from your podcast with a single stroke of the Delete key. You are crafting a *production*; the power is in your hands.

> Sometimes radio isn't radio. Ever wonder how everyone on National Public Radio (NPR) always sounds so darned smart? The broadcasters seem to effortlessly flow from one complicated subject to another without so much as an "ahh" or "um." And how come their guests are just as eloquent? You guessed it: beautiful editing. They record a lot of the interviews ahead of time and edit them before they are aired. If you ever want to sound like a real pro, hire a former NPR audio editor.

The editing process is the time for you to create your podcast out of the raw materials of your original master recording. Your original recording is like clay, and you are free to mold it any way you like. Elements can be shortened, moved, or removed. Segments can be rearranged to create a better flow or a clearer point.

When examining the various elements of your podcast, ask yourself, "Do I really need that?" If the answer is no and you don't think it's funny enough, insightful enough, or "whatever" enough, lose it. You can always refine it and then say it again in another podcast at a later date. Just remember, your podcast will be on your server being downloaded for months or years to come, so you need to be happy with what you put out there.

Be warned that you can labor over your podcast forever, taking out every hiccup, tightening every pause, and cutting and pasting until each segment sings like a bird. But do you need to? And if so, why? Be aware that it's a tempting pitfall. Sure, you want to create podcasts that you can be proud of, but nobody is expecting them to sound like they were produced by pros with a million-dollar budget.

Seriously, it's only a podcast. What's a stray "um" or "like" between friends? Actually, for some podcast users, the "ums" and "likes" that would never be heard in a "professional" broadcast are part of the allure of podcasting. Podcasters aren't professional broadcasters; they're real people, and some real people say "um" and "like."

If you're recording a 30-minute audio show and end up editing that show for three hours, you may want to tighten up your preproduction to give yourself a break in postproduction. Or rethink the standards that you're trying to live up to. If you want to sound like a seasoned pro and end up sounding too casual, maybe it's because you *are* casual. Is that such a bad thing? If you're editing yourself to such an extent that it's overshadowing the recording, you need to consider accepting what you're doing, instead of trying to live up to something you aren't. It's very easy to fall into the trap of over-editing your shows, because it's so darned simple to do.

File- vs. project-based editing

Before we even start looking at waveforms and pruning our podcast, let's talk a little bit about the two approaches to digital sound editing that you'll find as you search out the software that is best for you. Since the terminology seems to be a bit inconsistent from application to application when describing what they do and how they do it, let's agree on a couple of terms that we'll use throughout the rest of the book: **file-based editing** and **project-based editing**.

In what we'll call file-based editing, you open your original sound file (or a copy of it!) and make your changes, edits, and fades directly to the file. When you save the file, the original file is overwritten. This is how Audacity, BIAS Peak, and many other editing packages work. If you cut something out and save the file, the file has been changed, never to return to its previous state. Sometimes these apps claim to be "nondestructive" because they have an unlimited number of "undos," but the fact remains: you're messing with the actual file.

Project-based editing (what most people think of as true "nondestructive" editing) is different in that you don't change the file; you change *a reference* to the file, so to speak. You import a reference to the file into an editing/mixing project (see Figure 7-1), much like you would in a video-editing app. You can cut out what you don't like, rearrange the segments by sliding them around, and adjust volume settings using sliders or keyframes. When you're done, the application mixes the edits down into a new file, leaving all the old files intact.

Which is right for you? You'll have to be the judge of that. Many audio podcasters at one time or another have used both on each project. When Dan is putting together shows for the L.A. Opera, he edits the raw interviews in BIAS Peak (file based) but assembles and tweaks the shows in Apple Soundtrack Pro (project based). Read up thoroughly on any software you're considering. Some apps (such as Soundtrack Pro) have the ability to handle editing both ways. Either way you approach it, cover yourself by never editing on your original file.

Figure 7-1. Apple's Soundtrack Pro project timeline. Volume levels are adjusted, sound files are "edited," and effects are added, all without actually affecting the original file.

Editing the sound recording

Let's take a look at the waveform again and see what needs to be done to our recording before we start encoding it for upload. Figure 7-2 shows the waveform of a friend's audio podcast recording. Notice the almost flat area at the beginning of the wave; this is a bit of silence at the beginning of the show.

Let's do some cutting. We edit before we do any dynamics processing or start playing with the sound levels. This is because we may be editing out coughs or bangs that would cause spikes in the levels. These spikes, if left in, could have a dramatic effect on the dynamics processing. For instance, if there is a loud bang in the recording, the spike in the wave could trigger a compressor's attack, causing the more even parts of the wave to be compressed unnecessarily. The object is to first cut out everything we don't want and then process the sound we do want to get the best results possible.

Figure 7-2. A sample recording waveform, with silence at the beginning of the podcast

So, first let's tighten up this file by cleaning up the silence at the beginning of the recording. (For these examples, we'll mainly use the freeware application Audacity; however, the steps are almost identical in any other audio-editing application.)

1. Select the segment of silence at the beginning of the recording by placing your cursor at the beginning of the waveform and pressing down on your (left) mouse button. While continuing to hold the mouse button down, drag the cursor to the right, selecting the entire segment you are going to cut. If you find the segment is too small to easily highlight, use the zoom function to get a closer view of the waveform. When you have finished selecting the silence, release the button. The segment you are hoping to delete should remain highlighted (see Figure 7-3).

2. Click the Play button and listen, just to make sure you aren't about to cut something you didn't intend to cut.

3. If everything sounds OK (like silence), press the Delete key.

The silence disappears. With this file, we would follow the same process for the silence at the end of the recording. This cleanup process is also useful if you have any unwanted material at the end of a recording.

In the sections that follow, we'll look at different ways in which you can add to, take away from, and manipulate your recording to get it sounding just perfect before you think about encoding it to MP3, ready to be published on the web.

Figure 7-3. Select the silence at the beginning of a recording, and then "erase" it by pressing the Delete key.

Using the silence

The old adage "Silence is golden" definitely holds true in sound editing. The silent pauses in your recording are the places you will be able to cleanly cut material out, or add material in, without leaving a noticeable blip in the sound file. Since the general "noise" of your recording is going to be fairly uniform, cutting material out between two moments of silence will create almost undetectable edits. As long as the general timbre of your voice is the same and your recording technique is uniform throughout, you will be able to carve entire chunks out of your podcast or rearrange entire passages without anyone ever noticing.

> *Always cut immediately before sounds. Want to remove something? End the cut right at the beginning of the next sound to be kept. If it's speech, then cut immediately before the first syllable. The change in sound (from silence to speech in this example) will mask the edit. The same is true for any type of sound, either effects or music. The more sudden the change in the sound, the more it will mask the edit immediately before it.*

The simple technique presented in the preceding section to edit out some silence is the same one you'll use when you're trying to edit pieces of recorded voice, coughs, "ums," or anything else. The trick is to determine exactly what it is you want to cut and make sure that's all you're cutting.

In this next example, assume you want to cut a stray "um" from your original recording. To do so, you'll want to follow these steps:

1. Select the section you want to remove (see Figure 7-4).

Figure 7-4. Highlight the offending audio ("um"), and then delete, copy, or cut this section of the recording (being careful to start and end the selection in areas of silence).

2. Listen to the section by clicking the Play button, just to confirm that it is in fact what you want to cut. Only the highlighted section will be played.

3. When you're confident that you have the right section, press the Delete key.

The offending section will disappear, and the waveform will close up around where that selection *used* to be. Now, listen to your edit. You can always undo the action if you're not happy with the results. If it sounds good and seems to flow well, move on.

> *Be careful not to "overtighten" your show. When people speak, they often pause between words, whether for effect or simply to breathe. We've heard some podcasts where it's obvious the editor was trying to eliminate all the silent sections. Your ear will easily pick up that something just doesn't sound natural—how could a person speak for three minutes without taking a breath? Since audio editing with a computer is so easy, remember to use some restraint. This is why we keep reminding you to listen, listen, listen! You'll be able to tell whether you've gone a little overboard in your editing.*

Not only can you cut things out using this procedure, but you can also move things around. If something you really liked about those two seconds was just nixed and you want to simply put that segment elsewhere, all you have to do is cut and paste it to the appropriate point in your podcast as follows:

1. Highlight the segment you want to move and cut it (Windows: Ctrl+X; Mac: Cmd+X).
2. Find the place in the file where you want to paste in the extracted segment and single-click that spot.
3. Paste the cut segment into place (Windows: Ctrl+V; Mac: Cmd+V).

Voilà! The segment of sound has been moved to the new location. Listen to your new edit to see how it sounds. You can always undo it and try again.

Cutting on sibilant sounds: "S" marks the spot

Words are not always clearly separated in the waveform. When you speak, some words will flow into one another. This makes editing a little trickier, because you are trying to find a way to cut out something without a telltale edit sound (a clicking or popping noise caused by a bad edit). In such cases, you can experiment with cutting on **sibilant sounds**, or **"s" sounds** as they are more commonly known. Although people's voices vary greatly in tone and texture from word to word (or even from sentence to sentence) depending on their mood, delivery, and so on, we tend to always make the same "s" sound. While you could never expect to cut in the middle of a soft "a" or "m" sound, there is something unique about the sonic qualities of the sibilant "s" that makes it very handy in sound editing. As an example, if you said "Mike stands next to . . . ah . . . what was I going to say . . . oh yeah, stands next to the new bike," you might be able to cut together the two sibilant "s" sounds in "stands" and remove the entire "next to . . . ah . . . what was I going to say . . . oh yeah" part.

Cleaning up the audio

Sometimes you'll find yourself with audio that isn't quite up to your standards. Audio converted from a tape recording may have that familiar hissing sound. Perhaps the recording levels weren't properly set, and in order to get good audio levels you have to increase the gain so much that you also get a lot of ambient noise. Maybe you're stuck with the dreaded 60Hz hum that video users are so familiar with.

When this happens, you have a number of options. Obviously, you want to do your best to eliminate the noise interfering with your audio. A common solution is to apply what is known as a **notch filter**. This is a way of reducing the amplitude of the offending frequencies. Check the software you're using, because most will provide a tool for accomplishing this task.

Figure 7-5 shows an example of using a notch filter. In this figure, we have applied a notch filter to cause a –18.0dB reduction in amplitude at 10kHz. The Q value of 9.87 represents the amount the surrounding frequencies are affected by the filter (also referred to as **bandwidth**). Using zero as a reference point, Q values greater than zero reduce bandwidth and affect a narrow range of frequencies. Q values less than zero increase bandwidth and affect a wide range of frequencies as the numerical reference decreases in value. In this case, we have effectively reduced the amplitude of the 10kHz frequency so that we no longer hear the "noise."

Figure 7-5. A notch filter applied to handle a noise issue occurring at 10kHz using a four-band paragraphic EQ

For more complicated jobs, or to automate the task, many software solutions are available. One of our favorites is from BIAS (www.bias-inc.com). BIAS SoundSoap 2 (see Figure 7-6) is a stand-alone application available for both Mac and Windows that does an excellent job cleaning up audio. One of its best features is the ability it offers you to "listen" to your audio and learn the noise profile. This feature makes SoundSoap 2 both quick and easy to use. I was once forwarded a tape recording of an interview with one of my favorite film directors that had been made during the 1970s. Using both SoundSoap 2 and a notch filter, I was able to remove almost all the tape hiss. It turned the whole recording around so that the interview could be easily heard without noise distractions.

—Michael Geoghegan

Figure 7-6. SoundSoap 2

Using a multitrack setup to add music, sound effects, and comments

We mentioned earlier that you have the option to add music, sound effects, and other sound elements into your podcasts in postproduction using a multitrack recording and mixing application such as Audacity, Adobe Audition, or Apple GarageBand. Before you start adding additional audio elements, you should be confident that the editing process is finished. It's much easier to edit *before* you start adding music and sound effects than after you've added these elements. Also, once you add music and sound effects and do a **mixdown** (that is, combine all the layers of sound into one), it is nearly impossible to make further edits. Editing after the mixdown makes for nothing but disaster, because you can't cut without completely disrupting the musical elements.

Adding sound underneath your original recording

Music is one of the greatest ways to bring extra life to your podcasts, but sometimes it's tricky to get it cleanly into your show while you're recording. Depending on your studio setup, you may need to add all the musical elements of your podcast in postproduction. This is easily tackled by using a multichannel sound application that will let you record a new audio track while simultaneously listening to the others or allow you to add another track under your first, into which you'll paste some music.

You can add music as a short intro or outro to give the listener a quick sense of the tone of the show to follow or as a **music bed**. A music bed is music that plays under your recording or a section of your recording throughout. Adding a music bed to a podcast is a great way to give your program a signature sound.

> *Using a music bed is also a very handy editing trick. The underlying music will often mask room noise and can help to cover up some edits. If you find that either of these issues applies to your recordings, first try to rectify the problem, but know that a music bed may be a helpful tool for you. See our interview at* www.podcastsolutions. com *with Dave Slusher from "Evil Genius Chronicles" (*www.evilgeniuschronicles. org*) for some related conversation and techniques.*

For this example, we'll cover how to add some podsafe intro and outro music to your podcast, again using Audacity:

1. Go to Project ➤ New Stereo Track to create a new stereo track within your podcast project window. You'll paste your musical intro into this track.

2. Open the song/musical piece you want to use as your intro music from within the editing application.

3. Copy the waveform (or at least slightly more of the recording than you intend to use), and paste it into the new stereo track you created in your podcast project window (see Figure 7-7).

Figure 7-7. Create a new stereo track, into which you can paste some podsafe music.

Fading out your music

Now assume that you like the way the music segment begins, but you want the music to fade out sooner than the original song does. You simply need to use the Fade Out effect to automatically create a fade, as follows:

1. Select the section of music you want to fade. The length of the fade-out (and the speed at which the sound fades) is determined by the length of the selected sound you want to fade. The fade is created by leaving the volume of the beginning of the selected piece at 100 percent (full volume) and gradually decreasing it to 0 percent (silence) at the end of the selection.

2. Go to Effect ➤ Fade Out. The effect will immediately begin to process. When it is finished, your selection will have a smooth, gradual fade-out (see Figure 7-8).

Figure 7-8. The music track after applying a Fade Out filter

3. Use the Time Shift tool to slide the section of music back and forth within the timeline to position the music where you'd like it. If you want the music to start first and then play for a few seconds before the original speaking segment begins, use the Time Shift tool to shift the spoken-word recording on the upper track (see Figure 7-9).

You can apply this method of adding new tracks and pasting in music to sound effects, voicemail messages, prerecorded segments, or anything else you want to add to your podcast after the initial recording session. Odds are good you're not on a set schedule, so take as much time as you need to put together the show you want. Since you're the boss, you decide when you're finished.

Figure 7-9. Using the Time Shift tool, the original vocal track is slid to the right, so the vocal portion starts after the music begins to fade.

Locking and backing up your podcast

OK, **locking** is just a cool term we thought we'd throw out there so you'd know what to call this point in the process. When you're done cutting things out, cutting things in, and evening things out, and you know you're not going to change the actual content of your podcast anymore, you consider your podcast "locked." From here on out, it's just about improving the sonics of the show, not the content—the content is locked down.

But before we move on to discuss the aforementioned sonics, we should say a word or two about backing up your files. We know, we know—ever since your first day on your first computer, you've been constantly reminded of the importance of backing everything up. Saving copies of your podcast as you go through your production process is a must. A *must*. At each level, do your podcast the honor of saving a copy specific to that step in the process, and save that version somewhere that is *not* on your hard drive. When you've finished recording, save that version of your show (show.original_record); when you're done editing, save that version (show.edit), and so on, until your podcast is uploaded and the RSS is updated. The reasons for this are twofold:

- You never know when you'll want or need to go back a step in the process and start over.
- You never know when your hard drive will die and take its entire contents with it.

Mastering your podcast

Another great audio-production term is **mastering**. You've probably heard this term used in relation to mastering sound recordings for reproduction on CD or vinyl.

> *For our younger readers, there used to be these things called* **record** *or* **vinyl** *albums that were sort of like giant analog CDs . . . it's a long story.*

In the mixdown process (explained later in this chapter), you make your audio sound the absolute best you can in its pure digital form. In the mastering process, you make the audio sound the best it can given the characteristics and deficiencies of your target medium: CD, vinyl, cassette or, in our case, MP3.

Yes, we're dealing with MP3s. For us, then, the mastering process involves making the sound of the podcast as professional and as pleasing to the ear as possible, given that we're about to throw away a large amount of the original sound file for the sake of the file size. (You'll learn more about that in the next chapter.)

Doing a little dynamics processing

We touched upon dynamics processing in previous chapters when discussing possible studio setups and recording techniques. Just as you had an opportunity to add compression, limiting, sibilance reduction, and other processes to your sound as you recorded, you can also do much of the same processing in postproduction using plug-ins (audio filters). Depending on your system, using plug-ins to process the signal as you record may put too much strain on older or slower computers. Asking one computer to record new audio while also processing that audio and sometimes playing other audio sources can be a bit much. Knowing this, podcasters tend to fall into one of two camps: those who do much of their vocal/audio processing while they record using hardware and those who do most of it in postproduction using plug-ins.

If you're using a hardware processor, you may not need to do much processing at the mastering stage. Your signal may be just as even and snappy as you'd like. The extent of your postprocessing may just be making sure your levels are where you want them and calling it done. Serious podcasters tend to use a combination of hardware and software processors to get just the sound they want.

As we discussed earlier, there are many wonderful (and often free) plug-ins to load into your system and experiment with. But don't get too filter-happy: when it comes to processing sound, sometimes too much of a good thing is just that: too much. Forget about the Chorusifier filters and the Flanger—those are for music, not for speech (unless, of course, you are playing sound effects games to achieve some sonic goal for spicing up your podcast). Your main concerns will be a compressor, limiter, de-esser, and gate/expander (for an explanation of what each of these does, see Chapter 6). We highly recommend the use of a compressor and a limiter, in that order.

When you first use these processors, our advice is to experiment on a copy of your podcast (just in case), leaving each plug-in at its default settings (look for a Voice, a Speech, or even a Vocal setting). This way, you'll get a feel for what each one does and how it changes the specific sound of your podcast, and then you can start playing with them. We've found that the best way to get a grasp on how these dynamics processors will affect your audio is to just start adjusting the controls and then listen for the differences. That along with a bit of our general guidance from Chapter 6, and you should be on your way. Of course, you can always turn to the Internet if you are looking for exhaustive information on exactly how these processors work and the intention behind each control.

Sometimes the whole is less than the sum of its parts. Huh? Sometimes, listening to each process as it's applied doesn't give a clear picture of how the file will sound once everything has been applied. You might want to listen not to the direct results of these tools but to how the ultimate MP3 sounds. You might be surprised, for example, at how many digital artifacts are accumulated from all the different steps. Your added compression could actually make the final MP3 sound worse, even though the intermediate version sounds better. Never be afraid to experiment: go back a couple steps, tweak a setting, and try again.

In the sections that follow, we'll discuss some dynamics processing techniques and look at how to normalize a recording.

Applying processing to your recording

Something to keep in mind as you're refining your recording/editing/mastering process is that dynamics processing effects can be applied to the entire sound file at once or to specific areas or tracks, one at a time. This gives you amazing flexibility when it comes to tweaking your sound. Some sections of your recording may need a little extra compression, while others need none. If you've included a song in your podcast, it may not need any processing (since the producer and musicians probably already spent many thousands of dollars and several sleepless nights to get it to sound just right), while the rest of your recording needs a great deal of smoothing out. By selectively processing your podcast recording, you can maximize the quality of your sound without overprocessing it unnecessarily.

Whichever editing/mastering application you're using, the steps involved in processing your sound are going to be pretty much the same as in any other application: decide what part of the sound you'd like to add an effect to, select that part of the sound, and add the effect.

Again, keep in mind that as we go through the following example, the specifics may vary from application to application, but the principles of processing are the same across all applications. We use BIAS Peak in this example.

1. Determine what area of your recording you'd like to process, and highlight that area.

2. Now you'll apply some compression. Select the audio section to be processed, and from the Plug-Ins pull-down menu select Insert 1 ➤ VST ➤ BIAS Squeez 1.0 (BIAS Squeez is the compressor included with the application).

3. Set the appropriate settings based on your audio, and choose Bounce. (Other applications may use the term Apply or Process for this setting.) This will cause the compressor to process the audio.

You'll see that the variations in the dynamics of the sound wave are now reduced (see Figure 7-10), giving the audio a tighter, more even sound. The loud sections aren't quite as loud in relation to the quieter sections. This gives your podcast a more professional sound and makes it much easier to listen to, especially through headphones or ear buds.

> For the sake of this example, we've taken the same audio and repeated it three times over so you can see the differences the processing makes. The first section in Figure 7-10 (left of the first marker) is the raw audio with no processing applied. Notice that it is very dynamic.

Figure 7-10. Sample waveform. Left: Raw audio. Middle: After compression applied. Right: Final with Gain applied.

As a rule of thumb, dynamics processes are usually added in the following order to maximize sonic quality:

1. Equalization (EQ)
2. Noise gate
3. Compression
4. Limiting

Other effects will typically come in before compression, but sometimes after.

Now we will increase the gain to maximize the benefit of having used the compressor. Select the audio to be processed, and (in BIAS Peak) go to the DSP pull-down menu, select Change Gain, and set the amount of gain to be applied. In Figure 7-10, the gain applied was roughly 6dB, resulting in a peak of –0.2dB (more on that later). The final section (the rightmost section in Figure 7-10) represents the finished audio.

Remember that each of the three sections in Figure 7-9 is the same piece of audio repeated. Notice how the final section peaks at roughly the same level as the original piece but that the lower-level information has been increased to give the audio a full, rich sound.

Normalizing individual tracks or sections

Normalizing means adjusting the volume or loudness of a piece of audio to a specific level (expressed in dB). This process is incredibly useful when you're putting together a podcast using material from various sources or from multiple recording/shooting sessions where the recording levels may be completely inconsistent. By adjusting the levels of each piece to a uniform loudness, the overall sound of the production will be consistent and much more professional.

For instance, say you've added some music to your voice recording (see Figure 7-11), but the music has much higher levels than your voice track. In fact, the music track is almost clipping, yet the voice track maintains a level of between −12dB and −6dB, give or take. To even out the sound of the podcast, you'll need to normalize the tracks so they have a more unified sound (see Figure 7-12).

We've used a multitrack application for this example, but you can easily normalize sections of a continuous recording without using separate tracks. Simply select the area you want to normalize, and apply the process.

Figure 7-11. Example of normalization for a sample podcast where the music track (upper) is almost clipping, yet the voice track (lower) has nice, even levels

Figure 7-12. Example of normalization for a sample podcast after normalizing the music track to reduce its volume. The two tracks now mesh together beautifully. The change seems minor, but it makes a huge difference in sound quality.

Creating an audio mixdown

If you're using a multichannel workstation, you'll need to create a mixdown when your pieces are all in place. This is just a matter of taking your multitrack project and combining the layers into a single stereo or mono file. This file will be what you end up encoding into an MP3 and syncing to your final video edit. How exactly you get your system to do a mixdown will depend on the editing/mixing software you're using. (In Audacity, this involves simply selecting File ➤ Export as WAV.)

Before you do your mixdown, triple-check that the volume of each of your individual tracks is exactly where you want it and that the overall sound of the tracks, when played simultaneously, is what you want. You will not be able to make these kinds of adjustments to the resulting file, so do them now. Of course, if you're unhappy with the results, go back to your multitrack master, tweak your settings, and try again.

Adjusting the volume

Your podcast has come together nicely. There is just one last step in this final "mastering" process: you need to adjust the overall loudness. If the volume of your podcast is too low, it will be difficult if not impossible to listen to under anything but the most ideal circumstances. Since podcasts are meant to be enjoyed in just about any situation, it is critical that you ensure your show is loud enough (without being obnoxious).

The following sections discuss how to successfully adjust the volume of your recordings for the better.

Normalizing the entire podcast

Normalizing is also used to adjust the overall loudness of a file to a specific volume as the final stage of mastering. Something to keep in mind when doing this is that normalization doesn't have an effect on the dynamics of your recording in any way. It simply adjusts the volume of the section you are normalizing. So, if it makes the loud parts louder, it also makes the quiet parts louder and the noise louder. That is why a quality recording free of noise is so important.

Most compact discs these days are produced to be as loud as physically possible and are therefore mastered to as close to 0dB as possible. People think that if the space is there, they might as well fill it. With this same thinking, many podcasters will master their shows to as close to 0dB as possible so the file is as loud as possible. There are no solid rules for this and no set of podcasting standards, yet serious podcasters tend to try to stick to audio standards set forth by the broadcast community. With the increasing opportunities for podcasters to have their material broadcast, it never hurts to put your best foot forward.

If you have mastered your audio correctly to this point, you can use peak normalization or a gain increase (same thing) to set your finished audio to –0.2dB. We, and many other podcasters, have been using this standard with great success. Remember, this guideline is based on our assumption that you have followed our instructions to this point. For most podcasters, this setting will result in superior audio that will stand head and shoulders above the rest. Count yourself fortunate to have stellar audio from the get-go; not all podcasters can make this claim. (But then, that's part of the reason you bought this book.)

What—still around? Not satisfied yet? You say stellar audio is not enough—you want the best? Well, so do we. What we're about to cover is for the über podcaster. It is by no means required, but since we do it, we thought we'd share it with you. It's the kind of thing you don't tell your podcast pals because you'll get blank stares in return—they'll have no idea what you're talking about. Meanwhile, everyone will keep complimenting you on your audio. Ready?

Calculating root-mean-square

To really, really get the perceived sound levels right, you need to understand **RMS**. RMS stands for root-mean-square (look out, math majors, here we come!), and it's a way to measure the magnitude of a set of numbers or, in our case, the overall magnitude (loudness) of a sound recording over time. To calculate RMS, you take all of your peak sound level readings, square each one, find the average of all of those squared numbers, and then take the square root of that number. Confused? So were we.

7

Here's the bottom line. Peak normalization measures the difference between the current peak level in the audio and the desired final peak level and then increases the overall magnitude by that amount. As an example, in Figure 7-10 the peak level of the middle section of audio is –6.58dB. Peak normalization of the audio to a final peak level of –0.2dB simply increases all the levels by 6.38dB. The rightmost section of Figure 7-10 shows the results.

RMS normalization does something different. True RMS normalization looks at the average loudness of the audio and allows you to adjust that value. There are effectively three steps involved in RMS normalization:

1. Scan the audio to determine the current RMS loudness value.

2. Increase (or decrease) all samples so that the *average* RMS value achieves the new target.

3. As part of this process, compress or limit peaks that would otherwise exceed the selected threshold.

These steps result in gains that often can be seen as fattening up the lower and middle levels. While peak levels are easy to see visually, the average "loudness" (RMS level) is what your ear will hear. Thus, for the podcaster who wants to go the extra mile, having a set standard for RMS levels will result in consistent audio for all the shows that person produces.

> *Want to know what our suggested RMS settings are? Simple: –12dB RMS with a peak setting of –0.2dB.*

Be aware that there is a downside to RMS, though. Not all audio-editing applications will do true RMS normalization. Usually, this kind of processing is reserved for professional-level audio-editing applications. Sound Forge, Adobe Audition, and some plug-ins such as Ozone 3 from iZotope can assist with RMS normalization. Or, you can just download the Levelator.

The Levelator

One of the challenges with audio is that often in interviews you end up with people at different volumes. For the past few years podcasters have had to manually try to even out these variations, which is a tedious and time-consuming process. Enter the Levelator from GigaVox Media. It's a free utility (Win/OSX/Linux) that is a must for all podcasters, particularly audio podcasters; it adjusts the audio levels within your podcast or other audio file for variations from one speaker to the next. It's not a compressor, normalizer, or limiter, although it contains all three. It's much more than those tools, and it's much simpler to use. The UI is dirt-simple: drag and drop any uncompressed WAV or AIFF file onto the Levelator's application window to "levelate" (new podcaster verb) (see Figure 7-13), and a few moments later it outputs a new version that just sounds better. The results are remarkable. To get results from other software or hardware that are even close to those from the Levelator, you'd be spending upwards of $500 and countless hours of "learning time."

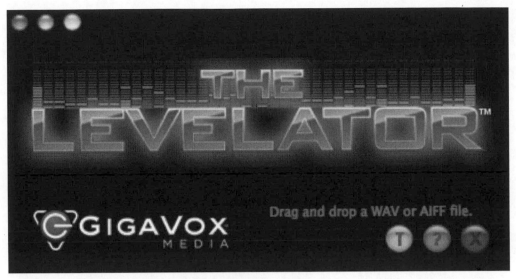

Figure 7-13. The Levelator is the most valuable free utility around.

Here is a quick example of an 11-minute-long interview with one microphone and ten interviewees (Figure 7-14). Originally this file took hours to fix so that you could clearly hear everyone. With the Levelator, we actually got better results, and it took less than 30 seconds to process. Trust us: download it, try it, use it. (http://gigavox.com/levelator).

7

Figure 7-14. The Levelator top waveform is before processing, and the bottom waveform is after processing.

> *Back in the early days of "IT Conversations," Doug Kaye provided us with a test file that output a predetermined RMS value. We (the staff) were expected to measure the file and subsequently use the resulting RMS value as a reference level for all produced content. Interestingly enough, we found that different applications on both the PC and Mac platforms provided inconsistent results. Needless to say, the staff submissions of produced content lacked consistency. The point is, it's difficult to set a specific reference standard. In terms of a recommendation, we have found that −12db RMS is much too loud and in some cases uncomfortable to listen to (this assessment is based on spoken-word processing). And, considering the lack of consistent measurement, it is possible that this −12dB RMS recommendation may result in audio that is processed at a much higher level than anticipated. It is for this reason that I suggest something like −16dB RMS as a reference standard. Keep in mind the Levelator processes files to −18.50 RMS. This setting was determined by a consortium of people involved in public radio, long-time audio aficionados, and the developer of the application who is quite savvy in terms of what may be best for the community at large.*
>
> *—Paul Figgiani, independent media producer and production engineer, "IT Conversations"*

Summary

We can't emphasize enough the potential to make your podcast really great in the postproduction and mastering stages. This is your chance to take out anything you don't like, tighten up anything you think is too loose, and add the connective tissue you'll need to make your podcast flow. These processes can make or break a podcast, turning a decent studio take into a piece of podcasting gold or an overproduced mess.

We'll end this chapter with a quick example of what finished audio should look like. The audio represented in Figure 7-15 was produced by our good friend Doug Kaye, who is responsible for "IT Conversations" (www.itconversations.com). When we first started podcasting, we used Doug's audio as an example of what to shoot for.

Figure 7-15. An example of what audio should look like

The production process is now officially over. You've done all to this episode you're ever going to do. You've buffed and polished your little baby until it shines like a diamond (well, shines like your first podcast maybe). Now it's time to encode your podcast to MP3 format. You don't really expect people to download your 250MB beauty, do you?

Before we get on with the task of encoding your audio program to MP3, we're going to take a detour into the world of video podcasting. We have to recommend that if you have any inclination toward video work of any kind, read Chapter 8. Just as we recommend that "video podcasters" read all the audio information, there is much to learn by learning it all.

Chapter 8

VIDEO PODCAST PRODUCTION

In the past couple years, YouTube has exploded into a "consumer-generated media" (and copyright infringement) phenomenon. Untold hours of video are being produced and uploaded to YouTube (and its illegitimate offspring) all day, every day. Whether it's kids in basements lip syncing to Maroon 5 or corporate concerns trying desperately to hit upon a viral marketing phenomenon, it seems everyone with access to a camcorder is shooting, cutting, and uploading. As far as we're concerned, anyone producing video with any kind of regularity should be enabling it for subscription. Yes, podcast it, kids!

Although video podcasting didn't really take off until Apple released the first video iPod, videos have been podcast since the very birth of the medium. RocketBoom was being downloaded by thousands of people daily, as far back as the autumn of 2004. Nowadays, they are hardly alone. The amount of video material currently being podcast is staggering, and the front of the iTunes podcast directory is regularly dominated by videos, from small independent productions (*Sam Has Seven Friends*, *Goodnight Burbank*) to segments of established television shows (HBO's *Flight of the Conchords*, *MTV News*) and material that could likely end up in the "bonus features" menu of the latest blockbuster's DVD (*Blades of Glory*, *Ratatouille*).

Now, this chapter of the book isn't quite as comprehensive as four years at USC film school, but we will cover all the basics (and then some) that you'll need in order to get a video production off the ground and ready for encoding (and, of course, podcasting).

We'll cover the following:

- Watching video podcasts on your television, in iTunes, and on the iPod
- Equipment such as cameras, microphones and cables, lights, and tripods
- Preproduction such as casting, locations, storyboards, and scheduling
- Production such as basic camera shots, lighting, "the line," and depth of field
- Postproduction such as importing video into your PC, editing basics, and the TV-safe and title-safe areas

Watching video podcasts on your television

Since our focus is on podcasting, we are not going to get into broadcast standards per se (since it's irrelevant), but we are concerned with our video programs being compatible with standard- and high-definition television. Downloading movies, television shows, and podcasts has become so common and the technologies are so advanced that it is more and more common for viewers to watch down-loaded shows on their televisions as well as their PCs or portable video devices. Media Center PCs, Apple TV, and dozens of other products are bridging the gap (or just plain closing the gap) between our computers and our televisions.

Even though the screen is only a couple inches wide, the Video iPod is designed to play back full-frame, full-frame-rate video. That being the case, more and more podcasts are being distributed at 640×480 pixels, 30 frames per second (full frame, full frame rate). We'll get into all that in more detail soon. First, let's watch some podcasts on our televisions. Why? So we'll be able to watch our own productions on a television to see how they stand up to a large screen.

There are several ways to watch video podcasts on your home television or media system. Let's look at the most common.

A simple cable connection

If you own and use an iPod, connecting your iPod to your television system is quite easy. Simply connect your iPod to audio-in and video-in jacks on your TV or VCR using a simple "AV cable." The Apple iPod AV cable offers an easy color-coded solution. Plug the mini-AV male directly into the iPod's headphone jack, and match the red, white, and yellow RCA plugs to the red, white, and yellow RCA connector on your television. Select the correct input on the TV, and you're ready to roll.

Keep in mind that the iPod handles audio and video differently. If you want to play video out to your television, you must tell your iPod that's what you want to do. Make sure to start from the topmost menu, and choose Videos ➤ Video Settings ➤ TV Out. Make sure that TV Out is set to On.

Also, the iPod will play both the audio and the video portion of a program only if you select it via the Videos menu. If you find a movie file in a music playlist or in a podcast without going through the Video Podcast menu first, only the audio will play. Always get to your videos by starting at the Videos menu item, and then choose from Video Playlists, Movies, Music Videos, and so on.

An Apple iPod AV cable or similar cable marketed as an iPod cable is not actually necessary. You may already have an AV cable lying around that came with your digital camcorder, and that cable will work just fine if you know one little secret: you need to swap the colors.

You can play audio and video from an iPod using a standard AV cable by swapping the red and yellow wires. Plug the red male into the yellow female, and plug the yellow male into the red female (white to white). No need to drop the extra $20.

An AV dock

Slightly more convenient are the various AV dock-style connections available, such as Apple's iPod AV Connection, Griffin's TuneCenter (Figure 8-1), or DLO's HomeDock Deluxe. They offer a small dock and remote control combo that plugs into your home AV system like any component would. The degree of functionality varies, but these are an attractive alternative for people who often connect their iPods to their televisions.

Apple TV

Apple TV actually streams audio and video content from your iTunes library via your home wireless network, bypassing the need to sync the files to your iPod at all. Sure, the interface is gorgeous and the usability is fantastic, but the system is designed to hook up to an HD wide-screen television, even though most of the material available isn't widescreen or HD. Still, as more and more Apple TVs are sold, we will see more and more video podcasters offering Apple TV versions of their programs. If Apple TV becomes as ubiquitous as the iPod (and you just never know), we as content producers need to plan for that now.

Figure 8-1. The Griffin TuneCenter allows you to watch and listen to your iPod through your home system, but the menu feature works only for audio and Internet radio.

8

Glossary of video basics

Let's take a moment to cover some very basic ground before we start planning our first shoot day. Do you need to know all of this? Maybe not. Still, it'll all come up eventually, so familiarize yourself with these introductory terms and concepts:

- **Aspect ratio**: This is the width of an image divided by its height, usually expressed as x:y. For example, standard-definition television is 4:3, which means no matter what size screen you're talking about for a standard-definition monitor, the measurements will be in a ratio of 4×3 units. Wide-screen high-definition screens are 16:9.

- **Standard definition (SDTV)**: A term used to distinguish digital television signals that have roughly the same resolution as analog television signals from high definition. 480i/p is 720×480, the same resolution as your digital video (DV) camcorder.

So, what size is full-screen, 720×480 (DV) or 640×480 (TV)? Well, both. They are roughly the same size, but DV pixels are rectangular and TV pixels are square.

● **High definition (HD)**: This is a relatively new set of television standards, offering much higher resolution and much larger picture sizes (see Figure 8-2). 720p is 1280×720 pixels, and 1080i/p is 1920×1080 pixels.

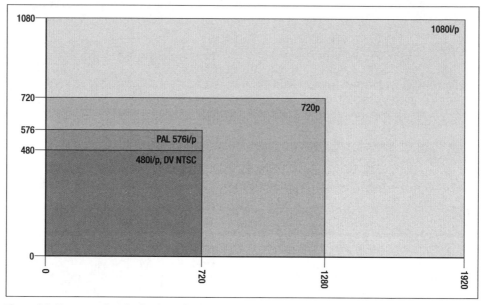

Figure 8-2. By comparing the horizontal and vertical pixel resolutions of standard and high definition, it becomes clear just how much more video information there is in a 720p or 1080i/p frame. Although this chart isn't pixel perfect, you also get a feel for the difference in the aspect ratios between standard definition (4:3) and high definition (16:9).

● **Interlaced (i) vs. progressive (p)**: With progressive scan, a video image is captured or displayed on a monitor from left to right, top to bottom. When the image is complete, the next image begins, again at the top left, scanning each line again to create the next image. With an interlaced signal, the image is scanned from left to right, top to bottom, but every other line is skipped. On the next pass, the remaining lines are scanned, completing the image. Each pass of every second line is called a field.

Video equipment

The truth is, nobody is expecting a video podcast to have the production values of *Spiderman 3*. Well, not most people anyway. As long as the picture is relatively sharp and the sound is clear, you will be fine. Remember: content is king. Of course, you *are* competing with network television, movie studios, and every amateur and semiprofessional filmmaker in the world for attention, so we always keep an eye on production value even when we're watching the bottom line.

> *If you live in or near a large city, you may be able to rent professional video gear. It will mean a tremendous savings over buying the equipment, especially the pieces that you won't use often.*

Video cameras

Of course, you don't have to buy a new video camera to make a video podcast, but if you're reading this section, we're going to assume you're in the market for one. Any digital camera will do the trick, as long as you know how to use its basic features (focusing, zooming, and ejecting the storage media). If you already own a digital video camera and are going to make a "passion project" as opposed to something that is a PR piece for your employer, use the camera you own. If you don't own a camera, consider checking out the cameras that follow (or cameras like them).

Small HD

We know, we know . . . we keep bringing up television and HD and all that when we're trying to make a video that will be watched most often at quarter-screen in a browser. True. Still, there are some very reasonably priced consumer-level high-definition cameras to choose from, and they may be worth considering as more and more people are looking for something to watch on that new 50-inch plasma they just bought.

Check out Sony's latest line of entry-level HD camcorders (www.sonystyle.com), recording in up to full 1080i, in stereo or surround sound, and recording to tape, hard disk, or DVD. Be warned: every so often Sony will release a camcorder with no audio-in jack. This makes it rather difficult to use non-Sony external microphones. Apparently on these simpler cameras, external mics must connect via the camera's hot shoe (the bracket on the top of the camera that can recognize connected Sony devices).

If the base unit seems too pared down, check out their prosumer products. The Sony HVR-A1U (US$3,100) is packed with features and accessories (pro audio inputs, external shotgun mic) but is still small enough to pass as a "tourist" camera if stripped. This is handy for shooting where you're not allowed.

Indie filmmaker cameras

Among indie filmmakers, who are forever on the quest for "film look" in video, the Panasonic DVX100 and DVX100A became popular for their wonderful handling of native "24p" recording: image capture that is full frame (progressive) and 24 frames per second, just like film. They're decent-sized cameras (big enough to impress clients and talent) without being overwhelming. The DVX100B ($2,999.99) is built for pros, so the zoom and focus is clear and smooth, and there are professional audio inputs and plenty of available Hollywood-grade add-ons.

Is 24p necessary? No. We do, though, highly recommend using a "three-chip" camera if you're shooting standard definition. Video color is RGB (red, green, blue), and a three-CCD camera has a special sensor dedicated to each of these three colors. If you want a great picture but don't feel you need HD or 24p, check out the Sony VX-2100 (Dan has one of these) or the Canon GL-2 (Michael has one of these). These are very high quality standard-definition three-chip cameras that are used by independent shooters and pros all over the world.

Microphones

You're going to need a microphone, maybe two. Sure, the camcorder you bought when your son was born has a microphone built into it, and that's perfect for recording school plays and soccer games. It's not good enough for your needs as a "content producer." Built-in mics record everything around them, so they're not directional enough for our needs here. Depending on what it is you're shooting, you'll want to use either a handheld microphone, a shotgun microphone, or a lavaliere microphone.

Handheld microphones

When we talked about microphones in Chapter 5, we touched upon handheld mics. Compared to the built-in mics of a camcorder, these units are very directional (even the omnidirectional models) and are ideal for on-camera interviews "in the field" (on location). Imagine the difference in sound between a mic that is five feet away from the sound source and three inches away from the sound source with a handheld.

Like we said before, if you are looking for a rugged handheld mic for on-the-go interviews, check out the Sennheiser MD46 (www.sennheiser.com/sennheiser/icm_eng.nsf/root/products_microphones_reporter_05172) or even the Electrovoice RE50b (http://electrovoice.com/products/105.html). Attach a mic "flag" with your logo on it, and you're ready to roll.

Shotgun microphones

As the name implies, shotgun microphones are long and slender, like the barrel of a shotgun. This design makes the mic incredibly focused and is ideal for recording voices in situations where the people speaking are also moving around. Professional-grade shotgun mics are very expensive, starting around $500, and need to be attached to a boom pole for proper placement near the on-camera talent but out of the frame of the shot. They are tricky to use this way, so a good boom operator is worth their weight in gold.

Small, camera-mounted shotgun mics are available (longer pro-mics, when mounted to the camera, tend to be in the shot) and are more reasonably priced for modest budget productions. The Rode Video Mic (Figure 8-3; www.rodemic.com/?pagename=Products&product=VideoMic) has a nice, clear sound and comes with a custom shock-mount and its own battery pack. It connects to the camera via a standard mini-stereo plug, so it will fit more consumer-level camcorders. It can also be mounted to a custom boom pole (sold separately) and even has an available "dead cat" (those furry-looking things you see on shotgun mics to reduce wind sounds).

Figure 8-3. The Rode VideoMic is an affordable, camera mountable shotgun that comes with its own custom shock mount.

Lavaliere microphones

Often referred to as **lapel mics**, these are the tiny little microphones you see attached to the shirts of newscasters and other talking heads. They are also commonly used in television and movie production, but their sound people do a better job of hiding them than the news people. They are available in omnidirectional and cardioid (did you read Chapter 5?) and are perfect for shoots that focus on seated subjects.

Again, we have to recommend Giant Squid Audio Lab (www.giant-squid-audio-lab.com) for inexpensive but high-quality lavaliere mics (see Figure 5-15 in Chapter 5). They are all handmade in a variety of configurations (mono omni, stereo omni, mono cardioid, stereo cardioid, and so on) and cable lengths. There is also a small power pack available so the mics can be used with devices that have only line level (as opposed to mic level) inputs.

Microphone cables

If you skipped it before, please take the time to read up on mics and microphone cables and connectors in Chapter 5. What we said there holds just as true here: when possible, use balanced cables with XLR connectors. Especially if your mic cable needs to stretch more than 10 feet, a balanced cable is a must. And, whenever possible, use XLR connectors, balanced or not. The resulting sound is far superior to phone jacks for mini-stereo.

If your camera has professional (XLR) microphone inputs, use them. If it doesn't, don't despair. You can pick up a small, professional "break-out box" for about $100 that will allow you to plug XLR cable mics into your mini-stereo input via a small mixer/converter. If that sounds like too much to handle, simply buy a mic adapter cable that goes from XLR female to mini (4mm) male.

Go wireless

Of course, this is the age of wireless. Wireless phones, wireless remote controls . . . why not wireless microphones? Most professional productions use wireless transmitters and receivers instead of cables to get sound from the mics to the mixers or cameras. Wireless handheld and lav mics rule the toolboxes of most sound recorders. We've never heard of a wireless shotgun, although we're sure it's possible. Unnecessary (since shotguns mics are meant to be off-camera anyway), but possible.

A wireless system will free your talent up to go anywhere while on camera. No more worrying about tripping on wires, and no more being saddled to a desk. With a wireless system you can use lav mics during a "walk and talk." Michael highly recommends the Sennheiser ew 100-ENG G2-A system (Figure 8-4; www.sennheiser.com/sennheiser/icm_eng.nsf/root/21418), consisting of a bodypack transmitter, omnidirectional lavalier mic, handheld mic transmitter, and camera mountable receiver.

8

Figure 8-4. The Sennheiser ew 100-ENG G2-A system consists of a bodypack transmitter, omnidirectional lavalier mic, handheld mic transmitter, and camera mountable receiver.

Camera stabilizers

Luckily for most of us, the "handheld" look became popular in the 1990s, and shaky footage is more acceptable now than it might have been in the past. Still, eventually you're going to want (or need) to keep the camera steady or have greater control over its movements than you might just holding it. Let's touch upon some of the options you have in stabilizing your camera.

Tripod

Obviously, a tripod is a must. Eventually you're going to need a tripod for *something*. Even if you're going for a handheld feel, you can still use a tripod to make the shoot less painful for your shoulder muscles. Any decent tripod is going to give you some amount of control over the height of the camera, either by adjusting the legs or by adjusting the central pedestal. Professionals and knowledgeable amateurs will insist you use a tripod with a "fluid head" to make your tilts (up and down movements) and pan (side to side movements) more, well, fluid. You be the judge of whether that's necessary, based on your production and your level of skill. The $24 tripods at your local electronics store may suit you just fine.

Monopod

Sometimes you just need a little support. A monopod is exactly what it sounds like it is: a third of a tripod. A long, extendible leg with a camera mount on the top, the monopod is very useful for quick, short-term stabilization, especially if you're trying to get a fairly steady shot in a place where you can't necessarily linger.

Steadicam

The word **Steadicam** (from "steady camera") is a lot like the words "Kleenex" or "Xerox." Casual usage has almost turned a trademark into a common word. Officially, Steadicam is a registered trademark of Tiffen (www.tiffen.com) for its brand of camera stabilizers. The Steadicam and Steadicam Jr. are so popular, the term "Steadicam" is now often used to refer to any such camera stabilizer. Specifically and in general, a Steadicam is a stabilizing mount that mechanically isolates the movement of the camera operator from the movement of the camera. The operator can walk, climb stairs, and turn corners, and the camera stays relatively steady on its horizontal axis. Steadicam rigs are pricey, but a Steadicam is a must for certain situations, since you can get camera moves that used to require laying "dolly track" on the floor of your set and pushing the camera on what is essentially a small train car.

Figure 8-5. Johnny Chung Lee's "$14 Steadycam" can be made from parts found at your local hardware store.

The $14 Steadycam

College student Johnny Chung Lee has made quite a name for himself as the inventor of the $14 Steadycam (Figure 8-5; www.steadycam.org). Sure, many people have created homemade camera stabilizers before, but Lee's just seems to strike a wonderful balance between simplicity and functionality. He includes on his site a complete parts list and step-by-step directions, plus some wonderful demo footage. The parts will set you back the aforementioned $14 at your local hardware store, or Lee will build you one for $39.95.

The Fig Rig

Sure, it looks like a steering wheel, but maybe there's good reason. Originally designed and used by acclaimed film director Mike Figgis (*Leaving Las Vegas*), the Fig Rig by Manfrotto (www.manfrotto.com/figrig/) is a modular support system that allows for smooth camera movements and acts as a frame to mount microphones, zoom controllers, lights, small monitors, and so on. The Fig Rig allows the director/camera operator to easily hold and "steer" the camera, while still monitoring other camera and sound functions (Figure 8-6). This is a good device to have when shooting in situations where a tripod or Steadicam just won't do the trick.

Figure 8-6. Seth Anderson (left) and Nathan Anderson (right) using the Fig Rig on the set of Tim Coyne's "The Hollywood Podcast." Nathan is shown adjusting the zoom on a Panasonic DVX100; then he will pan and tilt by holding the Fig Rig by the foam handles, right and left.

Lighting

Shooting video is all about light. Without light, you don't have an image. Without well-managed light, you don't have a decent-looking image. Let's talk briefly about lighting basics and how to make the most out of the equipment/time/money you have available.

When it comes to video know-how in the podcasting world, we always turn to one of two guys: Craig Syverson of VideoGrunt (www.gruntmedia.com) or Israel Hyman of IzzyVideo (www.izzyvideo.com). We highly recommend checking out both of their video tutorial podcasts: look at Craig's for a wonderfully clear introduction to video, aspect ratio, and podcasting, and look at "Izzy's" for covering all the basics of video lighting, shooting, and postproduction. Izzy covers far more in his fabulous series of how-tos than we could possibly cover in this book. If you're new to video (or need a refresher course), subscribe to IzzyVideo right now.

Before we talk light sources, let's go over the basics of the classic "three-point lighting" technique, with the generous assistance of Izzy himself.

Three-point lighting technique

The three-point lighting technique is the standard method of lighting for motion pictures and still photography. Yes, you can light with fewer lights, but you'll get the best results with three. The three lights are described next.

The key light

This is the main light used to light the subject. It is the strongest light of the three and is placed to either side of the camera, throwing light on one side of the subject and leaving the other side in slight shadow (see Figure 8-7).

Figure 8-7. The subject (Israel Hyman) lit with only the key light

The fill light

The second light is the fill light. Its function is to fill in the shadows left by the key. The fill light throws less light than the key and is usually a softer, more diffused light. If the light from your fill is too strong, move the light away from the subject or bounce it off a large white card (see Figure 8-8).

Figure 8-8. Subject with the key and the fill light. Notice that the fill light throws back less light (right) than the key light.

The backlight

At this point the subject is looking nicely lit, but rather two-dimensional, and he seems to blend in slightly with the background. This is where the backlight comes in. The backlight is positioned behind the subject, casting light on the back of the head and body (Figure 8-9). This creates a highlighting effect that helps separate the subject from the background (Figure 8-10). Next time you're watching TV or a movie, look at the top of everyone's head. There is always a small bit of light outlining their head. That is their backlight.

Figure 8-9. The subject lit with the backlight only. Notice the highlights it creates on the head and shoulder.

Figure 8-10. The subject lit with full three-point lighting. Thanks, Izzy.

Lights

Now that we know how to light, let's talk about what we use to light with.

The sun

As you know, the sun is a rather large star around which our planet revolves. It is also a wonderful source of light for your outdoor video shoots. Since it is such a large, bright light that is very far away, it offers a continuous source of relatively diffused light. On a bright, clear day, you will be dealing with so much light that you may need to block some of it by shooting in shade or by compensating for hard shadows by bouncing some sun light back up at the shadowy areas of the talent's face. In this way, you are using the sun as your key light and a bounce card as your fill.

Be careful: when shooting in shade, or indoors on a sunny day, you may need to set your shots so that the backlight of the sun isn't overpowering the light on your subject. Experiment with your camera's backlight compensation settings to even out light/shadows.

Work lights

Work lights are relatively inexpensive and easy to find at local hardware warehouse stores. They are built to light large, dark areas, so they throw a decent amount of light, and they are rugged enough to withstand the tortures of a shoot. The downside is that they're not built for delicate lighting situations and can be clumsy and dangerously hot. You have some control over how high the fixtures are and in what direction that light is thrown but little else compared to actual production gear. Still, they are a decent choice when budgets are tight (and you want to use them during a house remodel down the road).

Video/film lighting kits

Figure 8-11. The Lowel DV Creator 55 kit (around $1,200, depending on carrying case)

There are plenty of professional and prosumer lighting kits to choose from, so when we are looking for lights, we go back to our main advisors: Izzy and Craig.

Izzy recommends the Lowel DV Creator 55 kit (Figure 8-11, around $1,200, depending on carrying case), which includes four lights (one for the background!), a soft-box, an umbrella diffuser, barndoors, stands, gels, cables, and a carrying case. For a complete rundown of included lights and accessories, go to www.lowel.com/kits/DVcreator55.html.

Craig Syverson takes a different approach. He didn't want hot lights in the house when shooting his "VideoGrunt" and "PodcastGrunt" video podcasts. He decided to go with the Lowel Ego digital imaging light (Figure 8-12, $99 each, light only; www.lowelego.com). These lights are actually designed for still-life use but work wonderfully for "talking head" video shots, as long as the lights can be relatively close to the subject. Check out one of Craig's shows, not just for the content, but to see how wonderfully these lights work. Craig also admits that a little powder on the forehead doesn't hurt either.

8

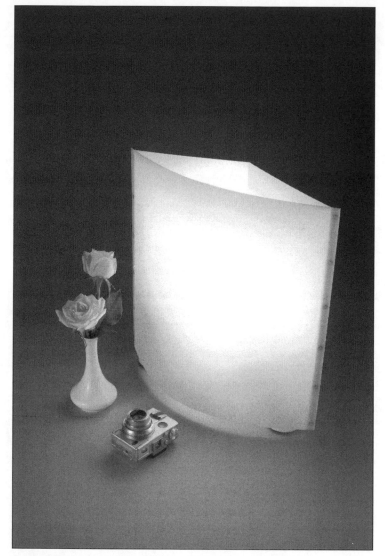

Figure 8-12. The Lowel Ego digital imaging light can be used for portrait lighting.

Preproduction

There is so much variety in the kind of video podcasts out there, it would be impossible for us to give you detailed advice about how to prepare for your shoot days. Yet, time has shown that all shoots are similar in fundamental ways. Before the cameras roll (we know you're anxious to yell "Action!"), go through a checklist of items to consider before you plow forth. Also, do yourself the favor of checking out Celtx (www.celtx.com), a great piece of cross-platform freeware that will help you organize and execute all the preproduction elements that follow.

Outlines, treatments, scripts, and storyboards

Eventually you'll need to write a script. Either you're going to write the script ahead of time and then shoot and edit that script, or you're going to shoot and have to write a script based on whatever made it on camera and edit that. One way or the other, you can't avoid it (unless your show is just a straight stream of consciousness).

At the very least, write down what you hope to shoot. This will put on paper exactly who and what you'll need. It's easy to get so focused on getting the camera and lights together and showing up at the set without the most important prop. There are several ways you can approach writing up (or down) your concept.

Outline

Just like you might outline a speech, write yourself a list of bullet points and basic actions so you can see who is doing what to whom.

Treatment

A **treatment** is a version of your idea written not in script form but in prose. This is between an outline and a full script, because it is more specific than the first but is not complete dialogue and action.

Script

You know what a script is. Don't get hung up on the exact layout of your script; just make sure you get all the action and dialogue on paper. Some types of shows will require a tight script to make sure certain facts get illuminated or certain plot points are hit.

Storyboards

Some directors don't believe in storyboards. Some do. The folks at Pixar storyboard every shot of the movies they make, over and over, rewriting and re-storyboarding until the story hums. Is it any wonder their films are consistently so successful? They put the time in.

Obviously, if you're shooting a talking head in front of a map of Idaho, you don't need to storyboard. In contrast, if you're shooting any kind of action, or a sequence that relies heavily on the shots coming together just so, take the time to draw it out (even with stick figures if you must). It is often the easiest way to communicate complex setups and moves to your crew.

Break down your outline/treatment/script/storyboard

Once you build up your idea on paper, it's time to "break it down." This means you need to make a list of all the characters, all the locations, all the props, all the vehicles, and all the equipment you'll need to make your video dream a reality. Keep adding to and updating these lists as your shoot approaches. Things will be popping up all the time. This will become even more important when you start to schedule the shoot. But first, you need a cast.

8

Casting

Odds are good you're going to need some "talent" (people in front of the camera or microphone) for your video project. If you live in Los Angeles, New York, or Chicago, finding talented actors and hosts will probably be a snap (ask your waiter for a resume). Outside of the top half-dozen major cities, it would seem more difficult, and it would be if it weren't for the Internet. Every city in the country—heck, probably every city in the world—is going to have some sort of theater community and some cache of folks who want to be newscasters or talk show hosts. All we need to do is find them. This is where the beauty of Craigslist comes into play. Not only can you find a new casting couch on Craigslist, you can find a cast as well (http://craigslist.org).

Post a brief but complete breakdown of all the roles you are looking to fill, including sex, age range, ethnicity if that is a factor, and any other traits that the roles require. Instruct respondents to send headshots and a resume to you either by e-mail or by snail mail. Many actors and hosts these day have websites where you can see their photos, their resume, and video clips of their work.

Send the actors you are interested in meeting with a set of "sides" (the section of the script you'll be using for the auditions), and set up audition appointments. Be sure to videotape each audition. This will minimize endless arguments among the producers later about who did what. This first round of auditions (especially when it comes to nonprofessional actors) is as much about seeing what the person looks and sounds like, and seeing whether they seem reasonable and sane, than it is about actual acting. Nonprofessional actors often (for better or worse) look nothing like their photos. This is your chance to see what the person will really look and sound like on camera.

From those auditions, you should feel free to call the people you liked back in for a "callback" audition. This is the time to get more specific about what you need the actors/hosts to do on the shoot day and see whether they can take direction and make adjustments to their performance. Videotape this round of auditions too, since this will be your last chance to see these actors before making your final decision. (If you are casting for a "starring" role, you might get away with meeting with the person again, but keep it to a minimum.)

This is where it can get hard. Now you need to go back through your cast list and decide who plays what role. Sometimes it's a snap, and sometimes it's a Rubik's Cube. Eventually, you will have your "talent."

Now, if you're producing a PR piece for a corporation, you may not have the luxury of casting for your podcast. You may be handed a product manager or corporate spokesperson who will handle hosting duties. That's OK. The most important thing you can do in those cases is to help the person forget there's a camera. Stand next to the camera and talk to the host, engaging them in real conversation so they can talk to you and not the lens. Odds are good they have more experience talking to people than to cameras.

Locations

As they say in real estate, "Location, location, location." If you're going to shoot, you have to shoot somewhere. Finding locations to shoot in is an art form all its own. Usually, for a video podcast, our options are limited, bound as they are by budget constraints and such. If you have access to a conference room, a friend's apartment, or a large garage and it can be converted into wherever it is you need to shoot, go for it. Just make sure it has enough room, enough power, enough parking, and enough quiet. Make sure you either have permission to shoot there or are ready to leave at a moment's notice (from the police). In most cases, you are technically supposed to get a shooting permit from the city to shoot anywhere (including your own home). As you can imagine, most video podcasts are not shot with permits. If you're shooting and someone tries to run you off their property or out of the street, go. If you have to go slowly, go slowly, but go. You have the constitutional right of free speech, but not of free videotaping.

Contracts

If you get permission to shoot your big dinner scene in a local restaurant, put together a location agreement. If doesn't have to be anything fancy; it's just an agreement between you and the owner of the location that says you are allowed to shoot on this day at this time and are allowed to bring in this much equipment, and so on. Be very specific about your rights, their rights, and their compensation (if there is any).

Also, get release forms from your actors, granting you permission to record their voice and likeness and to use such recordings to promote the project. Also, if you want to sell your podcasts later on DVD, spell out the actors' potential compensation in this agreement.

For boilerplate forms you can customize to your needs, go to www.megadox.com.

Production

OK, time to shoot. We've covered lighting, you have your talent (and their signed contracts), and you have all your gear. Let's roll!

To state the obvious . . .

Check the gear. Make sure the camera is working, your batteries are charged (even if you're working off AC), and the mics are plugged in properly and picking up sound. Have plenty of recordable media (whether your camera is a DV tape camera or DVD camera). Media is cheap; time on a shoot day is priceless. Make sure someone is monitoring the audio with headphones. If you have time, shoot it again . . .

Let's talk about some interesting (and rather simple) shooting techniques and rules that will help your frames be well composed and easy to cut together.

The rule of thirds

The rule of thirds is the belief that a frame is much more interesting and pleasing to the eye if the subject of the shot is not centered. Rather, if your frame were divided into thirds, horizontally and vertically, your points of interest should fall on one of the four intersections of these lines (see Figure 8-13). Like any rule it is meant to be broken, but you will be amazed how easily following this rule will make your shots look more professional. Keep the rule in mind next time you watch your favorite director's work. See whether you can find the thirds.

8

Figure 8-13. Commander Johnny from "ARFF! Animal Rescue Force Friends" (www.arff.tv) demonstrates the rule of thirds. The image is divided horizontally and vertically into thirds. Notice that the focal point of the subject (his unibrow) falls at the intersection of two of these dividing lines.

Don't cross "the line"

When humans speak to one another, they often look at each other. When we watch people talk on-screen, it is their "eye line" that helps us keep track of where the characters are in relation to one another, even when they are not both on screen. By maintaining the proper eye line and by keeping the camera on the correct side of the eye line, viewers are spectators of a coherent conversation.

Imagine when shooting that there is an invisible line that extends from one actor to the other (Figure 8-14). You must place the camera on one side of "the line" and *leave it on that side*. You can move the camera wherever you'd like to get your shots, as long as you never cross to the other side of the line. Doing this will disorient the viewer, and the characters will suddenly appear to be talking at random points in the room, and not to each other.

The shots

We'll briefly cover the basic shots you might use in your video podcast. There is often debate over where a long shot becomes a medium shot, and so on, so we'll stick to the definitions, as we know them, and as we'll use them in the book.

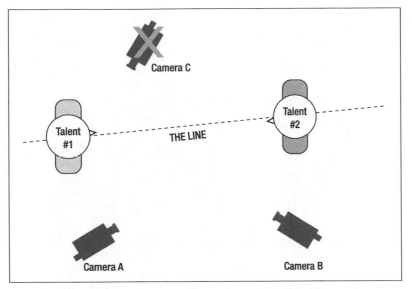

Figure 8-14. Camera A is set up to shoot a close-up of Talent #2. When setting up the camera to shoot Talent #1's close-up, you must place the camera in Camera B's position or some other spot on the correct side of "the line." If you use Camera C's position, you have crossed the line, and the resulting footage will not cut together to make a coherent scene.

Long shot

A **long shot** (or **wideshot**) includes the entire subject of the shot in the frame (Figure 8-15). Long shots and extreme long shots are often used as an *establishing shot* to orient the characters within the scene or reveal the location of the action.

Figure 8-15. Hudson from "ARFF!" in a long shot, apparently lost in the jungle.

Medium shot

A **medium shot** could be any shot that is tighter than a long shot but not quite tight enough to be a close-up (Figure 8-16). We like to think of a medium shot as starting around the actor's waist or so and including all of the top of the head.

Figure 8-16. Hudson in a medium shot

Close-up

A **close-up shot** is meant for dramatic effect, focusing on the face expressions and hand movements of humans or on the details of an object (Figure 8-17). They are often used to highlight a specific bit of action or detail that is important to the story or point at hand but that would be lost in a wider shot.

Figure 8-17. Our character in close-up

One shot or two shot

One shot and **two shot** refer to the number of principle actors on camera (meaning we don't count people in the background).

Over the shoulder

This is a useful shot when shooting a two-person dialogue, when the actors are standing close to each other face to face. It is set up exactly as it sounds like it would be (Figure 8-18), with the camera looking over the shoulder of one actor (from behind) at the face of the other.

Figure 8-18. An "over the shoulder" shot

Leave enough headroom

Unless you're doing a close-up for effect, make sure to leave enough headroom between your subject and the top of the frame. Not leaving enough headroom will make the frame look cramped. Too much headroom will give the shot a comical feel, especially if you place the subject in one of the lower corners.

Room to breathe

This pertains especially to one shots. Along with the proper amount of headroom, leave enough space between your subject and the side of the frame for them to talk and breathe. Assuming that we're following the rule of thirds, make sure the talent has their back to the nearest side of the frame so that they are talking into open space (see Figure 8-18). Only cram the talent's mouth against the side of the frame for effect.

8

Continuous action in and out of frame

What is the proper way to handle people exiting and entering the frame so that it looks like continuous action? This is something that you don't realize you need to think about sometimes until it's too late. There must be a guideline, like "don't cross the line," that would help keep shooters on-track. Well, luckily, IzzyVideo has covered this very topic.

The two main rules of thumb are as follows:

- If the action in the first shot is moving from left to right, the action in the next shot must also be moving left to right for the action to seem continuous.
- For the action to seem smoothly continuous, the person must completely exit the frame in the first shot and not be visible at the very beginning of the next until they enter the frame (again with matching left-to-right or right-to-left movement).

Depth of field

One element of moving picture photography that stands out as a signifier of "professional" video is the use of depth of field. Most amateur video is shot with "infinite focus," which means everything in the frame is sharp, from the subject to the background. The viewer's attention is drawn to the subject only by the composition of the frame and that the subject is either speaking or in extreme close-up.

A great way to give your shots a professional look and focus attention to a specific part of the frame is to use a shorter depth of field. So, instead of everything from 2 feet to 100 feet from the camera lens being in focus, only things (for example) 5 feet to 10 feet would be in focus. The result is a clear image of your subject against a blurry background (see Figure 8-19). Whether you realize it or not, depth of field is used in TV and film all the time.

Figure 8-19. A video frame with infinite focus (left) and a similar shot with shallow depth of field

So, how do we narrow our camera's depth of field to create this effect? Well, we'll skip all the technical talk about why this works and just say this: back up, zoom in, manual focus.

We need to trick most video cameras into reducing the depth of field, and to do this, you start by backing the camera away from your subject much farther than you instinctively would otherwise. Also, make sure you're using a tripod for best effect, since the more you zoom in, the better the blur but also the more you'll notice camera shakes.

Zoom in on the subject. You'll notice almost immediately that the background begins to blur out the more you zoom in. By pushing the zoom to its maximum magnification, you are reducing the amount of area it can keep in focus.

If you'd like to blur the background even more, reduce the amount of light entering the lens. You do this by adding a "neutral density filter" to the camera, either by literally covering the lens with a filter or by switching an NDF switch (if the camera has one).

On your mark

Because shallow depth of field and other shooting techniques require precise movements that must be repeated shot after shot, filmmakers routinely will "mark" spots on the floor where the camera needs to start or stop, where actors need to stand, and so on, to ensure clear and consistent action take after take.

For instance, if the host of your video needs to enter the frame and then stop to talk, he or she may be out of frame or out of focus if they misjudge where to stand. Make life easy for everyone on the set by putting an inverted capital *T* on the ground/floor, either with tape or chalk, precisely where the actor is to stand. Then you can have the host walk in and "hit his mark," confident that your "blocking" (predetermined movement of cameras and talent) will be carried out smoothly.

. . . Action!

So, time to roll tape, blow some lines, miss some marks, rewrite some lines, and have a typical shoot day. Make sure to label all your tapes or disks, keep you talent out of the sun when they don't have to be in it, have water on hand, and have fun. Remember, the blank media is cheap. Shoot until you get it, or at least get it close enough. You can always fix it in post.

Video postproduction

Everyone who makes movies is different. Many directors will tell you that the writing and planning is the best part of filmmaking and that shooting is just an arduous battle against time and money. Some directors love to shoot; they love the spontaneity and the potential for ruin. Regardless of which camp they fit into, eventually it's time to edit. Unless you have the time and resources to go back and reshoot, what you got on your shoot days is what you've got to work with to make your show. If you didn't get it, you ain't got it. That is the "glass half-empty" view, but you can also think of the editing process as a time of discovery. Your footage is a big lump of clay, and from this clay you hope to mold a masterpiece.

Video-editing applications

This is the era of digital video editing (yeah!). Finally it's here, after decades of waiting. Nondestructive, multilayered, nonlinear video editing has been the holy grail for pros and enthusiasts since . . . who knows, *I Love Lucy*? The applications available now are plenty, all offering full-screen, full-frame-rate

8

editing (often in standard and high definition), full CD-quality stereo sound (with add-ons to create 5.1 channel surround), every conceivable transition and image effect under the sun (few of which you should even consider using), and export functions to several different digital formats. Although the following figures are screen shots from Apple's Final Cut Pro (part of Final Cut Studio, $1299), the concepts and techniques of digital video–editing suites really don't vary significantly, so whether you decide to use Adobe Premiere Pro (Windows, $799), Avid Xpress Pro (Windows, $1495 and Mac, $1665), FCP, or iMovie (Mac OS, free with new computer; $79 with iLife), you will be able to easily apply these concepts to your editing projects.

Capture

Unless you're recording from your camera straight into a hard drive or onto a DVD, you will need to transfer all the footage you want to use from your DV tapes into a hard drive. Most apps suggest you run your video-editing software off your main hard drive but store your captured footage on a separate, dedicated hard drive. This is not necessary, but it will help alleviate dropped frames and crashed systems.

Video footage is captured by essentially rerecording it to your hard drive in real time. To minimize problems during capture, quit all other applications so that your editing software is the only thing running. This is no time to surf YouTube. As you capture each section of your video, name and describe your new files so that you will recognize them in a glance while editing. It is a huge waste of time to search your footage "bins" over and over for the shot you know you've got. Take advantage of any sorting and organizing functions of the app, because being organized is one of the keys to cutting.

Basics of digital video editing

Digital video is handled in "projects" much like we discussed with audio editing. You never actually edit the original captured files. Instead, references to the files are imported and dropped into a timeline to be organized, trimmed, swapped, and otherwise manhandled into shape.

For the sake of example, we're going to put together a little movie project where a giant lizard attacks a city, much to Dan's horror. This way we'll get to show you some basic (and universal) concepts of digital video editing using some footage we had lying around the hard drive.

Most people don't have footage of giant lizards attacking a city, and frankly neither do we. What we do have is some footage of a small lizard-like creature made out of clay, shot in shaky close-ups, static-filled footage of a high-tech-looking countdown we downloaded from www.istockphoto.com for a couple dollars, and some footage of Dan sitting in his car, looking out the windshield with a rather odd expression on his face. From these pieces, let's make our own little Godzilla movie.

By now it probably goes without saying that we are only scratching the surface of video editing. This is just a primer—something to get you on your way. Our biggest advice on video editing would be to find a decent book dedicated to the editing system you're using. If you will end up doing a lot of editing, you will find that really learning the system will save you untold amounts of time and frustration. We will, however, get deep enough into the basics that you will be able to easily edit fairly complex video projects.

In Figure 8-20, we have a typical project in Apple's Final Cut Pro. The footage we've imported for this project is listed in the top left panel. Next to that is the Viewer window for previewing our footage and the Canvas window for previewing what is on our timeline (bottom).

Figure 8-20. A project in Final Cut Pro

So, in our lizard movie, let's start with some static-filled countdown that ends with the "screen" going blank. Then we'll show the giant lizard stomping on the city and Dan watching from his car. This dramatic and silly scene will be "sold" by clever use of edits and sound effects. Sure, you may not be tackling something as ridiculous . . . uh, we mean involved, as this, but to put this project together, we'll be covering most of the basic concepts of video editing.

So, first, we drag the countdown to our timeline (Figure 8-21). Since the countdown has no audio, video is placed on track 1 (V1) but nothing is placed on the audio tracks. Don't worry, we'll fill the audio tracks soon.

Since we want the lizard footage to begin right after the countdown, we drag it into the timeline, just to the right of the countdown footage (Figure 8-22). Since giant_lizard.mov has sound, audio and video tracks are filled in our timeline. We want to make sure that the second clip is right up against the first to avoid unwanted black frames in the final movie. To help avoid creating gaps between clips, we turn snapping on; this "snaps" each clip up against its neighbor, ensuring clean cuts.

Figure 8-21. To add video to our project, we simply drag the desired clip from the clip bin onto our timeline.

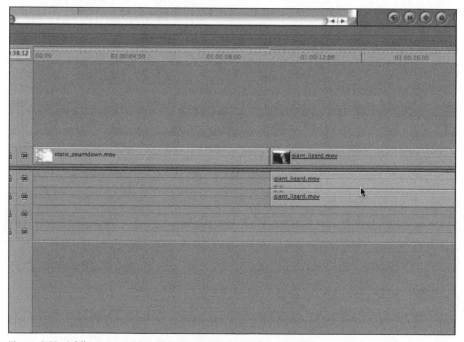

Figure 8-22. Adding more video, this time with synchronized audio

Our empty timeline had only two video tracks, and since we want to include the footage of Dan as inserts or cutaways, we need a couple more video tracks. Also, to really make this scene work, we're going to need plenty of room for sound effects (SFX). Let's add two audio and two video tracks (Figure 8-23) to give ourselves some room to work.

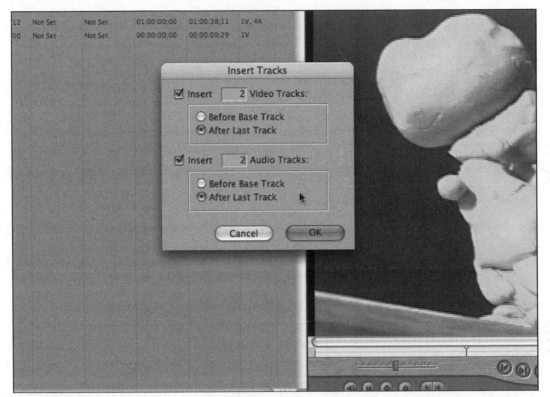

Figure 8-23. You may need to create additional audio and video tracks for your project. Odds are good you can create more empty tracks than you will ever need.

Now we can drag the footage of Dan in his car to the timeline, onto the new video track. Since we don't need the audio that is attached to that footage, we are going to select it and delete it from our project (Figure 8-24).

The beginning of the Dan footage isn't right for our movie. We need to start that cut with a shot of Dan looking out his windshield, not the city lights (which is how the unedited clip begins). So, we need to remove the first couple of seconds from this shot. We must move the playhead to the point in the video clip where we want the cut to begin by monitoring the Canvas window (Figure 8-25).

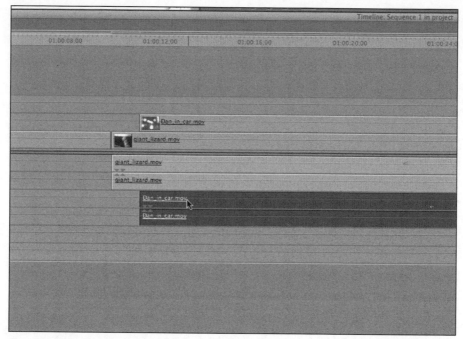

Figure 8-24. We continue to drag and drop additional footage into our timeline. Unnecessary audio can easily be deleted from a clip by selecting the unwanted audio and pressing Delete.

Figure 8-25. Move the playhead to determine where to cut by watching the Preview window as you "scrub" back and forth.

Now, with an edit tool (the razor blade in this case), we can cut the take where we want to make our edit (Figure 8-26).

Figure 8-26. Using the edit tool, we cut where we want to begin the clip we'll use.

Now the beginning of that clip is separated from the part where we can see Dan in the car. Now all we have to do is delete the unusable segment, like we did earlier with the audio tracks we didn't need (Figure 8-27).

Now, there is a problem with the lizard footage. At one point, the camera is just *too* shaky, and the lizard dips out of frame. It just doesn't make sense that such a gigantic lizard could possibly be out of frame. It lessens the impact of our 2-inch-tall lump of clay. So, let's take that part of the video out and cover our edit so no one will ever notice it was made.

First, we need to cut the footage at the beginning and end of the section we want to omit. Then, simply select that area and delete (see Figure 8-28).

Figure 8-27. Now that the footage of the city lights has been separated from the rest of the clip, we simply highlight it and hit Delete.

Figure 8-28. We need to cut out some unwanted footage. We'll then need to cover the gap this deletion creates.

Now, we simply slide one of the insert shots of Dan's look over the gap we've created in the lizard video (Figure 8-29). Why not just close the gap by sliding the lizard video over a bit? We could, but it would throw the audio out of sync. The lizard footage has sound that we want to keep, so we don't want to monkey with the audio unnecessarily.

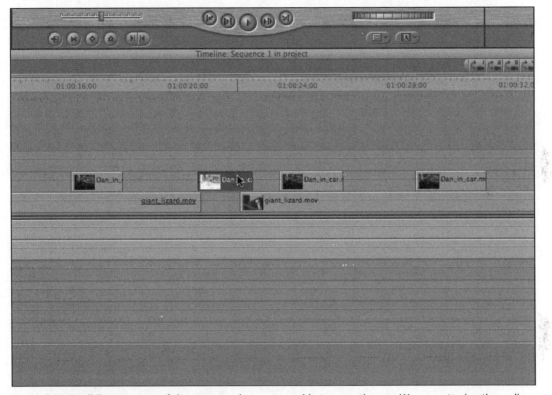

Figure 8-29. By sliding over one of the cut-away shots, we are able to cover the gap. We are not using the audio from this clip, so we don't worry about losing sync.

It will sound really great, and lead us into the terror of the scene, if we can hear the giant lizard stomping down Broadway *before* we actually see him. So, to do this, we're going to bring in the sound from the lizard video before we cut to the video. To do this, we've cut a section of the lizard's video track away and slid the countdown video slightly to the right to fill that gap (Figure 8-30). This is called a **J-Cut** because of the shape the edit makes on the timeline, and it is a common transitional technique. It prepares the audience for the next scene before they actually see what's happening. It is a wonderful way to build suspense, anticipation, or comic relief.

The sibling of the J-Cut is, you guessed it, the **L-Cut**, where a new video element is revealed before the accompanying audio. We've done this here at the end of our sequence by bringing the countdown footage back in before the sounds of the lizard end (Figure 8-31). Since the lizard is supposed to be a huge, hulking creature, it makes sense the sounds of his footsteps and the havoc he is creating would linger on long after you can't see him anymore.

Figure 8-30. A J-Cut. New audio elements are introduced before the accompanying video.

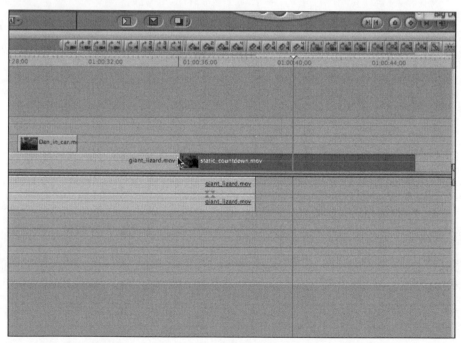

Figure 8-31. The L-Cut. The audio lingers on after a new video element is introduced.

Havoc? What havoc? We have a little green blob and a guy in a car, so what havoc? There's not even mayhem! Well, that's where the sound effects come into play. To add realism to our scene, and to make a lump of clay seem like a huge monster, we've added gorilla growls, metal booming for footsteps, explosions, police sirens, machine guns, fire, screaming, you name it (Figure 8-32).

Sound effects, music, and voice-over can be added easily on just about as many audio tracks as you need. Slide them around, match them to the picture, and tweak the picture to sync with the sound. Sure, too much is too much, but sound is an extremely important part of making video work. It's not all about the visuals.

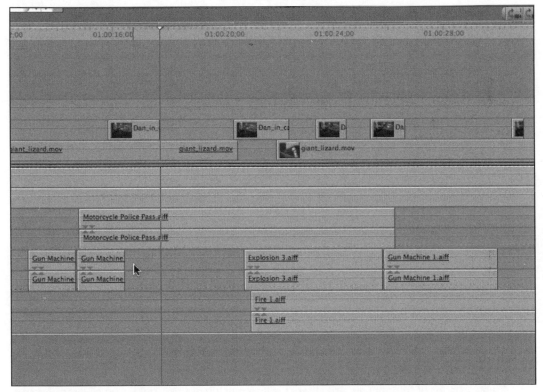

Figure 8-32. We add machine gun fire, explosions, and fire sound effects to add realism (and humor) to our project.

So, let's assume we're done with our giant lizard test project. The giant lizard has knocked out the television signals and crushed half of downtown, and a little boy is happy that we made a movie out of his lizard sculpture. So, now we need to take these layers of audio and video, these edit points, and several separate clips and export them into one unified video file.

Export your finished project so that it is compatible with your video equipment. In the United States, we export as DV NTSC 48kHz (Figure 8-33). This is your full-quality master file that you will save and back up and guard with your life.

Figure 8-33. Export your finished project as one unified video file. In the United States, we export as DV NTSC 48kHz.

So, we've got the first master file of our first video podcast. But is it a podcast yet? No. Is it ready to be podcast? No. It is not compatible with browsers, Flash Players, or iPods. Yet.

Summary

Wow. That was a lot of information. And, there's still so much more we could have covered. This has been enough of an overview to get you excited and started toward your first production. Take our advice and take the time to really prep, shoot until you know you've "got it," and feel free to experiment with the ease and versatility of your video-editing system.

Buying a book dedicated to your editing software may be essential. It is helpful to have something in print to turn to while your screen is full of timelines and preview windows.

In the chapters to follow, we'll take a final video and prepare it to be podcast, shrinking it slightly in size and resolution and then sending it out into the world. We'll not only talk about podcasting your show but also about getting it uploaded to YouTube, Revver, and other video community sites. Like we said before, video is everywhere these days. Let's make sure your video projects are out there with the rest.

Chapter 9

PREPARING YOUR FILE

The last few steps before you upload your podcast for the world to download involve converting your file to a podcast-appropriate format and **tagging** it so people know where the file came from, who was involved, and how to find more. Luckily, the hardest parts of preparing your show are over. Now you just have a little bit of processing to do, and you're ready to send your podcast off into the wild cyber yonder.

In this chapter, we'll cover the following topics:

- Encoding and compressing to MP3, M4A, MOV, and M4V
- Encoding audio with iTunes, Audacity, and LAME
- Encoding video with QuickTime Pro
- Adding ID3 tags and "album art"
- Following podcast naming conventions (or, not)

Encoding and compressing audio to MP3

Your raw sound file is just too darned big to expect people to download it. Frankly, it would take too long for you to upload it. Maybe someday it will be no big deal to upload and download a 250MB sound file, but not today.

Because of today's file size limitations, audio podcasts are compressed using the MPEG-1 Audio Layer-3 (MP3) format. MP3 is the audio compression component (Layer 3) of MPEG-1. All that really means to you is that by encoding a sound file using the **MP3 codec (compression/decompression standard)**, you can reduce the size of your sound files significantly. This compression is achieved by literally throwing out bits of information in the sound file. The codec is designed to balance file size with sound quality. It does this by trying to distinguish between those things that are important to maintain audio fidelity and intelligibility and those that are not.

Any way you slice it, compression deteriorates sound quality; however, a surprisingly good balance can be struck so that the audio is pleasing to the ear and the file is small enough for easy download. MP3 codecs do this by using **perceptual coding**, a process that uses algorithms designed to encode and compress the audio signal using psychoacoustic principles. In plain English, MP3 codecs try to compress the bits while maintaining fidelity for the human ear. Some do a better job than others, but with a little care, your sound files will come out sounding perfect for podcast purposes.

Now, MP3 is not the only compression standard available to use for audio podcasts. There is also MPEG 4, which is a "container format," that can store several different formats of audio and video files. Apple uses the M4A extension to signify that a file was non-rights-managed MPEG audio only and uses MP4 for files embedded with Digital Rights Management (DRM) restrictions built in. See www.M4A.com for a wonderful explanation of M4A, M4V, AAC, and other formats you'll see while poking around in iTunes.

We recommend you stick with MP3. MP3 audio files are playable on all standard music players, such as iTunes, iPods, Zunes, and so on, as well as Flash-based players on websites. Once you start messing around with other formats, you will quickly find where each format's compatibilities begin and end. Yes, down the road you may decide you want to produce an "enhanced podcast" (see the next section), but until that time, stick with the tried and true.

Enhanced podcasts

Once the iPod Photo was introduced, it was inevitable that podcasts would eventually have some sort of visual component above and beyond the standard podcast icon that shows up in iTunes while the show is playing. Thus began "enhanced Podcasts." Enhanced podcasts are audio podcasts that are embedded with chapter markers, hyperlinks, and/or artwork that is synced to the program, all visible on the screen of an iPod or in the album artwork panel in iTunes. It is a wonderful addition to a static, linear show, in that the listener can click directly to specific points in the program or see changing artwork as the content of the show changes from one subject to another. The downside of enhanced podcasts, of course, is that not everyone can enjoy them. If you don't have an iPod or are not listening in iTunes, you're out of luck. Enhanced podcasts are saved as M4A files, which are incompatible with many players and web browsers. If you are intent on producing an enhanced podcast (they are the perfect solution in many situations), you should strongly consider also publishing an MP3 version as well to give potential listeners an option.

Adam Christianson has been producing both a standard MP3 version and an enhanced version of his highly successful MacCast. Fearing that he might be laboring for extra hours to get a podcast out that no one was appreciating, he asked his listeners to chime in on whether he should continue with the "eMacCast." The response was clear: at the very least, Mac fanatics love his "e" version.

Also, with all our naysaying, we also have to take notice of the following: "The Ricky Gervais Show," the holder of the *Guinness Book of World Records* record for most downloaded podcast of all time . . . enhanced. Apparently millions of people are more than willing to download and enjoy enhanced podcasts. Don't let our pooh-poohing sway you.

How do you make an enhanced podcast? Well, for Mac users it's rather simple, thanks to the latest versions of Apple's GarageBand or other apps such as Übercaster, Podcast Maker, or RS Software's Chapter-Tool-Me. These apps make it simple to assign chapter markers or specific artwork to specific points in the show, based on the timecode embedded in the audio file. For podcasters using the Windows OS, we're not sure what to tell you. Information on creating true enhanced podcasts in Windows is scarce (nonexistent). There is information on the web regarding embedding code into Windows Media files, but our focus here is on podcasting MP3 and similar files. If you happen to find some information on the subject or finally crack the Windows barrier, *please* let us know.

Since the vast majority of PC users around the world are Windows users, we'll be focusing our audio attention on encoding and managing standard old (glorious) MP3s. With the right encoding parameters, your audio-only podcast will sound so good that nobody will want to distract themselves from it by looking at chapter art anyway.

Audio podcast encoding standards

Setting up iTunes to encode your audio file to an MP3 is easy, but you need to use specific settings to ensure that you are as likely as anyone else to have a great sounding and universally "compatible" MP3. Now, nobody is going to get an angry mob with pitchforks and torches together and come after you if you don't encode your podcast to what many are using as their "podcast standards," but why risk it? You never know!

The sample rate and bit rate at which you encode is completely up to you, but most podcasters stick to two relatively standard encoding settings, as shown in Table 9-1.

Table 9-1. General podcast sample and bit rates

Podcast Format	Sample Rate	Bit Rate	Compressed File Size
Talk	44.100kHz	64 kbps	≈ .5MB/minute
Music	44.100kHz	128 kbps	≈ 1MB/minute

Why these settings? First of all, they offer a great sound-to-compression ratio, providing wonderful sound reproduction considering their reasonable file sizes. Also, these bit rates and sample rates play well in the most players. Compatibility is key. New podcasters frequently wonder why their podcasts sound funny on some of the audio players that the podcast directories have set up for sampling new shows. The reason is simple: they are using sampling rates other than those we have suggested. Nothing turns off a potential listener more than when she samples your show and finds that you sound like a chipmunk. We're all about getting heard, and if encoding at a different setting is going to keep even a few potential listeners away, we're not interested.

For maximum player compatibility, always encode in stereo. Even if the source recording is mono, encode in stereo. Some players can't handle mono MP3s. Don't worry, MP3s aren't like WAV files: a stereo MP3 isn't twice as big as one that's mono.

Now, all this being said, higher bit rates (and therefore fewer artifacts) would actually make more sense logically for *talk* podcasts, rather than music podcasts, since music is so full of sounds that artifacts are easily masked. In voice files—especially those with no background music—artifacts of the encoding process are much more noticeable (and potentially much more annoying). It is because of this that we have some specific encoding advice (coming later in this chapter) that will all but eliminate artifacts, even at 64 kbps (if you're really worried about it, bump up to 96 kbps/44.1kHz; we won't tell).

So, let's get to encoding . . .

Encoding software

Many software packages available today will do a great job of encoding. You may even be able to export your file as an MP3 straight from your recording software. If not, a good place to start is with Apple's iTunes (www.apple.com/itunes) or Audacity using the LAME encoder. Both are free, easy to use, and available for both Windows and Mac OS X. Frankly, you may end up using both applications: Audacity to record, one or the other to encode, and then iTunes to manage the information stored within the MP3 as ID3 tags.

For the sake of demonstration, let's first encode your new podcast using iTunes, and then we'll show you how to incorporate LAME MP3 encoding into the iTunes system. After that, we'll go through the same process using Audacity with LAME. These steps differ from the steps you'd take in other applications, but the general concepts and settings are the same. If you know you'll be using Audacity, skip to that section now.

Encoding in iTunes

To encode in iTunes, follow these steps:

1. Launch iTunes.

2. Select iTunes ➤ Preferences to access the iTunes Preferences window.

3. Click the Importing button at the top of the Preferences window. The Importing panel will appear, as shown in Figure 9-1.

4. Set the Import Using option to MP3 Encoder.

5. In the Setting drop-down list, choose either Good Quality (128 kbps) for a music podcast or Custom for a talk show.

6. If you chose Custom, the MP3 Encoder window will open (see Figure 9-2). Set Stereo Bit Rate to 64 kbps and Sample Rate to either 22.050 kHz or Auto. Set Channels to Stereo, and set Stereo Mode to Joint Stereo. Click OK.

7. Check that the information in the Details area (shown in Figure 9-1) in the Importing window reflects the settings you were aiming for:

   ■ **Talk**: 64 kbps, 44.100kHz

   ■ **Music**: 128 kbps, 44.100kHz

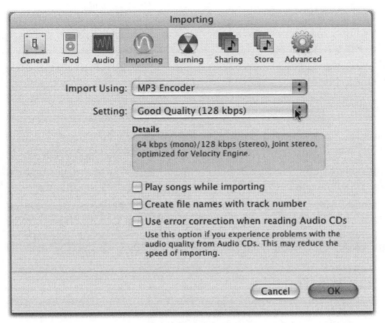

Figure 9-1. Settings for a podcast in the Importing panel in iTunes Preferences

Figure 9-2. Setting your bit rate and sample rate for a talk-style podcast in the iTunes MP3 Encoder

8. If everything looks good, click OK.

iTunes will use the settings you just established every time you encode a file to MP3 (until you change them).

Importing into iTunes

Now you need to import the sound file into iTunes. You can do this in several ways, but the way we recommend here will sidestep some of the idiosyncrasies of iTunes. When a sound file is imported into iTunes, it is automatically moved into the iTunes folder on your hard drive and renamed based on the ID3 tags (we'll get to those soon). At this point, it's likely that the file you used to be able to easily find is now buried deep inside the iTunes labyrinth on your hard drive. Instead of falling into a mini wild goose chase, simply follow these steps:

1. Create a new directory within iTunes (File ➤ New Playlist), and give it a unique name such as **Encode** or **Convert**. This playlist will be for sorting and encoding your podcasts.

2. Find your edited sound file, and drag it to the playlist window in iTunes. The file will then be imported, renamed, and so forth, but it will be easy to access through the playlist.

3. Change the name of your WAV/AIFF file to something easily recognizable, such as **My First Podcast**. Doing so will actually adjust the title in the ID3 tags for the file. We'll explain this in greater detail in a moment, but for now just know that you'll want to change the name of your podcast within the tags so it is easier to find within iTunes.

Encoding your file in iTunes

To encode your file in iTunes, follow these steps:

1. Highlight the file within the playlist. Go to Convert Selection to MP3 (Advanced ➤ Convert Selection to MP3) to start encoding your file. The encoding process will begin automatically. You will notice that a small orange Converting icon appears in the left column of iTunes.

2. When the encoding is complete, rename the original in such a way that you know it is the original, uncompressed file (by adding original, wav, or aiff to the title, perhaps).

Unfortunately, iTunes won't automatically put the new, encoded file into the same playlist as the original. Why? Who knows? That would be too easy. So, you'll need to go looking for it. Luckily, you took our advice and changed the ID3 tags before you encoded. Now a simple search of your iTunes Library will retrieve your podcast in a snap:

1. Click the Library icon within iTunes.

2. Click within the text field in the upper right, next to the magnifying glass.

3. Type the name of the podcast as you entered it in the ID3 tags.

4. All the other files within iTunes will fall away, leaving only your new podcast MP3 (see Figure 9-3). Drag that MP3 into the folder you created before encoding.

You've just successfully created an MP3 version of your podcast in iTunes. Now you're ready to get all the tags, the artwork, and the information for the Comments tag in order (you'll see this shortly). If you're interested in a slightly different way of encoding to MP3 using iTunes that will yield potentially superior audio after compression, read on. If you're happy with the results you've achieved in iTunes (you most likely are), skip to the section titled "Updating ID3 tags and artwork."

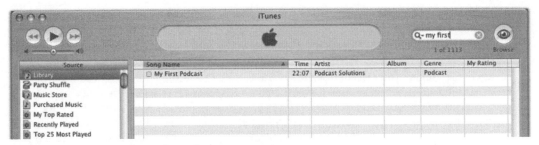

Figure 9-3. Searching the iTunes Library for your new podcast

LAME

LAME (which originally stood for **LAME Ain't an MP3 Encoder**) is an open source MP3 encoder that offers, in our opinion, superior compression. (A lot of MP3 encoder enthusiasts agree with us on this point. Entire discussion forums are devoted to how to squeeze every last drop of quality out of a file using LAME.) It is highly configurable, letting you manipulate how the file will be encoded. Because most standard MP3 encoders are built with simplicity in mind, they make some compromises in how they encode the file. They are usually optimized for music rather than speech, a preference that might be out of line with most audio podcasts. LAME allows you to select very specific settings for how you want it to go about its job. It is not a freestanding application, but it can be built into, or used in conjunction with, other applications. For geeks, it can also be accessed from the command line. (If that last sentence doesn't excite you or you don't know what it's referring to, just forget we mentioned it.)

In the steps in this section, we'll use iTunes-LAME to do a better job encoding than we just did with iTunes alone.

> *Throw away unnecessary audio. Is this necessary? No, but it will give you the best-sounding MP3 processing money can buy. Use an 80Hz hi-pass and a 13kHz low-pass filter. Even at 128 kbps, MP3s don't do a great job with audio in the highest octave of human hearing. Likewise at the very bottom. If you eliminate this information (data) yourself before encoding, you help the encoder's psychoacoustic model understand what's really important and what's not. More bits will be dedicated to what you really care about: the sound you can and want to hear. You can do this in the audio-editing software prior to encoding if you are using iTunes or a similar application. Alternatively, if you are using LAME as detailed next, you can do it with encoding options.*

iTunes-LAME

Follow these steps to use iTunes-LAME:

1. Install iTunes-LAME (available at http://blacktree.com/apps/iTunes-LAME/).
2. Launch iTunes-LAME.
3. In the playlist you created earlier in iTunes, make sure the radio button next to the name of the WAV/AIFF version of the podcast is selected.

9

4. In the text field within iTunes-LAME, type in your settings. To start, try -h -b 128 for high-quality, 128 kbps constant bit rate (music; see Figure 9-4), and -h -b 64 –resample 22.05 for high-quality, 64 kbps constant bit rate (talk). To change these settings, refer to the iTunes-LAME Encoding Options help by clicking the question mark button.

As we mentioned, you can control a lot in LAME. Here is a setting one of us has been using for a high-quality talk-format show: --preset cbr 64 -a --lowpass 15 --lowpass-width 1 --highpass 0.054 --highpass-width 0.04 --cwlimit 7 --resample 44.1 --noshort. As you can see, there is a lot of power built into LAME. The settings just presented are a jumping-off point. Frankly, if you dove into this section on LAME, then you'll probably want to experiment to find the best settings for your particular situation.

Figure 9-4. Using iTunes-LAME for superior encoding

5. Click the Import button. The encoding will begin, with progress being shown in a drop-down window within iTunes-LAME.

The good news is that when you encode this way, LAME puts the new, encoded version of the file into the same spot as the original. So, now both versions are in the same playlist, and you won't need to do any hunting. Phew!

Encoding using Audacity with LAME

LAME is not built into Audacity—you must download it and tell Audacity where it is. Then you can export your sound files as MP3s directly from your Audacity project window.

1. Download Lame.Lib (see http://audacity.sourceforge.net/help/faq?s=install&item= lame-MP3 for complete download information).

2. Unstuff or unzip the file, and copy it to your hard drive.

3. Open the file you'd like to convert to MP3. When it is open, go to File ➤ Export As MP3.

4. Audacity will ask you where you'd like to save your file. Choose the appropriate directory/folder, and click Save.

5. The first time you select Export As MP3 in Audacity, you are asked to locate the Lame.Lib file (you are asked to do this only the first time). Once you've found the file for Audacity, a window will appear for the ID3 tag information (we know, we know—we can't put off getting into it much longer!): Name, Artist, Album, and so on. Don't worry about those fields much right now. When you get to the next section, you'll really sink your teeth into using those fields to your advantage. For now, just enter your name and the name of the podcast.

6. Click the OK button. The encoding begins!

Here's how to change the bit rate and sample rate of your encoding:

- **Windows**: Go to Audacity Preferences (Ctrl+P), and click the File Formats tab. On the lower-left side of the tab, you can select a new sample rate from the Bit Rate drop-down (see Figure 9-5).

- **Mac**: Go to Audacity ➤ Preferences, and then click the File Formats tab. At the bottom of the Formats window, you'll see the MP3 Export Setup area. Within the drop-down menu, you will find several sample rates from which to choose. Choose the sample rate at which you want to encode, and click OK.

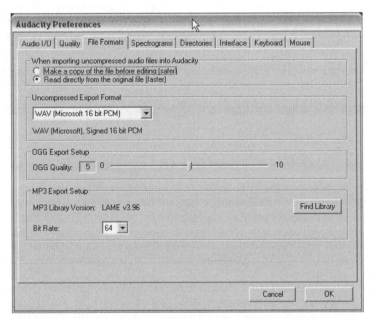

Figure 9-5. The File Formats tab within the Preferences window enables you to change the sample rate of your LAME encoder.

The encoding is finished. Now your rather large master sound file is a shadow of its former size. You have just a couple more small steps to perform before you upload: putting in the ID3 information and changing the filename.

Encoding and compressing video

Just like with audio, several video formats are available, with varying degrees of success when it comes to podcasting to the largest possible audience. Some formats are the video equivalent of enhanced podcasts and are appropriate only for iPod and iTunes users. Others will be more universally "viewable." The tricky part is deciding which format to use. This decision may be based on your computer's operating system, the software you have available, or the software you can afford (or justify purchasing to your boss). Also, because compressing video is so much more complex than audio, there don't seem to be standard bit rates and sample rates to adhere to like there are with audio podcasts.

That being said, several of the prominent video podcasters we've spoken to seem to think the majority of their podcast viewers use iTunes to download their shows and that non–iTunes users are viewing the programs (not as podcasts per se) on sites such as YouTube, MySpace, and the like. There seems to be little consistency about which format the biggest shows are using: "Mr. Diety" (M4V), "IzzyVideo" (MP4), "French Maid TV" (MOV), "Four Eyed Monsters" (M4V), "The Onion News Network" (MP4).

Brian Hogg of "dotBoom" (www.dotboom.ca) maintains separate MOV (regular video) and M4V (iPod video) feeds to maximize his podcast audience. He also has a separate audio-only feed for director commentary and weekly updates about the show, the characters, and the creators.

Since more and more viewers are watching podcasts on their home televisions, either through their iPod or via Apple's Apple TV, it's imperative that you offer versions of your shows that are iPod/Apple TV compatible. Yet, many *more* people are watching video on one of the dozens of burgeoning video/community websites. Therefore, we need to make sure you are encoding your video to ensure you'll get the best picture and sound from the encoders used by each of those sites as well. Yes, this book is specifically about podcasting, but while we're at it, we need to make sure you're remaining competitive in the nonpodcasting world too.

Formatting video for the iPod or Apple TV

Even though Apple's iTunes (the most common app for downloading podcasts) is able to play several formats (MOV, MP4, M4V), the iPod and Apple TV require very specific aspect ratios and encoding formats for playback.

According to Apple, the iPod supports up to 640×480 pixels (full screen, standard definition), while Apple TV supports up to 1280×720 pixels (720p). To optimize for both platforms, Apple recommends a source file of at least 640 pixels wide. We recommend using either Apple's QuickTime Pro (US$29.99, Windows/Mac) or iTunes (free, Windows/Mac), using the Movie to iPod or Convert Selection for iPod settings, respectively. Either solution will maintain the original aspect ratio of your original movie and spit out a super-clean M4V file containing H.264 video and AAC-LC audio. To "maximize the screen area" of your intended destination screen, Apple reminds us that the aspect ratio of a wide-screen TV is 16:9 (640×360) and a standard TV and iPod are 4:3 (640×480). Lastly, remember that a file encoded specifically for Apple TV will not play in an iPod.

Are you "anti-Apple?" That's OK. If you're using a non-Apple app to format your video, you should still keep the following information handy when setting up your encoding settings.

iPod can play the following video formats:

- H.264 video, up to 1.5 Mbps, 640×480, 30 frames per second, low-complexity version of the Baseline Profile with AAC-LC audio up to 160 kbps, 48kHz, stereo audio in .m4v, .mp4, and .mov file formats

- H.264 video, up to 768 kbps, 320×240, 30 frames per second, Baseline Profile up to level 1.3 with AAC-LC audio up to 160 kbps, 48kHz, stereo audio in .m4v, .mp4, and .mov file formats

- MPEG-4 video, up to 2.5 Mbps, 640×480, 30 frames per second, Simple Profile with AAC-LC audio up to 160 kbps, 48kHz, stereo audio in .m4v, .mp4, and .mov file formats

Apple TV can display H.264 video, up to 5 mbps, 1280×720, 24 fps, Progressive Main Profile. Apple TV supports AAC-LC audio up to 320 kbps. The gating factors for video are bit rate and frame rate. Table 9-2 shows some sample conversions generated by QuickTime Pro when choosing Movie to Apple TV.

Table 9-2. Sample conversions

Input	Output
640×480, 30 fps	640×480, 30 fps, 3 mbps*
1280×720 24 fps	1280×720, 24 fps, 5 mbps*
1280×720, 30 fps	960×540, 30 fps 4 mbps*
1920×1080, 24 fps	1280×720, 24 fps 5 mbps*
1920×1080, 30 fps	960×540, 30 fps 4 mbps*
1080i up to 60 fps	960×540, 30 fps 4 mbps*

*Represents an average bit rate.

For the most up-to-date info on Apple's podcasting specs, see www.apple.com/itunes/store/podcaststechspecs.html.

Encoding your video for the iPod or Apple TV

There are several ways to encode your full-screen/full-frame-rate video to a format that can be podcast specifically for use on the iPod or with Apple TV. Eventually, you may want to explore some of the more "professional-level" applications for compressing video, such as Apple's aforementioned Compressor or Sorensen Squeeze. For our purposes, Apple's QuickTime Pro (Windows/Mac) does a beautiful job of converting video to and from several formats and will always give us the most iPod-compatible files. At $29.99, it is an indispensable addition to your video toolkit.

So, here's all you really need to do to output an iPod compatible version of your podcast:

1. Launch QuickTime Pro.
2. Open your final edited master file in QuickTime Pro (File ➤ Open File . . .).
3. Go to File ➤ Export (see Figure 9-6).

9

Figure 9-6. Find Export in QuickTime Pro under the File pull-down menu.

4. Go to the Export pull-down menu, and select Movie to iPod (see Figure 9-7).

You'll notice that the Options button is grayed out. This is because Movie to iPod will automatically give you the latest/recommended settings for files for the iPod (assuming, of course, your QuickTime Pro is up-to-date). There is no need to tweak these settings.

5. Give the new file a unique name (QuickTime Pro will automatically chance the extension to .m4v), and click Export. Soon enough, you'll have the more compact, iPod version of your program (Figure 9-8).

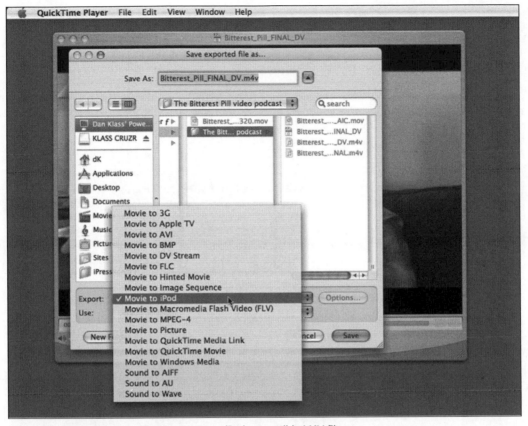

Figure 9-7. Choose Movie to iPod to export an iPod-compatible M4V file.

Movie Info		Movie Info	
Bitterest_Pill_FINAL_DV		**Bitterest_Pill_FINAL_DV.m4v**	
Source:	/Users/dK/Movies/Video Podcast promo f/Finals/The Bitterest Pill video podcast/Bitterest_Pill_FINAL_DV	**Source:**	/Users/dK/Movies/Video Podcast promo f/Finals/The Bitterest Pill video podcast/Bitterest_Pill_FINAL_DV.m4v
Format:	DV, 720 x 480 (640 x 480), Millions 16-bit Integer (Big Endian), Stereo, 48.000 kHz	**Format:**	AAC, Stereo (L R), 44.100 kHz H.264 Decoder, 640 x 426, Millions
FPS:	29.97	**FPS:**	29.97
Playing FPS:	(Available while playing.)	**Playing FPS:**	(Available while playing.)
Data Size:	1.14 GB	**Data Size:**	55.59 MB
Data Rate:	30.25 mbits/sec	**Data Rate:**	1437.50 kbits/sec
Current Time:	00:00:00.00	**Current Time:**	00:00:00.00
Duration:	00:05:23.85	**Duration:**	00:05:23.85
Normal Size:	720 x 480 pixels	**Normal Size:**	640 x 426 pixels
Current Size:	720 x 480 pixels (Actual)	**Current Size:**	640 x 426 pixels (Actual)

Figure 9-8. Here is the movie information for our sample file, before encoding the original DV file for the iPod and after. Notice that the original 1.14 GB file is now down to 55.6 MB, with only a slight change in screen dimensions.

Encoding your video for the non-iPod world

Yes, we agree: not everyone is going to watch your video podcast on an iPod, or necessarily in iTunes, or necessarily full-screen (although Dan loves hooking his iPod up to his TV to watch his faves). You may simply think a 640×480 file is just too much to expect your viewers to download no problem.

You can still use the power and ease of QuickTime Pro but output a file that is in the more universally accepted MOV format. This will give you plenty of leeway in choosing what setting you'll use but also will require more trial and error until you find the right balance of compression and quality for your needs.

1. Launch QuickTime Pro.

2. Open your final edited master file in QuickTime Pro (File ➤ Open File . . .).

3. Go to File ➤ Export.

4. Go to the Export pull-down menu, and select Movie to QuickTime Movie.

   You'll notice that the Options button is now grayed out. That is because you can adjust the setting of our MOV file until you hit upon the combination of compression and file size you're happiest with.

5. Click Options.

6. In the Movie Setting window, in the Video area, click Settings.

   For our example file, we're going to encode our file using Sorensen Video 3. This will give us some great results. We also recommend experimenting with Cinepak and 3 ivx D4.

7. Under Compression Type, choose Sorenson Video 3 (Figure 9-9). Click OK.

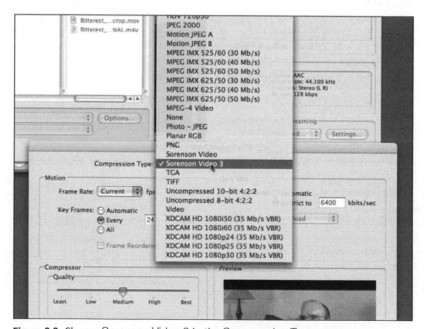

Figure 9-9. Choose Sorenson Video 3 in the Compression Type menu.

8. Back in the Movie Settings panel (Figure 9-10), in the Video area, click Size.

Figure 9-10. The Movie Settings panel in QuickTime Pro. Make sure both the Video and Sound radio buttons are selected, or your exported file will be . . . well, a bit lacking. This is the best place to make sure your settings are where you want them before exporting.

This is where you need to confirm that the output will be in the aspect ratio you desire. The most common 4:3 dimensions for podcast MOV files are 320×240 (the native aspect ratio for the iPod). In our sample file, Dan shot himself in 4:3, but then used a letterbox overlay in Final Cut Pro to simulate 16:9 (he prefers the wide-screen look). At this stage in the process, we can actually turn the 4:3 original into a podcast-ready file that is true 16:9, which is what we'll do in our example (there are plenty of folks shooting 4:3 who crave the 16:9 look).

> *Common native 16:9 dimensions are 960×540 [GeekBrief], 640×360 [GearMedia Tech], 480×270 [RocketBoom], and 360×202. Since the iPod is 4:3 and there is really no standard for Flash-based video players, no standard dimensions exist. To determine your own 16:9 measurement, determine a horizontal size, and divide by 1.78. For instance, if your image is 480 pixels wide and you divide 480 by 1.78, you get 269.66 and hence the properly proportioned 480×270 aspect ratio.*

9

9. In the Size Settings panel, in the Dimensions pull-down we choose Custom and type in 426×240. Since the original file is 720×480 (DV is actually slightly larger than standard 640×480), there are plenty of pixels to get to 426×240. Click the radio button next to Preserve aspect ratio using, and choose Crop in the pull-down. If you haven't deinterlaced your video yet, click the Deinterlace Source Video radio button (Figure 9-11).

Figure 9-11. The Export Size Settings window will allow you to export to any dimensions you'd like. If you haven't deinterlaced your video before this point, do it now.

10. Click OK. Now you're back at the Movie Settings panel.

11. Click Settings in the Sound area.

12. Confirm that your sound format is set to AAC, 44.100kHz. Set your Target Bit Rate to 128 kbps. These settings (Figure 9-12) will give you nice, clean sound without unduly creating a gigantic file.

13. Click OK.

14. Back in Movie Settings, Click OK.

15. Now, click Save, and your new MOV will export.

Our upload-ready file is complete. Notice that we're still at full 29.97 fps, but at roughly quarter screen, we've gone from more than 1 GB to 139 MB (Figure 9-13). This file will look fantastic playing in a browser and is ready to upload to MySpace, YouTube, Revver, or blip.tv.

Our final MOV file has been cropped from 4:3 to true 16:9 (Figure 9-14, not necessarily actual size). Sure, we still have tiny black bars on the top and bottom, but it looks better than a (vertically) larger file with letterboxing.

Figure 9-12. The Sound Settings panel. Make sure, no matter what compression you're using, that your audio bit rate is either 44.100kHz or 22.050kHz to be compatible with Flash-based video players.

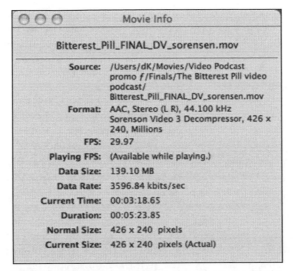

Figure 9-13. The final MOV file's movie information. Notice that we're still at full 29.97 fps, but at roughly quarter screen, we've gone from more than 1 GB to 139 MB.

Figure 9-14. Our final MOV file, cropped from 4:3 to true 16:9.

Updating ID3 tags and artwork

You can store plenty of information within the code of your podcast file. Since your podcast will be uploaded, downloaded, and potentially passed around the Internet, you want to make sure that when it ends up in someone's media player, it's easy to discover where the file came from, who was involved in creating it, and how to find out more information about the file/show/creators.

This information is stored in the form of **ID3 tags**, which are chunks of data that media players can read, making information about each MP3, MOV, M4A, or M4V file easily available. Since these tags were originally designed for handling music files, they are very music-centric: Name, Artist, Album, and so on. Still, as podcasters we use these tags to make sure people know the name of our podcast and podcaster, our URL, our voicemail phone number, our e-mail address, and any other information, including artwork, that we don't want separated from the file.

Creating ID3 tags

In this section, you're going to change the ID3 tags of your new podcast in iTunes. While many podcasters have come to rely on iTunes to manage their ID3 tags (remember, iTunes has a free Windows version), a number of good ID3 tagging applications have been built for all computer platforms, so just use whatever you are comfortable with. (Tag & Rename is a powerful ID3 editor for Windows only, for example.)

First, you must find your file within iTunes (assuming you've already dragged it into iTunes). If it is not readily available in a playlist but is in the Library, find it using the steps outlined in the "Encoding your file in iTunes" section (see Figure 9-3). Once you've tracked down your file, follow these steps:

1. Click the file from within iTunes to highlight it.

2. Go to File ➤ Get Info (press Cmd+I in Mac OS; press Ctrl+I in Windows). A window will open with several tabs to choose from: Summary, Info, Options, and Artwork.

3. Click the Summary tab. You'll want to double-check that you have the right file. If your original audio file is still in iTunes, for instance, at this point it will have the same title as the MP3 version. The summary information appears, giving you the file's size, sample rate, bit rate, format, and so on. Make sure the file format and sample and bit rates are what you expect from your encoding settings. If everything looks acceptable, click Info.

4. In the Info area, you'll see several text fields (Name, Artist, Album, and so on). These fields represent different metadata for the file. Obviously, you're free to put anything you want into these fields, but you'll likely find that conforming to the following guidelines makes your podcast more accessible (see Figure 9-15):

- **Name**: The name of that edition of your podcast.

- **Artist**: Your name/your group's name.

- **Album**: The name of the podcast (series).

> Please note that because MP3 devices such as the iPod and the Zen have small screens, you may want to truncate or abbreviate some words in your podcast's name to make the information easier to read on these players.

- **Track Number**: The number of that edition of your podcast (for example, if it is the fourth show, insert 4).

- **Comments**: Your URL, e-mail address, listener voicemail phone number, "Thanks for listening" message, or whatever.

- **Genre**: Insert Podcast, which is universally recognized as the appropriate genre tag for ease of sorting.

5. Click OK to save your changes.

Figure 9-15. Completing ID3 tags in iTunes

The Comments field is capable of holding quite a bit of information, so include in that field any and all information you want. However, the problem with inserting a lot of information into this field is that you can't add a line break from within iTunes. If you press the Enter/Return key, you will activate the OK button instead of putting in a carriage return. Oops. Since you will most likely be putting the same information in the Comments field for each show, we recommend typing your show information in a text-editing application and then cutting and pasting the information into the Comments field each time you do your tagging. Voilà!

Adding "album art"

You can add a piece of "album art" to your podcast file. This is a great way to include a visual representation of your show right in the file. For people who don't visit podcast websites, this may be their only exposure to any visual representation of your show. Make it good! The artwork pops up in iTunes, and it may appear who knows where else in the future, so use this feature to its fullest advantage.

Your album artwork can be up to a full screen, but it usually renders more clearly if you keep it reasonably small. There are no hard and fast rules about the size of your album art, so experiment and see what you like. We do not recommend using GIFs, because they don't render well if reduced in size for viewing.

Here's how to add album art:

1. Select File ➤ Get Info, and click the Artwork tab (see Figure 9-16).

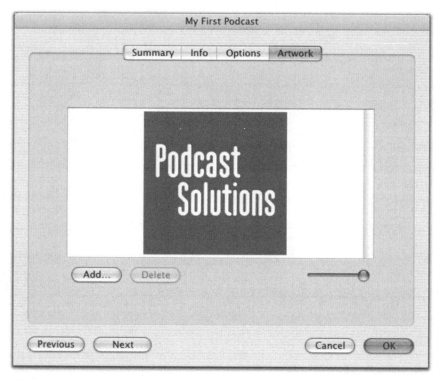

Figure 9-16. Inserting art into MP3 ID3 tags

2. Click the Add button.
3. Find the image you want to use on your hard drive, and double-click to select it. The artwork will be imported into iTunes and added to your ID3 tags.
4. Click OK to save your changes.

Naming your MP3 file

Apparently, some podcast listeners are picky. Not only are they picky about how the information is stored in the ID3 tags, but they want to have the podcasts named in a certain way, too. The name of your podcast has absolutely no bearing on whether it gets downloaded, but following podcast naming conventions makes podcasts easier to sort through on cluttered hard drives and keeps picky podcast listeners nice and calm.

> *Note that naming your MP3 file is different from assigning a name in the ID3 tags. One is the name "on the file," and the other is the name "within the file," respectively. As an example, in Figure 9-15 we named the podcast "Podcast Solutions – The iPodderX Team." When the file is downloaded and played in an MP3 application, that is the name that appears. However, the downloaded MP3 file itself is named PS-2005-05-12.mp3. As you can see, these names are quite different: one is designed for easy organization on the Internet, and the other is designed for easy organization once a listener has downloaded the file.*

Following naming conventions

You'll need to set up a naming convention for your podcast that includes the name of the podcast (or an abbreviation of the name) and the number of that edition or the date of its creation/publication. How you handle the naming is up to you, but most podcast listeners will demand that you are at least consistent.

One of the most common styles of filenaming is the classic **Podcast initials–edition number** method. So if your podcast is called "Podcast Solutions" and this is the sixth episode, you would name the file **PS-6**. This is a nice and clear way to name your show. The problem with this sample name is that once you get to the tenth show, the shows will be listed out of order on most people's hard drives. So, to compensate, change the name to **PS-06**. There, now the problem is fixed . . . as long as you have no intention of doing more than 99 shows. So, you may add another zero or two. Eventually, you realize that this is getting silly, and if you're doing that many shows, how will people remember which is which? If someone wants to refer to a previous show, how can they easily remember which show to look for?

This leads us to another common naming convention: the old tried-and-true **Podcast initials with date** method. So, with this in mind, the sample podcast becomes **PS-2005-04-12**, meaning it was published on May 12, 2005. Naming a file in this way seems to require that you begin with the year, then the month, and finally the date (although Europeans may do it year-date-month). This makes the podcasts easy to sort through on crowded hard drives and makes it easier for listeners to find an old show, as long as they can guess when they first heard it. You'll notice a lot of variation in filenaming among podcasters, but the vast majority includes the publication date in their filenames.

> *To make things easy on yourself, here's a tip if you're using iTunes to do your encoding and/or tagging. Instead of hunting through your hard drive for the finished MP3, simply drag it from a playlist onto your desktop. That way, it's at your fingertips. Rename the file there, and it will be easy to find for uploading.*

9

A word about foresight and files

We may have said this already, but either way it bears repeating: *save the master of your edited file.* You never know what the future brings, and you may want to repurpose that material later. Whether you want to syndicate the file's content to radio or television, press it onto CDs or DVDs, or simply make it available at a higher-quality download, you'll be glad you have the original file.

Summary

Well, that's it! You've made a podcast. From start to finish, from planning to encoding, you've done it all. Congratulations! (Is all this back patting getting sickening?) You've prepped your file by compressing it down to a manageable size and tagging it with all the information about your podcast that anyone might need. Now it's time to get that baby out into the world and globetrotting from media player to media player. You've raised it right—now it has to leave the nest and fly. Let's get the podcast onto the Internet in its own space, and then let's get it downloaded and into your audience's players.

Chapter 10

SERVING IT UP

It's time to get your podcast on the Internet and establish its web presence. The process is really pretty straightforward. First, you'll find a place on the Internet to host your files. Next, you'll upload your files and set up a website or blog to tell everyone what your show is about. Finally, you'll create the feed to let subscribers know that there is a new podcast available for download.

There are many ways to handle setting up a website for your show, and we'll offer several suggestions on how you can get set up without having to take a night class in web design. It is important to note that the decisions you make at this point will have an impact on how your feed is created and maintained as well as where your files will reside. While that might not sound like such a big deal, some of these decisions are akin to deciding to move to a new house. Once you get settled, deciding to move again can be a big hassle, so you need to plan carefully. We'll take things step-by-step so we don't get too far ahead of ourselves.

Here's what the chapter covers in a nutshell:

- Registering and securing your domain
- Hosting and uploading your podcast files
- Creating your website
- Setting up an RSS feed

Registering your own domain

You don't need to have your own domain to do a podcast. As long as your MP3s are on the web and people know how to find them, your podcast will be heard. Many podcasters have a **URL** (**Uniform Resource Locator**; the address you type in your browser) completely unrelated to their podcast. However, in our opinion, the best move is always to secure your own personalized domain name rather than choosing some less-than-ideal free hosting solution. For example, the location of your podcast will be much more memorable if it's at `www.myfarmingpodcast.com`, rather than `www.freeuserhosting.org/~user125448_ntvvvgh06/webfeed/default.html`.

A **domain name** is your "dot-com" (or dot-org, or dot-net, and so on). It's your personal address on the Internet that you control and maintain. You should be careful to choose and register a domain *before* you name your podcast. As hinted at earlier, we recommend coming up with as intuitive a name as possible. As another example, take one of our podcasts, "Grape Radio." Want to guess what its web address is? We made it easy: `www.graperadio.com`. As you might imagine, if someone were to hear the name of the podcast, it would be easy for that person to also remember its web address.

However, this late in the "Internet land grab," finding a suitable domain name is a bit of a crapshoot. You will be surprised at how many domains have long since been snatched up. If you wait until you have a few shows under your belt, you may find that the domain you want is taken. Instead, first think of several names for your podcast and see which domains are available. This is the reality of doing business on the Internet—to a certain extent, the availability of a domain name will dictate the name of your podcast.

> Unlike most of the early podcasters, I never had a blog or website before I started podcasting. Since most podcasters were using a blog as their launch pad, I went ahead and set up my site: `www.mwgblog.com` (easy enough to remember, right?). Things went swimmingly as I started doing my podcast "Reel Reviews—Films Worth Watching."
>
> As my show got more popular, I began to realize that it would be much easier if the name of my site were closer to the name of my show. Truth be told, I did not really even consider myself a blogger—I considered myself a podcaster. The only reason I had a blog was so I could podcast. I also had a few interesting reactions from movie studios when I called about getting advance copies of DVDs. Everything would go great until I gave them the name of my site, MWGblog.com. More than once I got the response, "Oh, it's just a blog." I knew that, right or wrong, my credibility had taken a hit.
>
> For a few months I toyed with new names for my site. The person who owned `www.reelreviews.com` would not return my phone calls, so I settled on `www.reelreviewsradio.com`. The problem was that I had thousands of people who had subscribed to my feed at `www.mwgblog.com`, as well as countless links and references in the press all pointing to the old site. To ensure that all the old links would forward correctly to the new site and, more important, that my subscribers would continue to receive the show, I had to have someone come in and help with all kinds of custom coding. It was a huge hassle.
>
> Learn from my mistake. Plan for success with your podcast, and take your time when naming your show, website, and domain.
>
> —Michael Geoghegan

To secure and use a domain name of your own, you need to register it and then have the domain hosted. Registering a domain name is easy and inexpensive. It wasn't long ago that Network Solutions handled all domain name registrations. The company continues to do a terrific job, but as you can imagine, when Network Solutions was the only one doing it, registration fees were rather high. Nowadays, dozens of companies handle domain registration, including Network Solutions, Register.com, Yahoo!, and GoDaddy.com (the service we both use).

Securing your domain

Once you've decided on several possible domain names, it's time to see what's available, choose an available domain, and register that domain in your name. It's a very simple process that is fairly uniform from site to site:

1. Go to a registration website (see the previous section for a selection of registration sites).

2. Search for your first choice of URL. Simply enter your prospective domain name into the Search field, and press Enter/Return.

3. The search will give you its results, showing the status of the domain you entered and offering up several similar options that you may also want to register. If the domain you want is available, select it, and proceed to the next step in the process.

   If the domain you want is not available, check over the list of proposed alternatives to see whether anything strikes your fancy. These options will most likely be less appealing versions of the domain you searched, with terms such as *online* or *site* tacked onto the end. Also, you may want to consider searching for the .net and .org versions of your domain name of choice, in case that would work better for you than the other names on your list. If not, proceed to the next domain name idea on your list, and repeat the search process. Continue until you find an available domain name that you like and that fits your podcast.

4. You may be asked whether you want to also register the .net, .org, .biz, and so on, versions of your domain to protect the name. Doing so is entirely up to you—it mostly depends on whether you feel not doing so would weaken your "brand."

5. If you are an individual (as opposed to a business), we recommend opting to have your domain listed as "private" in the WHOIS database. The database lists complete information on the registrar of every domain in cyberspace, including the registrar's address and phone number. Unless you want this information made available to everyone and anyone on the Internet, pay the extra couple of dollars for some peace of mind.

Once you own your domain, you can either have it point to an existing website or blog or have it hosted by a hosting service. This will all make more sense when we talk about websites and blogs in a moment.

Hosting your podcast files

You need to find somewhere for your podcasts to live. They need to be posted on the Internet and made available for download. How do you do that? Well, we're assuming you don't have access to Internet storage through your job or school and that you will need to get some of your own. To tell the truth, you may already have Internet space available for your use and you don't even know it.

10

Since we're talking specifically about podcasting, we'll forgo covering posting your video podcasts on other video sites such as YouTube and MySpace. That isn't really podcasting. New media? Sure. Podcasting? No. Using those services is mandatory if you want to ensure the largest audience possible for your programs. We are focused here on getting your files into the hard drives and portable media players of your audience.

Hosting through your ISP

We're going to take a leap of faith and assume you have Internet access at your home or office. You surf the Net, you check e-mail, and you pay a monthly bill or two. What you may not realize (because perhaps it was not a concern until now) is that many Internet service providers (ISPs) make hosting and storage space available as part of their service packages. Many ISPs include in their service agreements a set amount of Internet space to be used for a personal website, file storage, and so forth. That space is just sitting there, ready for your podcasts.

However, you have to be careful. Most of these ISP hosting plans are set up with the expectation that the user will be hosting only tiny web pages or the occasional photo album. They are usually not priced to accommodate the demands of a successful podcast (especially a video podcast, since the files are so much bigger). Read your ISP's service agreement carefully. There will undoubtedly be restrictions on the amount of traffic passing through the service (that is, **bandwidth**) that is allowed per month. Surpassing that bandwidth allocation can be very expensive.

We do not recommend you use this type of storage as the only hosting solution for your MP3s. It is too limited. But when you're just getting started, this might be an option, since it's there and already paid for.

Deciding on a web hosting provider

You will be much better served by finding yourself a bona fide web hosting company to provide file storage and hosting for your site. These companies offer domain hosting, e-mail forwarding (to you@yourdomain.com), storage, and a decent amount of allotted traffic per month. Depending on the service plan, you will be provided with enough storage and bandwidth to keep your podcast humming along for months.

Or will you? As your podcast becomes more popular, bandwidth will become an issue. If you're doing a 30-minute audio podcast that is a 15MB MP3 and 1,000 people download it the first month, that is 15GB of traffic for that month. As you can see, it can add up quickly, especially if your plan provides only 30GB of bandwidth per month. Do the math and get a rough idea of how much storage and bandwidth you'll need per month before settling on a plan for your hosting. It is important that you do some careful comparison-shopping here to find a plan that meets your needs and budget.

While we'd love to give you recommendations, there are just too many hosting companies to list here, and they change their plans all the time in order to remain competitive. One suggestion is to post questions to some of the podcast discussion boards we've mentioned in the book and find out what services others are using to host their files and would be willing to recommend. New and improved podcast hosting solutions seem to be popping up every week. You might even find that some of the more popular podcasters are hosting their shows from multiple sites to spread the bandwidth load of their shows.

If you don't carefully approach the bandwidth problem, you could easily get burned. Most plans charge subscribers exorbitantly high fees for going over their allotted bandwidth. It is crucial that you not only look at the storage and bandwidth offered by each plan (like anyone would, right?) but also *compare the cost for going over your bandwidth*. These costs can add up quickly, and you could suddenly be faced with a huge bill you didn't expect. It's like mobile phone overages—only worse.

One way to get around the bandwidth concern is to find a web hosting service provider that does not restrict your podcast traffic. Liberated Syndication (www.libsyn.com) is a web hosting company created especially to serve the needs of podcasters and is used by some of the biggest names in podcasting today. They seemingly originated the "no bandwidth restrictions" model of service, which means that (unlike most other service providers) you will not be penalized with higher charges if and when your podcast becomes popular. Regardless of the number of people downloading your files, you pay only for the amount of *storage* you want to use, *not the download traffic*. This is ideal for the needs of the average podcaster. Many of the video podcasters we've spoken to use Liberated Syndication; it's perfect for them, since their files are larger than those of the audio podcasters.

Whatever web hosting service provider you choose, make sure to read all the fine print, and make certain you understand everything you're signing up for. Most services involve no long-term commitment, but you don't want to end up with a surprisingly high bill that could have easily been avoided.

Uploading your files

You may be able to upload your audio or video files to your new hosting provider via the host's website. Most hosts have a way to easily choose files from your hard drive and upload them from your browser window. You will also have the opportunity to make new folders and subdirectories within your space. While this may seem like the easiest way to do it, it can actually be very frustrating, and it can be too big a burden for a browser to handle. Usually there is no way to monitor the progress of your uploads and no way to upload in the background while you take care of other business. Well, we're all about taking care of other business, so we recommend uploading through the browser only as a last resort. Instead, you should be using an FTP client.

A **File Transfer Protocol** (**FTP**) client is a software application that makes it easy to upload files to the web. There are many to choose from for every platform, all with the same basic functions. Check out Cyberduck (http://cyberduck.ch; open source and free to use), Fetch (http://fetchsoftworks.com), FTP Transmit (www.panic.com/transmit), and Yummy FTP (www.yummysoftware.com) for some reliable Mac FTP clients. If you're running Windows, you might want to look into SmartFTP (www.smartftp.com; free for personal use) and FileZilla (http://filezilla.sourceforge.net; open source and completely free).

The object of using a decent FTP client is to make uploading as effortless as possible. To get your FTP client running smoothly, you'll need the host name, the username/ID information, and the password your hosting service provided you (see Figure 10-1). This information will be stored in the FTP client so that each time you go to connect to your server space, you'll be able to connect easily. *If you have any trouble setting up the FTP client and getting it to connect successfully, contact your hosting provider*. They will give you all the information you need to get you connected properly.

10

Figure 10-1. The New Connection window in Fetch. All FTP clients will ask you for the same basic information: host, user ID/username, and password.

Once you are connected, you may see a series of directories and folders within the account window, many of which will have cryptic names. Check with your hosting provider about which folders to use for which files. Odds are excellent that if one of the folders is named public_html, that is the folder into which you should put all your files. (But check with your ISP to be sure!) Click the public_html folder to open it. Now you're ready to upload.

Assuming you've uploaded your podcast into a folder called MP3, your podcast MP3's address might be http://www.yourdomain.com/MP3/podcast1.mp3. This means your file podcast1.mp3 is within the MP3 folder on your domain's "root" directory. If anyone were to go to that URL using his or her browser, your podcast would start to play.

Creating your podcast's website

Don't worry, you're not going to have to learn HTML, PHP, or anything else to get yourself set up with a website. You don't need an elaborate website with pages and pages of information, links, shopping carts, and animated buttons. What you do need, however, is a place where your listeners (and potential listeners) can go to find out about you and your show. At the very least, you need a web page with the name of your podcast, links to the MP3 files, and information on how to subscribe to your show. You can accomplish this by setting up a blog or creating a standard HTML website.

A **weblog**, or **blog**, is a type of website (usually created using dynamic code linked to a database) where information can be posted to the web almost instantly. The person maintaining the blog (the **blogger**) can easily type in new text and, with little or no formatting, publish the text to the web. That text can then be read by web-based newsreaders, since most blogs are set up to output an RSS feed that these newsreaders can interpret and display. Converting a blog feed to a podcast feed is relatively simple; therefore, most podcasters (particularly audio podcasters who may be putting out a lot of material) maintain their podcast's web presence by using a blog.

Some podcasters prefer to use a traditional HTML website for their podcasts. (HTML is the standard computer language that website code is written in.) HTML websites are made up of static information, so to update them, you have to directly update the HTML pages, which can be more time-consuming than blogging. However, HTML is also easier to understand from a code point of view.

The choice is up to you regarding which to use, so let's look at a few pros and cons of each to give you an idea of which way you'd like to go. We'll also examine some of the tools you can use to get your site up and running.

Blog site vs. HTML site

In general, blogs are easy to update and usually require minimal knowledge of HTML. People with very little web development experience can set them up (or have their ISP walk them through the process), because they usually feature a fairly intuitive creation procedure. They also usually have fairly robust support communities.

On the other hand, serious HTML website creation tools can be a bit intimidating to novices, although once you get the hang of their basic functions, they are pretty straightforward. Also, with an HTML site your imagination is your only limit. You can do whatever you please, and you don't have to work within the framework of the blog service or software.

Table 10-1 shows a comparison of other considerations when choosing between a blog and a traditional HTML website for your podcast.

Table 10-1. Blog and HTML website comparison

Consideration	Blog	HTML Website
Uploading updated pages and images	Blogs upload pages with the click of a button. With some blogs, images can be uploaded from within the blog software; sometimes the images are uploaded separately.	Many web tools offer convenient, seamless uploading.
Layout and dating	Blogs will format your "postings" based on the format of the blog's template. Very little layout/design is required for each new post, and adding new postings, podcasts, and so on, is nearly foolproof. This comes at a price, however, in that it is often difficult to customize individual postings and pages, and changing the template of the blog changes the look of the entire website. To some, this is quite an advantage; to others, it is a hindrance. It all depends on the amount of control the user wants to have over the site.	Web tools offer much greater flexibility in creating different page layouts. With that flexibility comes the ability, of course, to mess things up if you are in a hurry and are not accustomed to web design conventions and standards. You have not only the luxury of designing each new posting but also the burden of making sure each posting is completely static, so it's much more difficult to make a mess of in general.

Continued

10

179

Table 10-1. Blog and HTML website comparison (continued)

Consideration	Blog	HTML Website
Feed creation	Most blogs will either create an RSS feed that can handle your podcast enclosure automatically or at least create a feed that can be converted to RSS.	If you create your site using HTML, the RSS feed must be created separately, either by hand or using a stand-alone application.
Feedback	Most blogs are set up to accept "comments" from readers/listeners. With the click of a button, people give you feedback about your podcast, chime in on your latest topic, and tell you about themselves. This is a great way to maintain a dialogue between you and your audience, and it's a must-have for any podcast.	HTML sites are not set up to accept comments as easily as a blog. If you choose to go the HTML route, look into setting up a message board or forum so listeners can "discuss" your shows online.
Price	Most blog software is free, although you may need to find someone to help you get it up and functioning properly.	A good, high-end web development application is expensive.

OK, from the comparison in Table 10-1, there doesn't seem to be much of a contest: an HTML site has its advantages, but a blog setup usually comes out on top. The use of blogs is so commonplace in podcasting that you really can't go wrong setting up shop that way. Ultimately, you may even choose to use both solutions: a blog for new podcast posting and feed creation and an HTML site for other areas of your website (links page, bio page, contact information, and so on). You won't regret it.

Building your HTML site

If you're serious about creating a website using traditional web development tools, we strongly suggest going with one of the two 800-pound gorillas in the web development game: Macromedia Dreamweaver or Adobe GoLive. Now, as we've said before, these packages can be intimidating at first. They are simple enough for a beginner to set up a basic page and robust enough to handle just about any requirement you'll ever have down the road. You do not need to know anything about programming to set up a professional-looking site. Adding pictures, creating hyperlinks, and embedding movies and Flash animations is all automated. As long as you know which button to click, you are set.

> For a good example of an HTML-based podcast site, check out our friends at "The Radio Adventures of Dr. Floyd" (http://doctorfloyd.com). In talking to "Dr. Grant" Baciocco, he pointed out that one of the advantages of an HTML-based podcast site is that you are not constrained by a template, as you are with a blog. Using HTML, you are free to make each page look any way you please.

Choosing your blog platform

While we wanted to be fair, it's probably clear that we are more in favor of using a blog as the launching pad for a podcast. You have many choices when it comes to picking your blog service or software. Like anything else, each has its pros and cons. In the sections that follow, we'll cover the three most common methods used by podcasters today:

- The fast and easy Blogger
- The just as fast and slightly more functional blog offered free to Liberated Syndication users
- The complex but rewarding "serious blogging" tools WordPress and Moveable Type

Blogger + FeedBurner = easy and free

If you want to create a blog quickly and painlessly and you already have a way of uploading and storing your MP3 files, then Google's Blogger (www.blogger.com) may be for you. There's almost nothing to set up, there's nothing to learn but some simple HTML (to include pictures and links within your posts, as shown in Table 10-2), and the service is free.

The Blogger homepage claims you can get a blog going in three steps, and it's true. All you need to do is create an account, name your blog, and choose a template for the look and color palette of your site. Blogger has dozens of templates to choose from, all created by professional graphic designers, so finding one that suits your needs is easy. Eventually, you may want to play around with the template of your blog to customize it a bit, but Blogger gives you enough choices up front to get you started.

You need to make sure your Blogger blog is creating a feed from your posts. A slight drawback to using basic Blogger is that (as of this writing) Blogger will automatically output only what is called an **Atom feed**. This is a type of news feed similar to RSS. However, since most of podcasting is built around RSS, you'll need to convert the Atom feed to a podcasting-friendly RSS 2.0.

> *All Blogger feeds are published in Atom 1.0 format. However, if you add ?alt=rss to the end of the feed URL, you will get the same feed in RSS 2.0 format.*

An alternative to adding code to your feed URL is to use FeedBurner (www.feedburner.com; also owned by Google) to convert your Atom feed to an RSS 2.0 feed.

For the sake of completeness, we're going to run you through the process of setting up a blog in Blogger and running the feed through FeedBurner. Do you have to use FeedBurner? No. FeedBurner will, however, give you a level of control and flexibility that you will not get from Blogger alone.

Setting up your blog at Blogger

To set up a Blogger blog, simply go to www.blogger.com, sign up, decide on a name for your blog, create a URL for your blog (typically http://yourpodcast.blogspot.com), and choose a template. Voilà! Your blog has been created. Once that's done, you're immediately taken to a window where you can type in the text for your first post. Simply type whatever you want into the text field, and press Return/Enter to break lines. Choose Compose to add images, links, and movies easily without being exposed to any unsightly HTML. Of course, if you want to see the code, you're welcome to by clicking HTML.

10

There may come a time when knowing even the tiniest bit of HTML is handy for creating blog posts or tinkering with your templates. Until you have `<a href=` memorized, Table 10-2 is a handy little cheat sheet to get things going.

Table 10-2. HTML cheat sheet for blog entries

Purpose	Tags	Example
Create bold text	`<strong></strong>`	Put it `<strong>under</strong>` the table . . .
Create italicized text	`<em></em>`	She was the `<em>only</em>` one who showed up . . .
Create links in text	`<a href="LINK URL"></a>`	For more information, go to `<a href="http://www.podcastsolutions.com">Podcast Solutions</a>`.
Open a link in a new window	Add `target="_blank"` to `<a href="LINK URL">` tags	Visit `<a href=http://www.podcastsolutions.com target="_blank">Podcast Solutions</a>`.
Add an image	`<img src="IMAGE URL">`	`<img src="http://www.podcastsolutions.com/images/logo.gif">`
Use an image as a link	`<a href="LINK URL">`	`<a href="http://www.podcastsolutions.com"><img src="http://www.podcastsolutions.com/images/logo.gif"></a>`

The only downside at this point is that your blog isn't yet set up to help you podcast. To do so, follow these steps:

1. Click the Settings tab above the new post text field.

2. Click Formatting. (You will eventually want to go through all of these tab choices and set up your preferences, but right now you're focusing on getting podcast-ready.)

3. Scroll down to the next-to-last choice, Show Link Field, and select that radio button. Now when you go to create a new post, you will see a Link field just below the Title field in the new post window (see Figure 10-2). This field is where you need to put the URL of your uploaded MP3. This URL is information that will eventually end up in the `<enclosure>` tag of your RSS feed, making automatic downloads of your podcast possible.

4. Within the main text area of the post, type in whatever information you want to post about your podcast: the topic, the length, the rating, whatever.

5. Click Publish Post. Within a few moments, your first post will be formatted based on the template you chose and ready to view.

6. Go back to Settings ➤ Site Feed. You need to note the information listed beside the heading Site Feed URL. That is the information you will need to input into FeedBurner. It should look like this: `http://yourpodcast.blogspot.com/atom.xml`.

Figure 10-2. In the Blogger Create Post window, make sure to include the URL of your podcast MP3 in the Link text field. That is what will eventually create the podcast enclosure.

Setting up FeedBurner

Now let's set up FeedBurner to take that Atom feed and convert it into not only a podcast-ready RSS feed but ideally an iTunes-ready feed as well. Don't worry if you still don't understand what we're talking about here—just follow along and everything will be fine, we promise. (We'll discuss RSS feeds in great detail later.)

1. Go to www.feedburner.com.

2. The site will ask you for your blog or feed address. Type the site feed URL you just got from Blogger. Check the radio button that says "I am a podcaster!"

3. Click Next. You'll be taken to a page asking you to create an account with FeedBurner and to give your new "burned" feed a title and "feed address." The feed address will be http://feeds.feedburner.com/ and then whatever you claim as your specific feed name. Remember to keep it simple and memorable. This is the feed you'll use to submit to podcast directories. Click Activate Feed.

4. FeedBurner will send you to a new page, shouting "Congrats! Your FeedBurner feed is now live. Want to dress it up a little?" Frankly, you don't need to worry about any of these items save one. All the others will give you this bell or that whistle, but that's not what you're working toward—you're working toward a podcast.

10

5. Click Next. This is where you insert information into your feed that is used by iTunes. Confirm that Create podcast enclosures from links to is set to the media type you'll be podcasting (it will keep FeedBurner from podcasting anything and everything you link to) or leave it on any rich media file in case you will be podcasting audio and video (Figure 10-3). Click Next.

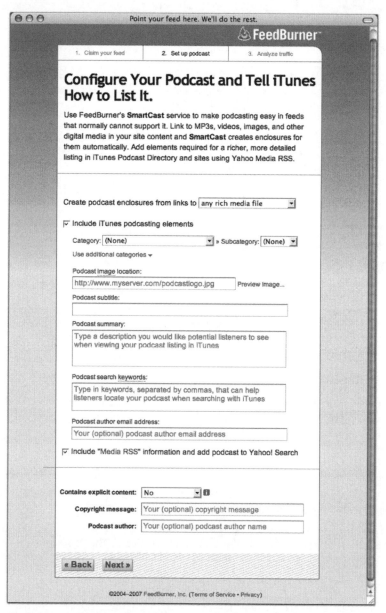

Figure 10-3. Setting up your podcast feed in FeedBurner is simple. Just fill in each field to ensure iTunes compatibility.

6. Now you're at the Analyze traffic page. Select the radio buttons for Clickthroughs and Item enclosure downloads. You may want this information when it comes time for monetization. Click Next.

And that's it—you're ready to go. When you've finished uploading a new podcast MP3, create a new posting, include the link to point to the MP3 as outlined previously, and publish the post through Blogger. Everything else will take care of itself. You will never need to worry about FeedBurner again—once it's set up, it continues to translate your blog feed to a podcast feed automatically each time you post.

Podcast hosting + blog = Liberated Syndication

To discuss Liberated Syndication is to jump around a little bit and talk about blogs, hosting your files, and the RSS feed all at once. Liberated Syndication is an ISP that was created especially to service the needs of podcasters. It has a rather inventive "no bandwidth restrictions" model of service, which means that (unlike with most other service providers) you will not be penalized with higher charges if and when your podcast becomes popular. As we mentioned earlier in the chapter, whether you have one person download your files or one million, you only pay for the amount of *storage* you want to use, but *not the download traffic*. Yes, that's right: it's the seemingly perfect ISP for future podstars.

But actually, it gets better. Not only does Liberated Syndication not charge for excessive traffic, but also it gives you a monthly allotment of storage space to use. So, instead of having 100MB of total space to use, you might have 100MB of *new* storage space each month to use. At the beginning of each billing cycle, you are automatically allotted fresh space. Your existing files are **archived** (that is, moved from Liberated Syndication's fastest servers to their less speedy but storage-rich brothers) and remain online until you stop using the service. Yes, it seems too good to be true (or it will once you have 100MB of podcasts to juggle), but true it is. Even better, each account comes with a foolproof blog built in that will automatically create your RSS feed for you. Simply choose whether it's a podcast or text post, upload your file right from the page, attach the file to the post using a pull-down menu, type in your text, and publish (see Figure 10-4). You can even easily add graphics and ping http://audio.weblogs.com.

"Real" blogs: WordPress and Moveable Type

If you want to be a "power podcaster," you'll want to set up a power blog. The methods outlined in the previous sections are great, and they certainly get the job done, but to have real control over your blog, you'll want to use a top-of-the-line blog platform such as WordPress (www.wordpress.org) or Movable Type (www.movabletype.org). WordPress is free, and a limited version of Moveable Type is also available for free.

Setting up one of these two powerhouses is complicated enough to exceed the scope of this book. However, there are extremely detailed, easy-to-follow tutorials available on the web that will take you through the entire setup process. Don't be intimidated. There is always the option of searching out a hosting provider that offers "one-click WordPress install" as part of their hosting package. If having total control over your podcast site is appealing to you, then you should check out these blog applications. Each is full of features and gives you the last word on the content and layout of the blog. Sure, using these applications involves more of a learning curve than the other two methods just described, but the difference in the results is night and day.

10

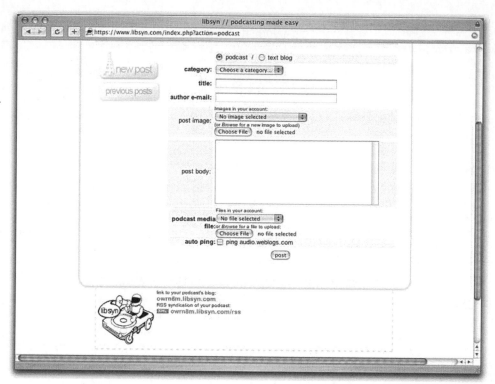

Figure 10-4. Liberated Syndication's blog tool, which is free with every account and handy for podcasters

Want our recommendation? We prefer and recommend **WordPress**. WordPress (which as its creators so eloquently put is "both free and priceless") is highly customizable, and developers are constantly creating new and improved plug-ins to further extend its flexibility. If you decide to use WordPress, there is a very active support community (www.wordpress.org/support). Also, because so many people use WordPress, you can easily find everything from step-by-step setup instructions to complex plug-ins that will allow you to do almost anything you can imagine.

> *Want to see some WordPress setups? Check out* www.reelreviewsradio.com, www.thebitterestpill.com, *and* www.podcastsolutions.com.

podPress

podPress (www.mightyseek.com/podpress) is the indispensable WordPress plug-in developed exclusively for podcasters by Dan Kuykendall of MightySeek.com. podPress automatically adds to your WordPress podcast post a customizable Flash Player that can play on the page or in a pop-up window, format-specific icons so visitors recognize that it's a podcast post, password protection of selected posts, complete iTunes compatibility, and a host of other features. *If you use WordPress for podcasting, explore podPress.*

Your domain, revisited

Now that you've set up your blog or website, whether it's hosted by Blogger or on your own server, you have a place on the Internet to call your own. It's time to set up your domain so that when people try to connect to it, they are taken to your site. All you'll need to do for this is go back to your registry service (GoDaddy.com, for instance) and make adjustments to your account there. Up until now the domain has just been "parked," sitting idly doing nothing. Now that you have someplace to point it, get it pointing.

If your site is being hosted by a hosting service provider (like Liberated Syndication), you will need to get that company's **Domain Name Service (DNS)** numbers. These are the magic numbers that tell browsers to go to the host's servers when looking for your web pages. Like we've said before, if you have any questions regarding setting up your domain to point to your host, contact your service provider for all the information.

If your site is a blog being hosted by a blog provider (like Blogger) or is uploaded to your ISP account, you may want to set up your URL to "forward" to that web address. Then when people type your URL into their browser, they will be forwarded to whatever URL you designate (your web page, your blog, and so on). That way, instead of telling people to go to www.podcastsolutions.blogspot.com, or to www.earthlink.net/~podcastsolutions/index.html, you just point them to www.podcastsolutions.com, and they are automatically taken to the correct page. Your registry service will have easy-to-follow instructions on how to set this up, which usually involve asking you for the URL you'd like your domain to forward to and whether you want the forwarding to be "hidden." Simple as can be.

The RSS feed

Gulp! You're finally going to have to learn to write code, right? Well, no. It's time to set up the RSS feed, but you still won't have to write any code. Yes, you may want to get to know the code a tiny bit, just to ensure that you have some idea of how it works. That way, if something ever goes wrong, you stand half a chance of figuring out why. For that reason we have included an uncommonly "geeky" (for this book), in-depth description of the RSS feed. It is here as a reference and is not required reading, but speaking from experience, we wish someone had laid it out for us like we have here so we could have avoided all the struggles we went through when we first started. So here it comes.

Really Simple Syndication (RSS) is written in Extensible Markup Language (XML), as we discussed earlier. The "feed" is simply a page of raw code that is stored on the Internet to be read by podcatchers and other newsreaders. So, let's take a look at the XML and see what it includes. If you find all this code stuff too mind-boggling, just skip to the section titled "Creating the feed"—you won't miss anything crucial.

OK, here's the XML code for a sample Podcast Solutions podcast, with one MP3 enclosure. This is a fairly straightforward version of a feed, created in Feeder (www.reinventedsoftware.com). We'll first give you the whole feed here, and then we'll talk about some of its key elements in the next section:

```
<?xml version="1.0" encoding="utf-8"?>
<rss version="2.0">
  <channel>
    <title>The Podcast Solutions Sample Podcast Series</title>
    <link>http://www.podcastsolutions.com</link>
```

```
<description>
  A series of sample podcasts, intended to make the RSS feed
  more easily understood.
</description>
<generator>
  Feeder 1.0.4 http://reinventedsoftware.com/feeder/
</generator>
<docs>http://blogs.law.harvard.edu/tech/rss</docs>
<language>en-us</language>
<copyright>
  Copyright 2005, Michael Geoghegan and Dan Klass
</copyright>
<managingEditor>
  Michael@podcastsolutions.com (Michael Geoghegan)
</managingEditor>
<webMaster>Dan@podcastsolutions.com (Dan Klass)</webMaster>
<pubDate>Tue, 03 May 2005 18:22:02 -0700</pubDate>
<lastBuildDate>Tue, 03 May 2005 18:22:02 -0700</lastBuildDate>
<image>
  <url>http://www.podcastsolutions.com/logo.jpg </url>
  <title>The Podcast Solutions Sample Podcast Series</title>
  <link> http://www.podcastsolutions.com </link>
  <description>Podcast Solutions logo</description>
</image>
<item>
  <title>#1: Trying to Understand the RSS Feed</title>
  <description>
  <![CDATA[
    <img src="http://www.podcastsolutions.com/podcast_icon.jpg">
    The first in our series of sample podcasts.  This one shows
    how the RSS feed looks when you look under the hood at the
    raw XML code.  It's not actually as baffling as you thought
    it would be, right?
  </description>
  <author> Dan@podcastsolutions.com (Dan Klass)</author>
  <pubDate>Tue, 03 May 2005 13:51:57 -0700</pubDate>
  <enclosure url=http://www.podcastsolutions.com/sample1.mp3
                  length="19908738"
                  type="audio/mpeg"/>
</item>
</channel>
</rss>
```

Before we get into how to effortlessly create your feed (like we did a bit when talking about FeedBurner), let's take a look at a few elements of the RSS code next so you understand how each element is important to not only getting the feed to work but promoting your podcast as well.

Examining the naked XML

Wow, that code listing in the previous section is a mess, right? Well, not really. Actually, it makes a lot of sense, and once we go through it and explain what's what, you'll realize that if push came to shove, you'd be able to update your code by hand without a hitch. Let's take a look, piece by piece.

We'll first present the code, and then we'll explain it.

```
<?xml version="1.0" encoding="utf-8"?>
<rss version="2.0">
```

These elements are simply an indicator that the particular version of XML/RSS that the following code is written in is XML, version 1.0, and RSS, version 2.0. Don't worry about the deeper ramifications. You'll never need to worry about this part.

```
<channel>
```

Everything in the feed must be between the opening channel tag, `<channel>`, and the closing channel tag, `</channel>`. In XML, like HTML, all tags that open (the opening tag is between angle brackets, `< >`) must close (the closing tag looks the same as the opening tag except it has a backslash before its name, `</ >`). This being the case, there is a closing `<channel>` tag at the end of the code, right before the tag that closes the RSS.

```
<title>The Podcast Solutions Sample Podcast Series</title>
    <link>http://www.podcastsolutions.com</link>
    <description>
      A series of sample podcasts, intended to make the RSS feed
      more easily understood.
    </description>
```

These tags establish the name (in `<title>` tags) of your series of podcasts, the main web address for the podcast (in `<link>` tags), and a description of the podcast series (in `<description>` tags). This description is more important than it seems: it shows up in podcatchers, directory listings, and online podcast players, so make sure it is a thorough, well-thought-out, and well-written description of your podcast. It will end up being one of your most valuable marketing tools.

```
<generator>
    Feeder 1.0.4 http://reinventedsoftware.com/feeder/
</generator>
```

The application used to create the feed is indicated within `<generator>` tags.

```
<docs>http://blogs.law.harvard.edu/tech/rss</docs>
```

This is a link to a Harvard Law School website, which includes in-depth information on RSS, including a very nice description of everything we're discussing right now! Why does it seem to end up in most RSS code? Who knows. Someone is just trying to be complete, we suppose.

```
<language>en-us</language>
```

10

This `<language>` tag tells the world that the feed is written in American English. If you are in another country and/or want to podcast in a different language, refer to the RSS specification at http://blogs.law.harvard.edu/tech/rss to find the right language tag to use here.

```
<managingEditor>
   Michael@podcastsolutions.com (Michael Geoghegan)
</managingEditor>
```

This line gives the e-mail address of the person to contact with questions or concerns about the content of the feed.

```
<webMaster>Dan@podcastsolutions.com (Dan Klass)</webMaster>
```

This line gives the e-mail address of the person to contact with questions or concerns about the feed itself.

```
<pubDate>Tue, 03 May 2005 18:22:02 -0700</pubDate>
```

This line gives the date and time when the material in the feed was published. Typically, this will be the same as the "last build date."

```
<lastBuildDate>Tue, 03 May 2005 18:22:02 -0700</lastBuildDate>
```

This is the date and time when the feed was last updated. For the podcatchers to know to download your latest MP3, it is crucial that this date is correct. If this dates ends up out of whack, your podcasts may not be downloaded by your subscribers.

```
<image>
      <url>http://www.podcastsolutions.com/logo.jpg </url>
      <title>the Podcast Solutions Sample Podcast Series</title>
      <link> http://www.podcastsolutions.com </link>
      <description>Podcast Solutions logo</description>
   </image>
```

Everything within the `<image>` tag is optional. This tag embeds an image (typically the logo of the podcast series) within the podcast that will accompany the feed when read by some readers/podcatchers. This series of subtags includes the URL of the image itself, the name of the image, a link that clicking the image would direct a browser to, and a description of the image.

```
<item>
```

Now, we are shifting from tags containing descriptions of the podcast series as a whole to tags containing descriptions of a single edition of that series. So, everything within the `<item>` tag pertains to only one particular podcast (in this case, sample podcast #1).

```
<title>#1: Trying to Understand the RSS Feed</title>
      <description>
       <![CDATA[
       <img src="http://www.podcastsolutions.com/podcast_icon.jpg">
        The first in our series of sample podcasts.  This one shows
        how the RSS feed looks when you look under the hood at the
```

```
        raw XML code.   It's not actually as baffling as you thought
        it would be, right?
</description>
```

So, this time the <title> and <description> are for our sample podcast, "#1: Trying to Understand the RSS Feed." Again, this description is important, because it will not only sell your podcast but it will also ensure the text within it will end up in newsreaders and other sites that aggregate these feeds, turning the description into text that search engines crawl through. Descriptive words you use here will get picked up in searches, and that could mean new listeners. Don't skimp on the descriptions!

```
    <author> Dan@podcastsolutions.com (Dan Klass)</author>
        <pubDate>Tue, 03 May 2005 13:51:57 -0700</pubDate>
```

This part is fairly self-explanatory, given what we're covered thus far.

```
    <enclosure url=http://www.podcastsolutions.com/sample1.mp3
                length="19908738"
                type="audio/mpeg"/>
```

Finally we come to the <enclosure> tag—the magic bullet that turns simple news feeds into podcast heaven. This is the tag that the podcatchers need, because it is the code that points to the location of your podcast MP3 file. Without it, the feed is fairly useless, consisting of titles and descriptions but no podcast.

The **<enclosure>** tag includes three elements: the location of the podcast MP3 (in the form of a URL), the length of the podcast in bytes, and the type of file the enclosure is. In the case of your typical podcast, it is an MP3 file. Truth be told, this exact code would work with image files and movie files. The images and movies would be downloaded by the podcatcher and sorted automatically (presumably, depending on your system).

```
    </item>
    </channel>
    </rss>
```

These tags close the item, the channel, and the RSS.

Now, if we were coding by hand and wanted to add another episode to this series, we would reconstruct all the information within the <item> tag, updating the information to reflect the new podcast. Cutting and pasting come in handy in these cases. Dan did his RSS for "The Bitterest Pill" by hand for almost six months, with very few glitches (and he's no computer programmer!). The main thing to remember when doing the code by hand is to *never use an ampersand*! Ampersands (&) are code killers. If you *have* to use an ampersand within your description, use the code-friendly version (&)—but don't worry, odds are you won't be handling the code in its raw state anyway. There are better ways to build a feed, as we discuss next.

The iTunes Music Store uses additional tags to get the host's name, artwork, and other information to appear correctly within their podcasting section. We thought about including the tags in this chapter, but they appear to be in flux currently. To take a look at the raw iTunes tags, see the PDF document at http://phobos.apple.com/static/podcast_specifications.pdf.

10

Creating the feed

A podcaster needn't write his RSS from scratch. Why waste the time? After prepping, recording, editing, and processing, who wants to sit and write code anyway? In the sections that follow, we describe a few different ways to get an RSS feed built effortlessly: using an automatic RSS creator, using a stand-alone application, and having your blog build the feed.

Using an automatic RSS creator

There are websites and bits of Java code floating around that will automatically generate RSS based on the information stored in your MP3's ID3 tags. Simply make sure all the information you want to end up in the feed is included within the appropriate tags (depending on the configuration set up by the particular creator), and run the MP3 through the website/code.

This may be an attractive solution for podcasters looking to shave some time off their production schedule, but it is so limiting it is hardly recommended for serious podcasters. "Real" RSS has the ability to include text links, images, and a lot more information than can be stored within the ID3 tags. By using this method, you are limiting yourself unnecessarily. You will find that including links and images within the RSS feed will enhance your presence within directories and podcatchers. This is where you'll attract listeners, so you must put your best face forward.

Using a stand-alone application

Several stand-alone applications are available that will create beautiful, robust RSS for you, without your having to use a blog to post your code. Feeder for the Mac OS is what Dan switched to after giving up on hand-coding, and he hasn't regretted it. Feeder works in much that same way as any blog platform, except that it doesn't publish blog posts—only RSS and RSS for podcasts (including iTunes tags). Still, the formatting and functionality is much the same, and Feeder, or another application like it, is an ideal choice for podcasters who choose to use a traditional nonblog website (or make the mistake of hand coding at the beginning like Dan did). We live, we learn. The only real downside of going this route is that you are potentially duplicating work: you are updating your website and your RSS separately.

Having your blog build it

Yes, your blog will build the feed for you, automatically. Any blog platform worth its bandwidth (WordPress) will be able to take your posts and add an enclosure fairly simply. The blog post becomes the contents of the <description> tag, and the title of the post becomes the <title> tag (see, aren't you glad we talked about this already?). You will be asked to designate a file to be attached as an enclosure, and that is automatically built into the feed code as well. When you publish your new blog post, it will create and post an update to your XML file. Simple. Just make sure that your blog is exporting an RSS feed and not an Atom feed.

> *Don't forget: put a link in each blog posting to the corresponding MP3 file so visitors can just click and listen.*

Displaying your feed

No matter how you create your RSS code, the one thing that every podcaster has to do is display the feed address. Until all podcatchers have seamless "one-click" subscribing, some podcast listeners will need to know your feed's URL. You don't want to alienate any potential listeners just because they are using one catcher rather than another. In fact, you may want to take this idea a step further and create a place on your blog or website that explains exactly how to subscribe to your podcast (see Figure 10-5). It can't hurt.

Figure 10-5. To make it easy for people to subscribe manually, Michael displays his feed URL prominently on his site.

Summary

There is this tremendous temptation to congratulate you at the end of each chapter, and it's getting a bit old. But let's be honest, you've come a long way. And now you're done. You have a podcast. Start to finish. Everything else we cover in this book from here until the end is gravy: promoting your podcast, getting listed in directories, making money at podcasting. All of that can be done or not, and it doesn't change the simple fact that you've been through the process, and you've put a podcast into the world. If you've followed along and followed through on each step, you could put your RSS feed into iTunes, and lo and behold, your podcast would download. Yes, you can deny it no longer: you are a podcaster! (Now all you need to learn is the secret handshake . . .)

Honestly, the thrill lasts only so long. Being a podcaster just isn't enough. You want to be a podcaster with an audience, right? Thought so. So, let's get the word out that there's a new 'cast in town. Let's get you known and generate a little buzz!

Chapter 11

GETTING HEARD

After all the hard work you've put into creating your show, it's difficult and possibly upsetting to imagine your podcast just sitting there on the server, being downloaded by only the two or three family members you can get to actually understand what you're spending your time doing. Let's be very clear about something right here and now: just because you think you're "podcasting" and there are millions of podcast listeners out there doesn't mean your podcast is going to instantly have an audience. People can't listen to a podcast they don't know about or can't find. You need to get your podcast out to the podcast community and out to the world.

As the number of podcasts continues to skyrocket (especially the number of big-budget corporate podcasts), it's becoming harder and harder to carve out a slice of the audience pie. However, there are ways you can generate attention and encourage people to check out your podcast. The key to building an audience is to *get seen and heard* (perhaps this seems too obvious, but bear with us). Sure, not everyone who checks out your show is going to love it, but *nobody* can love it if they don't find it first.

So, without further ado, let's look at how you can get your podcast the exposure it deserves. In this chapter, we'll cover the following topics:

- Listing your podcast in the major podcast directories
- Networking with other podcasters and using Web 2.0
- Getting your podcast reviewed
- Sparking interest in your podcast from the mass media

Getting listed in the major podcast directories

First and foremost, you need to get your show listed in the major **podcast directories**. Podcast directories are an essential part of any podcaster's promotional arsenal. Listeners go to podcast directories to find new shows, rate their favorite shows, and even to listen to shows. A well-put-together directory has the potential to be the virtual "town square" for thousands of podcast listeners and producers worldwide.

Podcast directories represent a growing and extremely competitive area in the podcasting universe. The creators and caretakers of these podcast databases know that podcast consumers (and the media) go to podcast directories when they want to search for new favorites. New audience members mean more traffic, and more traffic means potential increased revenue to the directories in the form of ad sales.

Most directories are on a tireless quest to better service their visitors and the podcasts they list, hoping to be *the* podcast directory. Podcast directories need podcasters as much as podcasters need directories, so the directories are constantly improving and streamlining their sites, inside and out, to make the experience of getting listed and getting discovered as easy and as powerful as possible.

In the following sections, we'll cover how to create your podcast directory listing, get your show information posted in the most popular and influential podcast directories, and ping podcatchers to let them know your show is out there.

Crafting your listing

Before you submit your listing to a single podcast directory, you'll want to do a little thinking up front about how you'd like to "position" your show. Not only will potential listeners see the name of your show, but also they'll be able to view a description of your show and the category in which your show is listed.

Just as with the description of your podcast within your RSS feed, the description you submit to a podcast directory should be concise and descriptive enough to entice people to audition your show. (In the case of some directories, the description of your show that gets displayed *is* the description from your RSS feed.) This is one of those golden opportunities to sell your show to potential subscribers. Make sure you tell them exactly what your podcast is about and who might like it, and give a feel for the overall tone of the show. Consider this your sales pitch in paragraph form. Make it count.

> *Here's an example of the description from Dan's show, "The Bitterest Pill":*
>
> *The Dan Klass Show: Examinations of life from a stay-at-home dad/shut-in.*

You will often be asked to list your podcast in a particular category. The category structure of the directories is an incredible benefit for both the podcaster and the podcast user. By breaking down the podcast listings by category, the directories make it that much easier for people to find the types of podcasts they want to find. By the same token, if you choose to list your show in the wrong category, it could mean that your podcast is overlooked by your target audience, which is a bad thing. Choose the categories you want to be listed in carefully. Most directories use a wide enough array of categories that you're bound to find one that suits you. If not, drop the directory in question an e-mail and suggest a new category.

We aren't kidding about suggesting a new category to a directory—we've each been the first in a category on a directory. For example, "Reel Reviews" was the first movie-oriented podcast at the time I created it, so I asked Adam Curry to create a "Movie" category (node) in iPodder.org since I thought that category title was a better fit than "Entertainment."

If the category makes sense to you, then it will probably make sense to the kinds of people you are trying to reach.

—Michael Geoghegan

Submitting your listing to the main directories

We talked a bit about specific directories in Chapter 2. As we examine directories in this chapter, it's from the point of view of a podcast creator, as opposed to a podcast consumer. In the sections that follow, we'll look specifically at the iTunes Store (www.apple.com/itunes/store/podcasts.html), PodcastPickle.com, and Podcast Alley (www.podcastalley.com). We want to make sure you get your show listed in at least these three directories, because they're the biggest currently on the scene. If you aren't listed in these directories, you aren't really listed at all. We'll also cover other available directories that are definitely worth investigating.

Apple iTunes

The Apple iTunes Store is the 800-pound gorilla of podcasting. iTunes is responsible for bringing untold numbers of new listeners and viewers to podcasting every week, and its importance to podcast producers is immeasurable. Since so many people already use iTunes to manage their music collections, there is no need for them to download new software or search the web for podcasts. If users are already familiar with the iTunes Store, they are halfway to your podcast.

You need to be listed in the iTunes podcast directory without question, and to get listed, you'll need to play by the iTunes rules. You need to use an iTunes-compatible feed, using iTunes RSS tags (see Chapter 10). Feedburner and podPress can help with this immensely.

Luckily, submitting is the easy part:

1. Go to the Podcasting section of the iTunes Store from within the iTunes application.
2. Look for the Publish a Podcast area, and click the link there. Or, direct your browser to https://phobos.apple.com/WebObjects/MZFinance.woa/wa/publishPodcast. The browser will open iTunes and take you directly to where you need to be.
3. You are now at the Publish Podcasts to the Music Store page. Type or paste the feed URL of the podcast you are submitting into the text field at the bottom of the page (see Figure 11-1), and click Continue.
4. On the Review Podcast page, you can see how iTunes will interpret your feed. As it says on the page (see Figure 11-2), you cannot make changes from this page. This page only reads your code; it cannot help you change your code. For that, you need to go back into your feed and make the appropriate modifications, either to clean up the code itself or to add missing information.

11

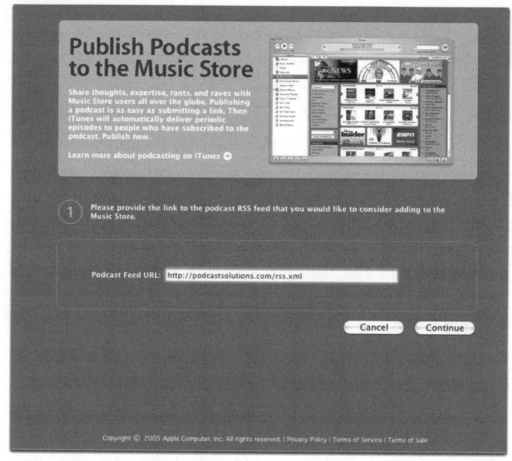

Figure 11-1. Type or paste your iTunes-compatible feed information here.

5. If/when the information displayed looks right to you, click Publish.

6. Then wait. As of this writing, iTunes is very slow to add podcasts, very slow to update changes in podcast information, and very slow to update podcast episode listings for each show. When iTunes looks for new episodes of podcasts a user has subscribed to, it seems to read the current version of the feed. But when it displays the podcast "page" within iTunes, it relies on a cached version for some time.

> *Here's a great iTunes-related trick: you can easily create a link on your blog or website that will take listeners directly to your "page" within iTunes. Simply go to your podcast page and right-click (Windows) or Ctrl-click (Mac) your podcast's artwork. A pull-down menu will appear with the choices* iTunes Help *and* Copy iTunes Music Store URL. *Choose the latter option to send the URL of your show's iTunes page to your clipboard. Go to your website and create a link to that URL. Now whenever someone wants to find your show in the iTunes Store, it's just a click away!*

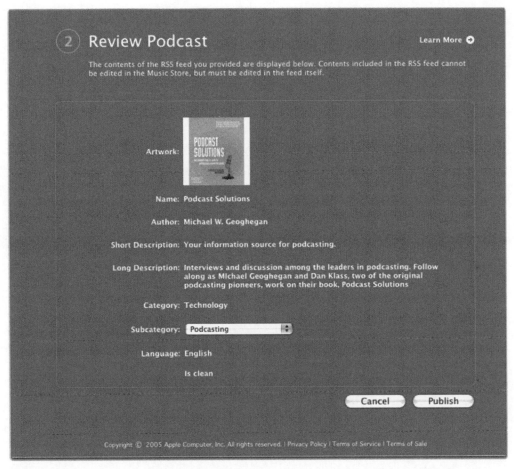

Figure 11-2. iTunes reads the feed and shows you how the information will be displayed within the iTunes Store.

PodcastPickle.com and Podcast Alley

The other main directories you'll want your show to be listed in are PodcastPickle.com, and Podcast Alley (www.podcastalley.com). These sites have become incredibly popular places for podcast fans to go looking for new shows. As such, they are an essential submission for all podcasters. Each has become a town square of sorts for the entire podcasting community, with listeners and producers stopping by daily to see who's hot, who's not, what the discussion topics are for that day, and much more. The power of these sites' "Top Ten" lists is quite impressive, as exposure on the Top Ten has led directly to national and international press coverage for many podcasters.

> *See our interview with Podcast Alley's Chris McIntyre at* www.podcastsolutions.com.

To give you an example of how to submit your show to one of these directories, let's submit a show to Podcast Alley:

1. From the Podcast Alley homepage (www.podcastalley.com), click the Add a Podcast link.

2. On the submission form that appears (Figure 11-3), insert your podcast title, website, feed (RSS), and e-mail address. You'll also be asked for a description of the podcast and some "keywords" to further describe your show. Podcast Alley warns, "Add keywords and a good description. Good search results on this site depend on it," and we couldn't agree more.

Add a Podcast
If you have a podcast you create, or a podcast you like, please submit the information to us below. We are trying to create the best index of all the availalbe podcasts on the internet. All podcasts will be reviewed before being made public to ensure link accuracy.

* *PLEASE* <u>do a search</u> and make sure the podcast is not in the library already.
* *PLEASE* Add Keywords and a good Description. Good Search Results on this site depend on it.

Title of Podcast:

Podcast Website:

Podcast Feed Link (RSS, XML, PHP):

Description:

Your Email:

Keywords:

Pick a Genre: Technology

Submit Podcast   Clear Entries

Figure 11-3. Podcast Alley podcast submission panel

Other directories

There are perhaps dozens of other podcast directories, all vying to be an alternative to iTunes Store and Podcast Alley. Time will tell which ones make it in the long run and which don't. Still, it never hurts to get listed in as many directories as possible. The other directories we recommend checking out are as follows:

- Yahoo Podcasts (www.podcasts.yahoo.com)
- Odeo (www.odeo.com)
- Podfeed.net (www.podfeed.net)
- PodNova (www.podnova.com)
- Podcast Bunker (www.podcastbunker.com)

We'll all have to watch how the relationships between the directories and the podcatchers change over time, especially now that Apple's iTunes has podcast features built in and as some directories are inevitably swallowed up by corporate concerns.

It seems that almost every day we receive notice of a new directory that claims it will soon be the best. When you start submitting your show information to directories, do yourself a favor and search around a bit. The situation is fluid enough at the moment that by the time you have digested the contents of this book and are ready to publish your podcast, new "must-list" directories might be available.

Pinging podcast trackers

A great way to let the world know you have just posted a new episode of your podcast is to **ping** podcast trackers (that is, make them aware of you) such as http://audio.weblogs.com, a service run by one of the original podcasters, Dave Winer. This service keeps a running list of the "freshest podcasts in the known universe." When you visit the homepage, you will see a list of the 100 most recently posted podcast episodes on the Internet, along with their RSS feed links (represented by the white-on-orange XML buttons).

Most blog software allows for pinging of tracking services such as this. If you are not sure how to do it with your blog software, you can manually let http://audio.weblogs.com know you have a new podcast up by visiting http://audio.weblogs.com/pingform.html. Enter the name of your podcast and the address of your RSS feed. The service will then respond by letting you know whether it sees your podcast as new. If not, it probably just means the service has already logged it. How did it do that? Magic.

The list moves pretty quickly these days, because new podcasts are posted now at an alarming rate (we remember when it took a day or two to cycle off and be dropped from the 100 most recent list!). Even so, this service is used by many to see what is new in the podcasting world. In addition, the site features a great tool, a podcast feed debugger, which you can access through a link in the checklist of common problems at www.podcatch.com/howToPing.

11

Networking with other podcasters

A great way to generate new subscribers is through networking. Nobody understands what it's like to try to connect with an audience quite like your fellow podcasters. They have been there and done that. Other podcasters can be a resource for attracting new subscribers, or they can at least give you advice on how best to build some awareness. In the next few sections, we talk about how to network effectively.

Sending show promos to other podcasters

This pertains mostly to audio podcasts, but you never know. Back when we discussed how to find podcasts in Chapter 2, we talked a bit about listening to or viewing the podcast promos being played on your favorite shows. Well, now you're on the other side of that audience/podcaster fence, and it's time to listen again, but from a new angle. Now when you hear a promo for a podcast being played on another show, take special note: what is it about this promo that works or doesn't work? Does it make you want to check out that show, or does it make you want to write a nasty e-mail to the podcaster who played the promo?

You should definitely consider developing your own podcast promos to send to other podcasters. When you're putting together your own promos, keep in mind that you're targeting two very distinct audiences: the other podcaster's audience and the other podcaster. Get to know the other podcaster's audience and understand what they've come to expect from that podcaster's show. You can't send an adult-themed promo to a family-friendly show and expect it to get played. We hope you're sending your promo to a podcaster whose audience is similar to your own, so that sort of consideration is moot. Still, consider every angle. More important, consider the other podcaster. Does he or she ever play promos? If so, what are they like? Are they long or short? Funny or serious? Is the other podcaster more likely to play the promo if it's written in iambic pentameter? If so, break out your quill, Shakespeare!

When you send a promo, send an MP3 file, and be sure to maintain your usual post–*Podcast Solutions* sound quality. Keep in mind that your promo MP3 will be played, recorded, and then reencoded for the other podcast. That is a lot of encoding and decoding for one file. To maintain your promo's sound quality and the sound quality of the podcast you hope will play your promo, encode your promo at *twice the bit rate* of the receiving podcast. For instance, if the receiving show is usually encoded at 64 kbps, encode your promo at 128 kbps. Your promo should be relatively short, so file size isn't a concern (compared to the lousy sound of sending something at a lower bit rate); in fact, you could even send a WAV file. The other podcaster will appreciate your forward thinking, technically speaking.

The art of promoting without promoting

If you send a popular podcaster a three-minute promo extolling the virtues of your new show, she may not play it. Why not? A better question is, Why should she? That podcaster's time is precious, and she is probably not in the promo-playing business. You need to approach promoting your podcast through other podcasters with some stealth. Everyone knows everyone else is doing it; it just needs to be done with tact.

> *I don't play promos where the people go on and on about how great they are. I play promos where the people go on and on about how great I am.*
>
> —*Dan Klass*

Promote yourself by promoting the other podcaster. Now, this should really be done only if you truly enjoy the work of the podcaster for whom you've recorded the promo. A simple, minute-long recording of how much you enjoy said podcaster's show sprinkled liberally with your own podcast's URL is a perfect way to kill two birds with one promo.

Keep it short and simple

Great things can come in small packages, especially when it comes to podcast promos. You're asking another podcaster to give up time on his show to promote your podcast. Exactly how much time are you willing to ask for? Five minutes? No way. Three? Too much. Remember, those seemingly endless commercials you used to listen to on the radio were only 60 seconds long. (Apparently, 60 seconds can seem like forever if you go about getting people's attention the wrong way.) Shoot for a minute, give or take. If you can't say what you need to in 60 seconds, you're trying to say too much. This is another benefit of having come up with a short, snappy description for your podcast. Let's take a look at a standard, no-frills (and easily acceptable to other podcasters) promo you might send (or phone in) to a show:

> *"Hi, this is (your name) from (your podcast), (one-line description of your podcast). I really loved your show about (a topic you sincerely liked). (Your take on that same topic, or more congratulations to the host for being such a genius.) Keep up the great work! Bye."*

You're mentioning your name and the name of your podcast, and you're even telling a little bit about it. But, most important to the other podcaster, you're adding to the content of his show in a constructive way. Rest assured, "Hi, this is (your name) from (your podcast), (one-line description of your podcast)" will start to roll off your tongue in no time. That is who you are now, so you need to introduce yourself that way.

Bulletin boards and user groups

If you're going to be a podcaster, you might as well become involved in the podcast community. Checking the new forum topics at PodcastPickle.com and Podcast Alley will keep you up to date on what's at the top of many podcasters' minds. Sure, the bulletin boards can sometimes turn into gripe-a-thons, but they can also be an invaluable source of podcasting dirt. Also, several podcasts have thriving online communities of their own, built on blog comments and bulletin boards. If the podcasts you enjoy have bulletin boards, don't hesitate to get involved.

By contributing to a bulletin board or blog thread, whether it's asking a question, helping answer someone else's question, or just chiming in on a topic, you're getting your name (and the name of your podcast) out into the world. (But be careful not to make a nuisance of yourself.) Legitimate discourse and interaction within a bulletin board community will help spread the word that there is another legit podcast out there worthy of a listen.

The same holds true for user groups and mailing lists. We both belong to the Yahoo! Podcasters Group (http://groups.yahoo.com/group/podcasters) and receive list mail all day long on topics including how to market a podcast, what equipment to use, and decency and censorship issues. Contributing to these mailing lists, as well as bulletin boards, will get your name out there. If you seem to be an expert on a particular subject or you're just especially insightful or humorous, people will be moved to check

11

out your show. Joining various mailing lists can also be a big help in putting you in touch with other podcasters to share promos with.

In addition, bulletin boards and user groups are great sources of information, news, interaction, and advice about all things podcasting. The community as a whole is very helpful, particularly to newbies, and there are no "bad" questions when it comes to getting involved. Yes, there are threads on boards where people can get snotty with each other and have month-long disagreements and flame wars, but these are the exceptions rather than the rule. The podcasting community is by and large a positive, hospitable group to be part of. Welcome.

Web 2.0

Web 2.0 is a term coined in 2003 by O'Reilly Publishing that refers to web-based communities and the proliferation of "user-generated media" and a move toward web-based applications that behave more like desktop applications, rather than traditional website experiences. The term does not refer to a change in the basic technology of the web as the name would imply, but rather the way the web is now being used and the zeitgeist of the web in the 21st century.

Huh?

Web 2.0 is MySpace. It's YouTube. It's Flickr.

The web is now littered with social networking sites that you should use to help build your podcast community and create strong, lasting bonds between you and your audience. As your audience grows, the exposure your podcast gets on their pieces of Internet property grows. In the world of getting noticed, we all need to shoot for "omnipresence," and being involved in as many web 2.0 sites as makes sense will certainly help. Let's look at a few examples.

MySpace

MySpace (www.myspace.com) is the king daddy of social networking sites. With accounts numbering in the hundreds of millions and new membership rates of more than a couple hundred thousand a day, MySpace is in many ways the epicenter of social networking on the web, at least for the young and young at heart. MySpace incorporates user profiles, blog posts, photos, embedded music and videos, and networking groups, all with an easily maintainable user interface. Yes, MySpace is also littered with self-portraits of teenage girls sucking in their cheeks, dating ads featuring the latest hot babes of stock photography, and a decent amount of spam, but MySpace is mostly an indispensable means of getting exposure and networking with your audience.

In MySpace (like you don't know this already), you accumulate "friends." Each time you add a friend to your MySpace page, their personal profile icon shows up within your friends list. And, yours ends up in theirs. So, for every friend you have in MySpace, that is an extra page on the Internet where your show's logo appears.

Also, MySpace is simply the way many of your younger audience members communicate. They may not send you e-mail or leave a post on your blog, but they may leave you a MySpace message or post a comment there. That's just how they do it. Give them the option.

Also, check out Facebook (www.facebook.com), which is kind of like a MySpace for adults.

Flickr

Flickr (www.flickr.com) is a social networking site built around sharing photographs. Users upload shots, and visitors can view them, leave comments, or whatever. Photos can be tagged with key search words, which makes it easy to find photos of any subject. Maintaining a Flickr account revolving around the subject of your program or just the program itself is another way to bring like-minded people to your show. It also gives your existing audience more exposure to you, your life, and your program.

YouTube

This is a no-brainer, but it must be said. If you're going to all the trouble of producing video for your podcast, you would be foolish not to also put it on YouTube (www.youtube.com). YouTube is the MySpace of online video. Many people would argue that if your video is not on YouTube, it's not online. YouTube is the first place many videoholics go when they need information, a laugh, a TV clip—you name it. YouTube is not just a database of video; it's also a social networking platform, where users can subscribe to each other's "channels" and create playlists of their favorite videos to post on their own blog or MySpace page. Exposure is everywhere, as long as you're willing to do the work to maintain your YouTube presence. And, while you're at it, make sure to upload to Blip.tv, Revver, and any other video site you can find. Blip.tv and Revver actually seem to be more focused on quality content than the whatever-is-hot-is-hot mechanism of YouTube. These competing sites are more likely to give a well-produced show some invaluable showcase space.

Twitter

Twitter (http://twitter.com) is a strange little midpoint between blogging and instant messaging. Users post short, 140-character "tweets" into a field on Twitter labeled "What are you doing?" that can be viewed by friends or followers. You can view a constantly updated list of all the twits coming from everyone you've added as a friend or click a specific profile to see only the twits that user has posted. Yes, some are as mundane as "I'm eating a pork chop," but some users use the service to easily post little comments and asides to keep their audience up to date about their podcast or just to spread a little cheer between shows. An excellent feature is the ability to embed a small Twitter window on your blog or web page that displays your latest twit. It's a great way to post something that is not quite important/permanent enough to warrant a full blog post.

11

Getting your podcast reviewed

There are surprisingly few podcast review sites, especially when you consider just how many podcasts there are to weed through these days and how many new listeners are doing the weeding. Back in the old days there was "The New, New Podcast Review," but now most podcast reviews are audience reviews on the podcast directory sites. There has yet to emerge a Roger Ebert of podcasts. Still, the directories are littered with reviews (some not as well thought out as others), and they'll most likely serve as your first bit of audience public recognition.

If your reviews are glowing, don't hesitate to pull a couple of quotes and feature them front and center on your website. This is a great way to quickly add credibility to your podcast for new site visitors (and it will do wonders for your ego). The truth is, people sometimes need the affirmation of others, whether it's a trusted friend or a known critic, before they're willing to try something new. If you have the opportunity to give them a gentle push, why not do so? Be as proud of your reviews as you are of your podcast.

Even if the reviews are lukewarm, you can often do a little creative cosmetic surgery on the text in the form of copyediting to make the review seem more glowing, and your podcast will appear to be the greatest thing since Thomas Edison. Don't feel guilty; Hollywood does it all the time (and worse) in movie marketing, so why not learn from the experts of promotion? Now, we're not suggesting that if a review reads "It's a shame this podcast isn't the least bit funny!" you should edit it down to say " . . . funny!"—you can't make an outwardly bad review great—but we are suggesting that it's not unheard of to cut and paste a little. This is promotion, after all. Promote!

Why let those great comments on Podcast Alley go to waste? If people are leaving comments about your show on the directory sites, in bulletin boards, or wherever, why not pull from these? True, your website might start to look a bit cheesy and self-aggrandizing if you have hundreds of glowing quotes on the front page. So, create a separate "What People Are Saying" page, and stow them there. People love to be involved with something successful.

Getting your story to the mass media

If we've learned one thing about the media, it's that they need a good story. Every day in every city in the country—no, strike that: every city in the *world*—news directors, magazine editors, and book publishers are looking for the next hot topic, the next great story. What's the up-and-coming technology? Who's an up-and-coming celebrity? Who's cashing in? Who's crapping out?

Podcasting was still in its infancy when the media outlets arrived, smelling a story. And the stories are there. They've covered the technological side of podcasting. They've covered the business side of podcasting. They've covered the celebrity side of podcasting. The mass media will continue to cover podcasting as long as there is something *newsworthy* to say. At the rate podcasting is growing and evolving, it will be an awfully long time before they run out of things to report.

Press coverage translates directly to an increase in listenership. It's that simple. If you're on television, talked about in a newspaper, or mentioned in a magazine, that's guaranteed to drive traffic to your show.

You may be lucky enough to have the media come to you. Whether your podcast is on the PodcastPickle.com Top Ten list or your show happens to have a particularly catchy title, you may suddenly get a call or an e-mail from someone in the media. Or, if you want some coverage and are sick of sitting by the phone, there are things you can do to stack the deck and help usher the press in your direction, as we'll discuss in the following sections.

> *You know who always needs a good podcasting story?* Podcast User Magazine (www.podcastusermagazine.com) *and* Blogger & Podcaster *magazine* (www.bloggerandpodcaster.com). *Read them, know them, submit to them.*

Hand them a story

What better way to get someone's attention than to make that person's job a whole lot easier? For your show to get noticed, there has to be something to notice—some reason you get the call over another podcaster. What is it about your podcast, or you as a podcaster, that might make a good story? What sets you and your show apart and makes you "newsworthy"? Depending on your show, it might be quite simple: you may be the youngest podcaster or the oldest. You may podcast every day from your car on the way to work (it has been done). You might podcast from your bathtub (ditto). News writers and their editors are always looking for an angle—a bend in the story that actually makes it a *story*.

You'll hear a lot of people say, "Hey, you should write a press release about your podcast and send it around," but they never follow that up with advice about how to actually *write a press release*. A good press release is your gift to a news editor. We said "hand them a story"—well, this is it. Your press release needs to tell who you are, what your podcast is about, and, most important, why you are newsworthy. You do this by skipping over the news writer and writing the story yourself. Hand them the story, written, typed, proofed, and ready to roll. Will they print it as is? No, but that's not the goal. The goal is to help them see that an interesting, engaging news story can easily be written about you and your podcast.

News stories are written with a very particular flow. First, you put the most important and specific information up front. This is not a "story" story; this is a news story. You are not trying to build suspense or slowly develop a character. You are hooking the reader with a strong lead, for example:

> *"From a small apartment over a dry cleaner on Crest Avenue, with only his PC and a microphone, Poddy Caster does a new kind of radio show that is heard in 17 different time zones around the world . . . "*

Holy cow, really? Over the dry cleaner? Seventeen different time zones around the world? OK, now you've got my attention. What is this story about? How can I hear this show? How did this guy even know he could do something like this?

Your story's lead must be specific; it should probably be the single most specific and narrow sentence in the entire piece. After the lead, keep the story as specific as possible while slowly introducing more and more general information. Think of the structure of your news story as being like a pyramid, with the lead being at the tip, and the story getting broader and broader as you continue along. Think about the reader and the questions she may have as she reads, much like in the example just shown. Have all the answers flow from the questions that logically follow your lead. Continually ask yourself, "What is interesting about my podcast, podcasting, and everything else relevant to this story?"

> *When I was in college, I had a very hard-nosed journalism professor who would always berate his students with the same two words: "Who cares?" He would read our stories aloud, stopping after every sentence to ask, with great disgust, "Who cares?" These are the last two words in the English language you want to hear after someone's just read your story, but their brutality is revealing.*
>
> *Ask yourself the following two questions when you write your story to keep you grounded: "Will someone care about this, or is it extraneous information that does nothing for the news I'm trying to relate?" and "Am I leaving out something that people would care about?"*
>
> *—Dan Klass*

11

Think globally, start locally

One of the easiest ways to get a little coverage is to start at home. Podcasters are spread out all over the world, and since we're not producing shows from huge corporate studios (we're likely creating our shows in spare bedrooms and empty conference rooms), nobody knows where we are. There could be podcasters right there in your hometown and nobody would know it. Hey, you're a podcaster in your hometown! Nobody even knows! Tell them.

> *I took this "start locally" approach early on. I had been featured in a number of articles on podcasting but none that had run locally. I contacted a reporter from my local newspaper and explained that I was involved in something that was getting national media attention and thought the paper might be interested in covering the local angle. Sure enough, that initial contact led to local coverage and a large photo "above the fold" on the front page of the paper's business section.*
>
> *—Michael Geoghegan*

Make it easy to contact you

A reporter from the *New York Times* isn't going to leave a comment on your blog. That's not how this sort of thing works. That reporter wants to get someone on the phone. Right now. If he can't get the first person he tries to reach on the phone, he'll try the second. There is no shortage of podcasters to interview, but there is almost always a shortage of time the reporter has to put a story together. Make sure you have some sort of contact information prominently displayed on your blog or website. This is another great reason to set yourself up with a voicemail account. With a voicemail account, people can contact you by phone, without the hassle of having your home phone number posted on the Internet.

Be yourself

The truth is, if someone in the media does contact you, you may not know why. You never know what the angle of the piece the reporter or producer is working on is until you see it on the air or in the paper. She may be looking for someone who is taking podcasting to the limit with thousands of dollars' worth of equipment and a determination to make millions, or she may be looking for a lonely guy in his basement who uses a tube sock as a pop filter. You never know. All you do know is, as on your podcast, you have to be yourself.

Summary

Always keep your eyes and ears open for new ways to promote your show to new listeners. Make sure your podcast information is in the signature of all your e-mails. When you post on a bulletin board, don't forget to say what podcast you're from. Mention your podcast at every turn. Yes, you may call your doctor's office to make an appointment and accidentally address yourself by your URL, but, hey, your doctor could be a podcast subscriber, right?

Get a MySpace account, a Flickr account, a Twitter account . . . they're all free. Jump in—the water is great.

Once you feel like you have a good-sized audience and you see that it's steadily growing, you may decide it's time to try to turn some of those listeners into income. Yes, it may sound a bit crass to the more artistic, but is there anything wrong with trying to lessen the financial burden of bandwidth and new mic cables? No. So, unless you're doing this solely for self-expression, read on, and we'll discuss how to make money through podcasting.

11

Chapter 12

MAKING MONEY WITH PODCASTING

Before too long, your podcast will be up and running. You'll have your production process down to a science, your content will be focused and inspired, and your audience will be growing at a nice, steady pace. There's nothing like the days of your podcast's youth, watching what was recently a mere concept bloom into a full-fledged ongoing concern. You're busy now with your new offspring, checking download stats, answering e-mails, and worrying over your ranking on your favorite podcast directory.

When your show has matured a bit and you've gained some experience as a podcaster, you'll start to wonder, "What's next?" The show is going well and you're getting great responses from your listeners, but in what ways can you grow the show and mobilize your newfound audience? Like many before you, your mind may turn to—dare we say it—*money*.

Plenty of podcast purists (especially from the early days) strongly believe that podcasting is an art form and that a person should do a podcast for its own sake. Bravo to someone so selfless, because podcasting is hard work. The prep is hard work, the recording/editing/mastering is hard work, and the encoding and updating of blog entries is hard work. OK, maybe it's not *hard* work, but it's a lot of work nonetheless. Since podcasting is work, why not get paid for it?

There has been a lot of talk about "monetizing" podcasting. Apparently, **monetizing** is a business term for "turning it into a business." Fair enough. People have been fretting over how to monetize this new medium since moments after its inception. So, why all the fretting? Podcasters can easily borrow from the tried-and-true business models that have served radio, TV, and independent artists for decades. Now, if you have an advertising sales staff in your basement, you're probably fairly clear on how you could sell some time on your podcast. But for everyone else, we'll start slowly with a few simple ways to earn, well, perhaps not millions but at least enough money to cover your expenses.

In this chapter, we'll look at a few ways you can take podcasting to another level. We'll discuss the following topics:

- Making media money
- Learning about your audience
- Implementing donations/memberships and paid subscriptions
- Selling your own merchandise
- Selling other people's merchandise
- Understanding advertising and sponsorships
- Finding advertisers and sponsors
- Becoming a podcast producer for hire
- Moving beyond podcasting

Making media money

Before we get into the specifics of how to monetize your podcast, let's be very clear about how making money in the media works (since that's what we're actually doing here). Not to be too blunt about it, but for you to make money, you need to get someone to give you his or her money. Simple, right? Well, just how do you do that? You leverage your audience.

Your audience is your greatest asset, bar none. Without your audience, it's just you and a mic and some audio equipment. Your audience is that hundred or that hundred thousand people who subscribe to your show on a regular basis. They actively participate in your podcast, whether by e-mailing comments, phoning you, or simply downloading your show.

So, how do you leverage your audience to make money?

- Offer your audience something they would pay money for.
- Offer your audience as a target market to someone who is dying to pay for them.
- Offer your audience to businesses as proof that you know how to reach and build an audience, and hire yourself out as a podcast producer.

We'll discuss these points throughout this chapter. We'll start by covering ways you can learn about your audience, which is the basis for any marketing and advertising steps you take next.

Learning about your audience

Who is your audience? This is an important question to be able to answer, because from this answer comes all of your marketing, all of your merchandising, and every sales pitch you will make regarding your show, whether it's to your audience or to the head of a media company. As you sit back and enjoy your daily barrage of fan mail, take note of where it's coming from, who's sending it, and what they're attracted to about your program. Are they mostly male or female, or is it an even mix? Are they married, single, American, European, Asian, tech-savvy, tech newbies? If your show has a narrowly defined focus, you'll be able, with a little work, to define your audience. If, for instance, your podcast is a movie review show (like Michael's "Reel Reviews"), it's safe to assume that your audience is made up of movie lovers, right? Here again is the advantage of the narrowly defined concept we talked about in Chapter 4. For the podcasters who do shows about religion, movies, sports, beer, sex, Windows, Mac, Linux, sci-fi, and so on, it's easy to make certain assumptions about their core audience. For others, you have to ask.

Survey says . . .

Don't be afraid to ask your listeners to fill out a survey. It doesn't need to be a 13-page opus or anything fancy; you just need to gather enough information from your listeners to get a sense of how you can market them and market *to* them. Ask for your listeners' gender, age range, and annual income range (we know, that sounds a bit personal, but you haven't asked for their names!), and ask any other questions specific to your podcast that might yield helpful answers. A slower, less aggressive approach is to just hang loose and get to know your listeners naturally. In due time, you will get a sense of who's who and what your show means to them.

Keep in mind, though, that if you take the time to do a "formal" survey, potential advertisers will know you're serious. They'll be able to glean the demographics of your show, which they need to make a decision about whether to advertise with you. Remember, you are now competing against print, radio, and TV for ad dollars. Potential advertisers will appreciate that you are taking it seriously. Surveys also help you to ensure you are aligning with advertisers/sponsors who will provide a real benefit for your listeners.

The easiest way to get a survey into action in no time is the take advantage of PodTrac's (www. podtrac.com) wonderful podcaster tools. PodTrac is an ad placement company that secures sponsorships for shows. You don't need to have PodTrac represent your podcast to advertisers to take advantage of its survey and demographics tools. Just create an account, and fill out the thankfully exhaustive podcast information pages. PodTrac gives you code to put on your site that links to an audience survey prepared especially for advertisers' favorite demos and separate code to include in your RSS feed so PodTrac can act as an impartial third-party to monitor your show's downloads. Within a month or so you should have accumulated enough audience and download metrics to have "statistically significant" information to pitch to advertisers, including feedback on audience satisfaction (see Figure 12-1).

12

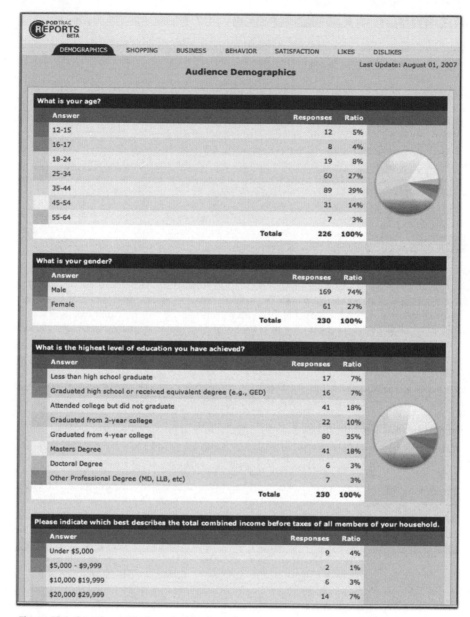

Figure 12-1. Sample results from PodTrac's audience survey

Determining what your audience is willing to pay for

Pinpointing exactly what your audience is willing to pay for may seem impossible at first. Luckily for us, it doesn't actually take much effort to figure it out. Setting up donation links or offering an array of merchandise may have once required a considerable up-front investment in time and money. These days, thanks largely to the Internet, we can set up online transactions in no time.

Ask yourself what sorts of "stuff" your audience would want, given who you believe they are. Can you think of something to offer, at a reasonable price, that they would really like and enjoy and that is a natural extension of your podcast? Or is offering the podcast itself enough?

Implementing donations/memberships and paid subscriptions

Going straight to your subscribers for donations or membership fees is something you may have mixed feelings about. Asking for money is something that some people just aren't comfortable with. The flip side of the situation is, however, that your audience may be more than happy to help subsidize the show. Whether it is to feel more connected to the podcast, show their appreciation, or just help to avoid your having to look for sponsors, your audience may be willing to share a bit of your new financial burden. Let's take a look at some of the ways you can seek support directly from your audience, whether through donations, memberships, or paid subscriptions.

Donations and memberships

In mid-June 2005, Jason Evangelho from "Insomnia Radio" (www.insomniaradio.net) sent a dollar to Dan's PayPal account out of the blue. Why, you might ask? According to Jason, "I'm sending a dollar each month to all the podcasts I listen to. Maybe it will catch on." Now, yes, this is a testament to Jason's good nature, but it's also a shrewd and forward-thinking move. What does it cost Jason each month to send $1 to each of the podcasts he subscribes to? Five dollars? Ten? Twenty? Most of us are paying well over $20 a month for the cable TV we barely watch (not including premium channels and Pay Per View), $15 a month for Netflix, and more than all that put together to go to the movies (especially if you have kids). Yet we're paying nothing for the hours and hours of podcast entertainment we download each month. Not a cent. For the form of entertainment that for some of us has taken up all the time many other kinds of entertainment once dominated, *we pay nothing*.

Now, Jason isn't the first podcaster to have this type of idea. Many podcasters have had a PayPal (see the next section) "tip jar" on their podcast sites for ages. The striking thing about Jason's gesture is that it is a small but regular contribution to his favorite podcasters (Dan is honored to be among them). And because of Jason's (and other podcasters') kind gesture, eventually some money will start coming back to him. If all of Jason's listeners did what he has vowed to do, he would no longer have to cover his storage and bandwidth costs out of his own pocket. Actually, if we can guess at Jason's listener base, he could devote *a lot more time* to working on his fantastic podcast and a lot less time to, well, working.

For a podcaster, that $1 a month per listener could mean the difference between needing a second job or not. It's a movement worth pushing forward. In the meantime, asking for donations is not unheard of. You're offering your listeners a wonderful program and asking for very little in return.

Instead of asking for donations, you could consider taking a cue from the folks at National Public Radio (NPR) or the Public Broadcasting Service (PBS). These organizations rely heavily on donations to continue to produce and broadcast some of the most interesting news and entertainment programs available (sounds like podcasting, right?). One way that they have maintained a certain level of donations flowing in is through offering memberships and conducting membership drives. Listeners/ viewers pay a certain amount of money to become a member, and in return they get discounts on

12

merchandise and are eligible to win sweepstakes and prizes. Also, for joining, members get a little free swag (for example, a magazine subscription, a logo mug, and so on) and a good feeling from knowing they've contributed to a worthy cause.

As we talk more later about creating and selling your own merchandise, keep the idea of member gifts in the back of your mind. It's a great way to build community and offer an incentive to give.

PayPal

PayPal (www.paypal.com) is an online service whereby you can send money over the Internet. The money is withdrawn from your checking or credit card account and "sent" to another PayPal user. PayPal is a great way for smaller websites to accept payments or for individuals to pay for goods and services. PayPal is owned by eBay (www.ebay.com), and it's a secure and well-protected service. You might use PayPal if you're accepting donations, selling merchandise that you stock at your home or office, buying equipment through the eBay auction site, or doing any other transaction that doesn't involve a major online retailer.

PayPal makes it easy to set up a donation button for your website (see Figure 12-2). People can simply click that button and send any size donation they choose.

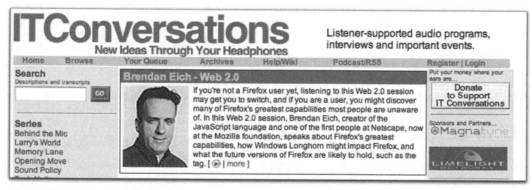

Figure 12-2. A donation button in action in the top-right corner of the "IT Conversations" homepage

Paid subscriptions

You always have the option, of course, to directly charge listeners to receive your podcast. At the time of this writing, there is no clear-cut way to easily set up a paid subscription feed without having some serious technical savvy. That being said, now that Audible (www.audible.com) is charging for the "Ricky Gervais Show" and Apple has included podcasting functions in its iTunes Store (emphasis on "Store"), the day may be close at hand when a podcaster can easily set up a subscription channel that requires a per-download payment. (In fact, we're positive this functionality is coming—it's just not yet available.) How much will listeners be willing to pay for a podcast? That remains to be seen. People all over the world are paying the equivalent of $.99 for a single three- to four-minute song from iTunes. What might they pay for a 30-minute podcast?

Although there are not any current subscription-only services for podcasting in widespread use, some podcasts do offer a "subscription" model where the subscription fee is more akin to a membership than a gateway to the content. The most successful of these services at the time of this writing is "This

Week In Tech" (www.thisweekintech.com), a show hosted by Leo Laporte and a number of other former TechTV hosts. They have a recurring $2-per-month donation choice, as well as an annual $20 donation option. Of course, listeners are free to donate any amount they are comfortable with, and as we mentioned, donations are not required to listen to the content. Because this show is produced by people who make their professional living talking about technology, it is an interesting experiment to see whether they can use a pseudo-subscription model to keep traditional advertising out of the show and still succeed in reaching their revenue goals.

The best use of a paid subscription in the long run may be to charge for a "premium" feed that is an alternative/addition to a standard, free feed. The free feed is there to hook new listeners and to maintain the listener base that will not pay for the show. The premium feed is for the hard-core fans and offers more content than the free feed ("best of" segments from shows no longer on the server, outtakes, special editions, and so on), at a much higher sound quality.

The podPress plug-in for WordPress (among its other features) simplifies the process of creating a custom "premium" feed. Listeners who become members of your blog and have "premium content" access are the only people who can view/subscribe to the premium feed. To site visitors who don't have the premium access, the extra content is invisible. Managing a member's status is done from within WordPress, in the Users ➤ Authors & Users menu.

Selling your own merchandise

We assume you don't have a bunch of stuff sitting around your house that you'd like to unload on your unsuspecting listeners, which is good. When we talk about selling to your listeners, we aren't talking about selling anything and everything you can get a digital photo of. We're talking about offering something to your audience they might want—something connected to the show. Whether it's a T-shirt with your podcast name on it or a bumper sticker that reads "Kill Your Radio: Podcasts Are Better," you'll want to offer your listeners something they connect with (sound familiar?).

Products on demand

For those of us with a do-it-yourself mentality, this has got to be the best time in history to put together our own swag. Gone are the days of having to pay to silk-screen hundreds of T-shirts in varying sizes or getting stuck with boxes and boxes of unsold *How to Care for Your Pet Rock* paperbacks. Now there is the Internet, and with the Internet and the advances (and advantages) of the digital world, we now live in the age of **products on demand**. You could be selling T-shirts, buttons, coffee mugs, hats, books, and bumper stickers in a half hour with no cash outlay at all, thanks to the relatively new on-demand services available on the Internet.

In the sections that follow, we'll discuss a couple of options for offering your merchandise to your listeners.

CafePress.com

If you don't know about CafePress.com, you need to. CafePress.com (www.cafepress.com) is the premiere on-demand product service, and through the CafePress.com site, you can set up your own online store selling shirts, hats, sweatshirts, CDs—you name it—in no time, free of charge.

12

You pick which products you'd like to sell, upload graphics according to the site's specifications, and determine the amount of profit you'd like to make. CafePress.com handles order taking, printing, packaging, receiving payments, and shipping. You pay nothing. CafePress.com's payment comes from shipping and handling costs and the base price of each item, upon which you add your profit.

There is no inventory for you to pay for and maintain. When someone orders one of your products, CafePress.com produces the item on demand. Because there is no inventory, there is no initial investment on your part.

Setting up a basic CafePress.com store (see Figure 12-3) is free, but you are restricted to selling only one version or design of each item at a time (that is, only one design for the basic T-shirt, only one design on the trucker hat, and so on). The site also offers upgraded "premium" stores for a monthly fee, where you can sell as many variations of each product as you desire. The choice of products is extensive, and new seasonal products are added regularly to keep things fresh.

Figure 12-3. Setting up a store at CafePress.com

The print quality of CafePress.com products is good, though not perfect, but for what you're getting for no up-front cost, CafePress.com is a perfect solution for the podcaster who wants to offer some merchandise.

Lulu

Lulu (www.lulu.com) is similar in concept to CafePress.com, except it specializes in on-demand books and comics. You upload your manuscript in the form of a PDF, and you upload graphics for the front and back covers. Lulu sets up a sales page for your book on its site, and it prints and binds each copy as it's purchased. Lulu also can make your book available through the Amazon and Barnes & Noble websites to give your book a "professionally published" appearance.

Lulu's print quality and binding is top-notch, and the prices are quite reasonable. As with CafePress, there are no up-front costs. The final price of a book is determined by combining four figures: each item has a base price (based on the dimensions and binding of the book), a per-page cost (a few cents per page), whatever profit you'd like to make, and an additional 25 percent of your profit that Lulu keeps (if your profit is set at $4, Lulu charges an additional $1). It sounds like a lot, but when you add up the actual charge (and compare that to the alternative), it's not a bad deal to have an entire book published.

Now, yes, we understand that not many podcasters have books cluttering their hard drives. We also realize that anything a podcaster might write, she could just as easily publish on a blog and have people read it for free. But, from the point of view of the listener, a blog entry doesn't make a very good birthday gift; it's not a tangible keepsake of a podcast that has become a regular part of someone's life. Publishing something for your listeners to enjoy and treasure is not such a crazy idea, especially, obviously, if you're the writer/producer of a **podiobook**. Podiobook writer/producers are hitting the mainstream (Scott Sigler signed a multibook deal with Penguin in 2007), so give yourself a boost in your credibility with the publishing world by selling printed versions of your work. Who wouldn't want a signed copy of the *7th Son* trilogy anyway?

> *Dave Slusher of the "Evil Genius Chronicles" (www.evilgeniuschronicles.org/wordpress) has put together a real win-win way of providing revenue for his podcast. Dave offers listeners a chance to support his podcast and the band Gentle Readers, which graciously allows Dave to use its music as his theme song and music bed, through the purchase of a "stuff package." The package includes an "Evil Genius Chronicles" shirt and a Gentle Readers CD (www.evilgeniuschronicles.org/stuff). Everyone wins: the listeners, the band, and Dave. Now that is a great way to monetize. Best of all, Dave continues to keep up the interest among audience members by posting on his site pictures of listeners wearing their "Evil Genius Chronicles" shirts.*

Selling other people's merchandise

You can also capitalize on your podcast through **affiliate programs**, which are arrangements with major online retailers for you to sell their products through your website. Here's how it works, generally speaking: you post an ad for a specific company or product on your site. If someone clicks through that ad link and makes a purchase, you get a cut of the action. Sound simple enough? It is.

In the sections that follow, we discuss a few of the major affiliate programs you can participate in.

Amazon.com Associates program

You use Amazon.com. We use Amazon.com. Presumably everyone who shops online at one time or another purchases something from Amazon.com. The site carries not only books and CDs but also things like professional audio equipment, clothing, and kitchen appliances. You name it, Amazon.com sells it. The benefit of having such a wide array of products for sale is that it makes it easy to find things on Amazon.com that you own, use, and recommend. If you talk about a new CD or DVD that you particularly enjoy on your podcast, why not include a link to Amazon.com's listing of that CD or DVD on your site? If you've recommended the item that highly and the listener is moved to purchase it because of your recommendation, why shouldn't Amazon.com give you a piece of the pie?

Signing up and being approved as an Amazon.com Associate is relatively easy (https://associates. amazon.com/gp/flex/associates/apply-login.html). In practically no time, you are given an affiliate code that is embedded into the URL of the items you want to promote. When someone clicks an affiliate link on your site, they are taken to that product on the Amazon.com site just as they normally would be. What the user doesn't see is that their every move is being tracked with the help of your affiliate code. After they enter the Amazon.com site from your affiliate link, a percentage of *anything* they purchase, whether it is the linked item or not, is put toward your affiliate earnings.

Amazon.com makes it easy to set up links with your embedded code, and you can choose from general-category ads (that is, "All import CDs 10 percent off!") to item-specific displays. With Amazon.com's performance fee structure, associates stand to earn as much as 4 to 6.5 percent on the sales of electronics, audio and video, and camera and photo items. This is above and beyond the standard 1 percent for "Easy Link" items (general category banner ads) and 2.5 percent for "Direct Link" purchases.

Family shows can have links to kid-friendly movie recommendations. Political shows can link to biographies and tell-all books. A great example of the use of the Amazon.com Associates program is the common practice of podcasters posting links to the audio equipment they use. Any podcaster doing a decent show will get e-mails asking what hardware and software she uses to record her podcasts. What a great way to display the equipment, maybe help a newbie out with some information and insight, and help pay for the show.

CD Baby

When it comes to music in podcasts, it's all indie. Since most podcasters doing music shows are almost exclusively playing independent artists on independent labels, they can't promote the music they play through affiliate links to Amazon.com's exhaustive catalog of major-label CDs.

The good news is that many independent artists sell their CDs through CD Baby (www.cdbaby.com), which offers a wonderful affiliate program through which podcasters can promote and sell the music they play. Whenever Dan is putting together a new edition of "Old Wave Radio," he checks to see whether any of that week's artists have CDs listed with CD Baby (see Figure 12-4). If so, he makes sure their album is prominently displayed on that podcast's blog entry, complete with affiliate links. Why not? Everybody wins.

Figure 12-4. A posting from "Old Wave Radio" featuring several affiliate links to artists on CD Baby

CD Baby also offers rudimentary shopping cart functions and several ways to set up and style affiliate displays. Be aware that the site is not as professional-looking as Amazon.com; it's indie, and it looks it.

LinkShare

Easily the mother of all online affiliate marketing companies, LinkShare (www.linkshare.com) manages affiliate programs with some of the biggest retailers in the country: Target, Netflix, KB Toys, Disney Direct, Apple, Delta Air, TimeLife.com, and Champion, just to name a few. LinkShare clearly offers something for everyone. Determining which participants are currently involved can be a bit confusing, and each participant requires separate registration and approval. LinkShare is not one-stop-shopping to sign up for affiliates, but it's a great resource for finding major companies that offer affiliate programs you never knew existed.

Understanding advertising and sponsorships

Clearly, one way you can capitalize on your podcast is the way most media does: through advertising and sponsorships. Since you are a podcaster with a podcast and a website, both of which get a lot of traffic, you are in the enviable position of having two potential revenue streams: selling time and selling space.

Before you can really get started acquiring advertisers, though, you need to know a bit about how advertising works money-wise and how ad rates are calculated. Then you'll need to find advertisers looking to market to your audience. To do this, either you can use a service that will bring the ads to you or you can find your own.

How ad rates are set

Selling time is fairly straightforward: you determine how much your show is worth, based on how many listeners you have (or realistically expect to have) and how targeted your audience is in marketing terms.

Ads rates on web pages are slightly more complicated. Payment and charges for web ads are usually based on either **click-throughs** or **impressions**. A click-through is exactly what it sounds like: someone sees a linked ad on your site, clicks it, and you get paid. Payment for impressions is based on how many times the page with the ad is loaded in a given period of time. Think of it as a very accurate Nielsen rating. The advertiser pays for exactly how many people see the ad.

Cost per click

In a **cost per click** (**CPC**) arrangement, the person hosting the ad (in this case, you) is paid only when someone clicks that link. Our theory is that CPC ads are most beneficial to the person placing the ad, not the person hosting the ad. The ad sits on the page and is exposed to every viewer of that page. Visitor after visitor sees the name of that product, service, company, or whatever. It's free advertising every time that page is loaded, except on those occasions when someone clicks the ad.

In what other ad medium is the advertiser charged only if the media people can prove that the ad actually grabbed viewers' attention and moved them to action? Radio stations get paid for their air-time whether or not the ads they air get listened to. The same is true for magazines, TV shows, you name it.

As you might imagine, CPC is an invention of the Internet age, dating back to the early days of online ad placement. Since so few people believed that advertising on the web would be worth paying for, the CPC structure was devised to prove to advertisers and their agencies that there was value in advertising on the Internet. But those days are over. We've long since proven that Internet advertising works.

CPC ads really work for you only if the ads are so targeted (that is, a link to an affiliate program where you are literally choosing the products being sold) that they are almost guaranteed to be clicked. Although CPC may not be ideal for a primary revenue source for your podcast, it is certainly something to consider on your site. Many people use Google AdSense, which is a CPC-based system that features targeted ads (see the "Google AdSense" section).

The flip side of the CPC coin is that if and when *you* decide you'd like to start advertising your podcast on other websites, the right CPC setup might be the perfect way to get a lot of exposure for your podcast at very little cost to you. Remember, you are not paying every time someone sees the name of your podcast or the URL; you are paying only if someone clicks that link.

Cost per thousand impressions

Having links on your site, particularly large graphic links, exposes visitors to your page to the message those links convey. That should be enough, and you should be compensated for it. In this way, you are being paid using a structure similar to that of any media outlet: you are compensated based on the size of the potential audience for the advertiser's message. Now, this is not to say that every *cost per thousand* (**CPM**; the "M" stands for the Roman numeral for "thousand") impressions arrangement is fair, but it looks inherently more so than a CPC agreement.

CPM is how all ad rates are determined in the real world for print and electronic media. You will eventually (if you decide to go looking for sponsors and advertisers) need to determine your *podcast's* CPM and use that to calculate what you would charge for an advertisement on your podcast or to sponsor your podcast.

As traffic to your website increases and the number of people downloading your shows rises, more and more advertisers and sponsors will be willing to pay to get their message in front of your audience. That much almost goes without saying. The challenge is finding those advertisers and sponsors.

Google AdSense

When you're looking for something on the Internet, if you're anything like us, you probably go straight to Google (www.google.com). Through Google, you often can find everything you need on the web in little to no time at all. And, yes, Google can even find advertisers for you. Not only is Google the search engine of choice for many, but also it offers an easy-to-set-up and fairly unobtrusive system of including ads on your website. You choose between text and graphic ads, the ads' dimensions, and their placement on your site. Google gives you code to cut and paste into the appropriate section of your site and uses that code to push fresh ads to your page whenever it is viewed. The ads displayed are chosen by Google's system, which scans the text of each page for keywords and then uses that information to determine which ads might work best for your site. For instance, if you mention Johnny Depp, The Ramones, and Australia in a blog post, the Google ads on that page might be for movie posters, MP3 downloads, and travel packages.

Google AdSense (www.google.com/adsense) income is based on CPC. Each time a page with Google AdSense ads is loaded, an invisible auction takes place behind the scenes to determine which ads will be the most profitable to display on that particular page. For this reason, Google does not pay publishers a fixed amount per click or impression. Revenue varies based on the actual CPC or CPM impression paid by the specific advertiser for each ad that ends up appearing on your site. Some ads have higher CPCs or CPMs than others; therefore, it is not possible to say precisely how much someone might earn for a given number of clicks or impressions.

12

Revver

Revver (www.revver.com) is a viral video–sharing platform and community, similar to YouTube, but with one huge difference: ad insertions. Content creators upload videos to the Revver site and get in return "Revverized" versions of their video to podcast or embed in MySpace, blogs, and so on. These updated versions have a single-frame targeted advertisement at the end and embedded code that pings Revver every time someone watches the video, even in the podcast version passed around from viewer to viewer.

Each ping is a paid "impression," generating ad revenue that is shared between the content creator and Revver in a 50/50 split. Even users simply sharing other people's videos earn money: 20 percent off the top, before the 50/50 split. Not bad for just spreading the word. Revver is used by many of the biggest entertainment video podcasts and is well worth checking out.

Kiptronic

Kiptronic (www.kiptronic.com) offers automated ad insertion for audio and video "downloadable media." As with Revver, it maintains the relationship with the advertisers and automatically inserts five-second spots into the media upon download. The system can change/swap ads on the fly and can even target ads by geography and demographic.

Finding your own advertisers and sponsors

By now, you've figured it out: to be a successful podcaster, you need to be a radio host, an audio engineer, a blogger, and an advertising sales rep. Hey, nobody said this was going to be easy. To be clear, attracting and keeping potential advertisers and sponsors is *work*. You need to make sure that the revenue you are expecting to produce is in line with the amount of work you are going to put in. Interestingly, it takes as much time to attract a $500 sponsor as it does a $5,000 sponsor. Don't undersell your podcast's value. Luckily for all of us, when we go looking for sponsors and advertisers, we're at least selling a product we believe in: our podcast.

Advertisers vs. sponsors

It may seem like a fine line between someone being an advertiser on your podcast and a sponsor of your podcast. To split the hair, an **advertiser** is someone who gives you money to promote his or her products, goods, services, or what have you. In exchange for money (well, we hope money), you spend a certain amount of time on your podcast or set aside a certain amount of space on your website to promote the advertiser's wares. A **sponsor** is a person, group, or organization that supports your podcast and/or website financially, in part or as a whole. In exchange, you are expected to tell everyone who is sponsoring you.

So, what's the big difference? Well, the difference definitely seems semantic at best. Typically, non-profit ventures and public media outlets (that is, PBS and NPR) have sponsors, whereas corporate endeavors such as major TV networks and radio stations have advertisers (and lots of them). Since podcasting is still so young and still adjusting to life with advertisers and sponsors, it is commonly expected that if you are accepting money from someone for "promotional consideration," it is in the form of sponsorship. Still, we are not naïve enough to think that podcasting will continue to grow and thrive forever without an influx of ad dollars. Therefore, we will continue talking about advertisers and sponsors and, for the sake of our convenience, not worry about which word we use.

Selling the category

At the time of this writing, one of the major stumbling blocks to selling a podcast show to potential sponsors is the fact that too many people still don't know enough about podcasting. It is astounding that so few people are aware of this movement, though this is also changing at a pace that is astonishing to all. Before anyone is going to buy your podcast, they have to understand what podcasting is. That is why it is so important for all podcasters to get out of the podcast community every once in a while and out into the general public to start spreading the news. Until more people know what podcasting is and how it can be used for marketing, we will only be selling the category, not the individual shows.

The great thing about podcasting, and the thing that puts it head and shoulders above most other media out there today in terms of reaching an audience, is that the audience pays attention to the *entire program*. Most podcast listeners will tell you that they start a podcast, they listen to a podcast, and then they listen to another podcast. Since there is no expectation of long, horrible ads and no expectation that some part of the program won't suit their tastes, they listen intently to each podcast in its entirety. This is the great advantage of the audience getting exactly what they want, when they want it.

You could go to an advertiser right now and say "Listen, I can get your new sales message into the ears of 3,000 people by Tuesday" and actually do it.

Understanding your audience

Go back to the survey of your audience and your endless checking and rechecking of your download statistics. You know how big your audience is, give or take. You know who your listeners are—perhaps not as individuals, but as a group. That is a group to market to. Recognize that and offer it up to those who are dying to reach that particular market.

From that bit of market information, ask yourself, "Who is most likely to benefit from reaching my audience?" Computer sales websites? Sport drink manufacturers? DVD rental companies? In the case of today's on-demand culture, and by virtue of the nature of podcasting, the more narrowly defined your audience is, the easier it will be to attract advertisers desperate to reach that audience.

Creating a sales kit

You'll need to put together a sales kit, which is a collection of information that tells about you, your show, your audience, and why it would be a great opportunity for advertisers to get involved in your podcast. Tim Bourquin of the "Podcast Brothers" and founder of the annual "Podcast and New Media Expo" put together a superb sales/media kit for his "Endurance Radio" podcast. He made sure it looked great, sounded professional, and included Arbitron information (Arbitron is the company that handles quantifying the ratings of radio stations), listener stats, and contact information. He was selling not only airtime on his podcast but also the banner at the top of every page of the Endurance Radio website. He prepared mock-ups of the site for prospective clients, showing them what it would look like if their ads appeared on his site.

12

> *Tim was gracious enough to make his sales kit available to download for reference and inspiration at* www.enduranceradio.com/EnduranceRadioMediaKit.pdf.

Then Tim started pounding the pavement with his sales kit. Much to his surprise, he wasn't getting any offers. His media kit looked great, he had the sales pitch down, and his ad rates were affordable, but still no one was interested. Eventually he realized his ad rates were too low, and they were working against him. According to Tim, "Big companies just don't write checks that small, especially for advertising buys." So he adjusted his rates and approach. Rather than selling multiple ads at $250 apiece to various advertisers to appear on the shows, he bundled the whole package and sought a sole advertiser/sponsor for monthlong periods (see Figure 12-5). He set the rate at $4,000 per month and landed Gatorade as the sole sponsor of "Endurance Radio" for several months.

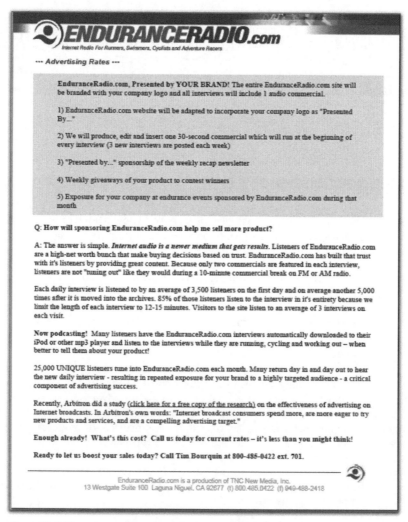

Figure 12-5. The ad rates page from the "Endurance Radio" media kit

Strength in numbers

For smaller advertisers, spending a couple hundred dollars to sponsor a podcast may be a big deal, but the real money is going to be found with big companies—companies so big, in fact, that they may simply dismiss your podcast because you couldn't possibly offer them the audience size they'd need to make it worth their while.

This is why several podcasting "networks" have sprung up over the years where podcasters band together to provide a larger audience to advertisers and potential sponsors. After all, there's power in numbers. The Tripod Network, BackBeat Media, the Podcast Network, and many others have had varying levels of success attracting sponsors to the varied stable of shows.

If joining a network isn't your style, there are several services you can use that will help find advertisers for you using the same "strength in numbers" approach as the networks.

Most notably perhaps, PodTrac is approaching advertising executives and media buyers in major markets around the United States, offering podcasting as the ultimate "new media." The promise of podcasting is clear: tell us who you want to reach and how many of those people, and we can get your message directly to them in a matter of days. Well, even hours. Whether the advertisers need 10,000 sci-fi geeks or 20,000 music lovers, podcasting associations can deliver them almost instantly.

Developing advertising and promotion policies

A podcaster's most important currency is the trust of her audience. Once you start accepting money for advertising or sponsorship, you need to deal with the reality that some listeners may view your credibility with a little more suspicion. Are you talking about how much you love that computer program you are using because you genuinely like it, or is it because the maker happens to sponsor your show? Of course, you are an honest person who would never sell out—never! As such, it is a good idea to develop a policy regarding these issues. One approach is to segregate paid announcements and disclose them as such, both in your podcast audio and on your website. How you choose to develop your advertising and promotion policies is entirely up to you, but you should address these issues well in advance of signing on advertisers and sponsors.

> *A good example of an advertising and promotion policy is the one we developed for "Grape Radio" (www.graperadio.com). At "Grape Radio," we often get wine producers and vendors who offer to send us samples of their wine. Although we're happy to accept these samples, we decided it was important to develop a written policy that disclosed our "sample wine policy." When vendors offer to send samples, we forward the following disclosure to them:*
>
> *"Grape Radio, Inc. (Grape Radio) does not solicit samples of wine-related products. Should a vendor decide to send samples, Grape Radio's acceptance of such samples does not imply an evaluation will be conducted. In addition, should Grape Radio decide to evaluate a sample, vendors are advised that Grape Radio does not warrant such reviews will be made public, nor that such reviews will be positive."*
>
> *We post this policy in the "About Grape Radio" section so that anyone—including our listeners—can read it. As a point of interest, we have had some vendors who ended up not sending us a sample after receiving our notice.*
>
> *—Michael Geoghegan*

12

Managing your own ad insertions

If you're not using a service such as Revver or Kiptronic, you will be managing your own ad insertions. You'll sell some time, either on your own or through PodTrac or the like, and then you have to get the spot into (and out of) your podcast.

The easiest way to handle this is just to record the spot read live during your show or permanently embed the footage into your master podcast file. That way you know it's there, and you know that every time the show is downloaded, so is the ad. The problem with this approach is that advertisers often pay for their ads to run between specific dates, based on a special event, product update, offer, and so on. So, you make sure the ad is included in all your shows produced between those dates. Great. The downside is, of course, what happens when those dates have passed, and the ad is permanently part of the shows? Audience members continue to download those shows, and the advertiser continues to benefit from the ads being there, but you don't continue to be compensated.

The solution is to use a service such as GigaVox Audio Lite, developed by GigaVox Media (full disclosure: Michael is CEO of GigaVox and one of the masterminds behind GigaVox Audio Lite). GigaVox Audio Lite is a service for podcasters that automates the updating and publishing of audio podcasts, so your podcasts are always up to date and your sponsors are getting everything they're paying you for (and no more). GigaVox Audio Lite works on a component system, where your shows are broken down into static and dynamic building blocks. The static elements (intro music, segue, production company ID, and so on) stay in the system as permanent elements. When you publish a new show, you unload only the body elements of your program that are new and specific to that episode. Placeholders are created for the ads that are managed by the advertising campaign system. The system takes these individual elements (for example, preroll, theme song, body of show, sponsorship, outro, company ID), assembles them, and publishes them as an MP3. When it is time for the current sponsorship message to stop running, the system automatically reassembles and republishes the show with the next sponsorship inserted in its place. And, the new sponsorship ad will run in all of the episodes being managed by GigaVox Audio Lite, so you can offer to your sponsor's ad exposure in your back catalog as well. (At time of press, the GigaVox Audio Lite technology was sold to Podango for integration into its P2 publishing platform. Refer directly to Podango.com for further information.)

Becoming a podcast producer for hire

Unlike you, not everyone is willing to plow through a 250-page book about RSS, RMS, and XML to get the word out. They may want to put a podcast together but lack the time, skill, patience, and/or wherewithal to do so. That is where you come in. Once you've established your own show, you may be presented with the opportunity to produce other people's podcasts, your show being the ultimate proof of your podcasting savvy. This may be a great way for you to earn some money without the sweat and heartache involved in looking for sponsors and designing T-shirts.

If you have the knowledge and expertise to put a podcast together for yourself, you surely could be doing it for others as well. At the time of the original writing of this book, the most prominent (and possibly the most lucrative) podcast/producer-for-hire relationship was forged by our own Michael Geoghegan. Michael secured a contract with Disneyland in Anaheim, California, to podcast its entire 50th Anniversary celebration, complete with behind-the-scenes "sound-seeing tours" and celebrity red-carpet interviews. Two years later, the "Official Disneyland Resort Podcast" with Michael as host and producer is still going strong.

You should approach projects such as this with your eyes wide open. Large companies are not used to dealing with small operations; as a result, if you are interested in pursuing corporate podcast consulting and/or production, we suggest aligning with a public relations (PR) agency or company. That way, the PR company can offer your services to their current clients. They will also be able to better deal with the complications of negotiating with and getting paid by larger companies.

The Disneyland podcasts Michael produced turned out to be a podcaster's dream (see Figure 12-6). The vice president in charge of the event certainly understood where podcasting fit into the coverage of Disneyland's 50th Anniversary celebration and gave Michael exclusive access to interviews with celebrities, Disney executives, park guests, and others who help to make Disneyland such a special place. This experience was a highlight of Michael's podcasting career so far. You can find the Disneyland podcasts at www.disneyland.com/podcast.

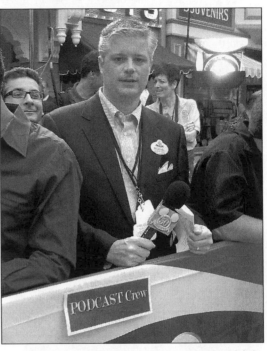

Figure 12-6. Michael is getting ready to do celebrity interviews on the "gold carpet" for Disneyland's 50th Anniversary celebration. Over his shoulder is Greg Cangialosi, who was helping out with the podcast.

Not all corporate podcast hosting experiences may be as positive as Michael's was with Disneyland, however. Some companies may be interested in just getting in on the "newest" or "hottest" thing. We know of other podcasts where the client companies would not post the podcast prior to a review of a transcript and in some cases demanded postproduction edits. This is big-league stuff. No one is fooling around at this level. When money and corporate reputations are involved, the sensibilities of the podcaster are not the primary concern. Make sure you are clear well ahead of time on exactly what is expected regarding content, timeline, review process (if any), and music rights issues.

If you can balance producing an exciting and entertaining podcast with fulfilling the needs of your client company, you've got yourself a business. Think about how valuable this type of production is to the company hiring you. To have countless customers and potential customers listening to 20, 30, or even 45 minutes or more of content specific to the company or its products and services is an advertiser's or publicity person's dream.

Let's do some math. What do you think it would be worth to Ford Motor Company to have a podcast available of a recent Mustang promotion event where celebrities and professional race-car drivers were invited to drive the newest Mustang GT on a racetrack? Let's say that in addition to inviting traditional media outlets, Ford also hires a podcaster to produce a podcast based on the event. Just imagine the audio the podcaster could get—in-car audio of the cars going around the track and the sounds of screeching tires as cars accelerate away. Interviews with celebrities the listeners would identify with describing how much they enjoyed driving the cars, all the while speaking with the excitement of someone who just experienced something that got his adrenaline flowing. Professional race-car drivers talking about the handling characteristics of the car on the track and how that would carry over to

12

street performance. Perhaps interviews with a person who helped design the car describing the design decisions made and an engineer discussing some of the innovative technology behind the performance increases. Anyone from Ford listening? We think we may be onto something here.

Now here is the kicker: unlike with TV or radio, there is no requirement to get all this information conveyed as quick sound bites to fit before the next segment. The podcast could be 45 minutes long if there were enough material and quality content (though this often has more to do with the skill, planning, and execution of the podcaster than anything else). Most important, unlike a two-minute spot on the evening news seen by everyone, including people who couldn't care less about performance cars, who do you think is going to subscribe to and download this podcast? Obviously, the people Ford would be most interested in: Mustang fans and potential customers who can listen to it over and over if they want.

Now back to the math. What is it worth to a car manufacturer such as Ford to have 50,000 potential customers who by choice listen to 45 minutes of podcast audio like this? We leave that question to you, as we're sure you get the point.

Using the Ford Motor Company example, you'd think every company would be getting involved in podcasting and producing great audio content. The reality is, though, that most of the corporate-backed podcasts available today are, for lack of a better term, terrible. Why? They are produced by ad agencies and PR people who try to turn the podcast into a 45-minute ad that the company will like rather than something listeners will enjoy and share with their friends. Listeners can hear the inauthenticity from a mile away and instantly get turned off by it. This might change over time, but most companies have the wrong people helping them try to attract a podcasting audience—they just don't get it yet (but you always hear that, don't you?). A perfect example is some of the earliest corporate attempts at podcasting, which were podcasts of audio from "visual" events. We remember one of the first that got some hype, where in the first few minutes of the podcast, a new product was unveiled. The hosts kept referring to how beautiful the item was and asking the audience to "gaze upon it" while an executive read from a prepared speech—not very compelling listening.

Clearly, there are some great opportunities for aggressive yet professional podcasters who can plan, produce, and execute compelling content that listeners will enjoy and corporate clients will appreciate. Approached correctly, corporate podcasting may prove to be a profitable addition to your podcast production abilities.

Moving beyond podcasting

We're just beginning to see some of the more entrepreneurial people involved in podcasting put together companies based on products and services inspired by or at least related to podcasting. For example, some new companies are trying to syndicate audio advertisements in podcasts or are attempting to create podcasting associates. Podcast networks are forming, and people are trying to figure out ways to make the sale of podsafe music more efficient for the bands involved. Then there are more specialized uses of the underlying technology, such as Michael's newest venture, PrivaCast (www.privacast.com), which is an enterprise-level solution for secure corporate and educational communications among organizations and their employees or constituents.

The bottom line is that new businesses as well as a new media segment are emerging. It's an exciting time to be involved in podcasting. If you get bitten by the podcasting bug, you'll find a way to make your passion your business.

Summary

If you are interested in monetizing your podcast, the key is to consider it all: T-shirts, magnets, trucker hats, advertisers, sponsors, click-throughs, and affiliate programs. But again, we have to stress that you start with your podcast and your audience and let them dictate how you approach making money with your podcast. Keep trying and revamping your strategy until you find the combination of advertising and merchandising that's right for you and your show. It could be that you're better off just asking for a monthly donation and leaving well enough alone. Or you may end up with a huge online superstore. You never know.

12

Appendix A

GLOSSARY

The following is a list of terms used in the book. For each term, we have provided a definition and, optionally, some links to follow for further reading about the subject.

AAC

Abbreviation for *Advanced Audio Coding*. AAC is a new breed of codec for encoding audio that provides more efficient compression than older formats such as MP3. It is used by many modern Internet, wireless, and digital broadcast systems. Apple heavily supports AAC in iTunes. For more information, see www.vialicensing.com/products/mpeg4aac/standard.html and www.apple.com/mpeg4/aac. See also **codec**.

aggregator

A piece of software or a website (service) that collects disparate content and presents it in one place, making it much easier for users to keep up with important news stories, websites of interest, or the latest edition of a favorite podcast. Podcatchers such as iPodder Lemon and iPodderX (which you'll find on this book's companion CD) are aggregators focused on retrieving podcasts. An aggregator is also often referred to as a *feed reader* or *feed aggregator*.

AIFF

Abbreviation for *Audio Interchange File Format.* A file format (similar to WAV) that is popular on the Mac platform for storing digital audio waveforms. It is widely used in professional audio production programs such as BIAS Peak, Sound Forge, and DSP Quattro. Like WAV, it is a lossless format. For more information, see www.borg.com/~jglatt/tech/aiff.htm.

AMP

Acronym for *Association of Music Podcasting.* An association of podcasters and independent record labels that seeks to promote new music through podcasting. The group operates with agreements stipulating that the music is to be licensed to allow it to be legally played on podcasts. For more information, see www.musicpodcasting.org.

ASCAP

Acronym for *American Society of Composers, Authors, and Publishers.* A for-profit performing rights society. ASCAP licenses public performing rights for musical compositions, so if you want to perform someone else's song on a record or television show, for example, and the original composer/artist's song is licensed under ASCAP, you have to pay a fee to ASCAP for legal permission to do so. For more information, see www.ascap.com.

aspect ratio

The width of an image divided by its height, usually expressed as x:y. For example, standard-definition television is 4:3, which means no matter what size screen you're talking about for a standard-definition monitor, the measurements will be in a ratio of 4 units by 3 units. Widescreen high-definition screens are 16:9.

Atom

An XML format and HTTP-based protocol for syndicating web content. An Atom feed describes web content (such as a podcast) and allows it to be collected by an aggregator. Proponents suggest that it is supposed to solve some of the problems with RSS (by offering improved security and interoperability), although some critics have argued that it just creates more confusion. For more information, see http://en.wikipedia.org/wiki/Atom_(standard) and http://ietf.org/html.charters/atompub-charter.html. See also **aggregator**, **RSS**, **XML**.

bit rate

The speed at which digital information is transmitted or stored, measured in bits per second (bps).

BMI

Abbreviation for *Broadcast Music, Inc.* A for-profit performing rights society. BMI licenses public performing rights for musical compositions, so if you want to perform someone else's song on a record or television show, for example, and the original composer/artist's song is licensed under BMI, you have to pay a fee to BMI for legal permission to do so. For more information, see www.bmi.com.

capture

A term used in video and film production to refer to the transfer of digital "footage" from the original media (often DV) to a hard drive for editing.

casting

The process of finding and securing on-camera talent for your production.

clipping

An effect that happens in a recording when the recording level of an audio signal (be it musical or vocal) is too high and exceeds the ability of the digital system to represent the waveform (you just run out of numbers!), causing a loss of audio signal information in the recording and a horrible distortion of the sound. You need to avoid clipping at all costs when recording a podcast.

close-up

A camera angle that is meant for dramatic effect, focusing on the face expressions, hand movements of humans, or details of an object. They are often used to highlight a specific bit of action or detail that is important to the story or point at hand that would be lost in a wider shot.

codec

Acronym for *compressor/decompressor*. An encoding algorithm run on a piece of hardware or as software that compresses audio or video files into a format suitable for transportation over the web or for storage. The codec is also used to then decompress the file again at the end.

CPC

Abbreviation for *cost per click*. The method of determining how much an Internet ad costs, based on how many times people click the ad link.

CPM

Abbreviation for *cost per thousand exposures* (note that the *M* in the abbreviation represents the Roman numeral for "thousand"). The method of determining the cost of advertising based on the number of people potentially exposed to the ad.

Creative Commons

A nonprofit organization dedicated to allowing creative types to share their work through the use of free licenses known as *Creative Commons licenses*. These licenses offer a flexible range of protections and freedoms for authors and artists alike. For more information, see www.creativecommons.org and www.creativecommons.org/licenses/by-nc-sa/1.0.

dB

Abbreviation for *decibels*. The logarithmic units used to describe sound amplitude or intensity.

DOF

Abbreviation for *depth of field*. The distance in front of and beyond the subject of a shot that appears to be in focus.

domain name

The unique identifying name of a server or site on the Internet that allows web browsers to find it. For example, the domain name of the website found at http://www.podcastsolutions.com is podcastsolutions.com.

DSP

Abbreviation for *digital signal processing*. Audio processing (usually to improve clarity or for a specific sound effect) carried out through the use of hardware or software such as can be found on this book's companion CD.

A

DV

Abbreviation for *digital video*. A standard used for amateur and professional video production. Much that we refer to as DV is actually its smaller form factor, MiniDV.

EQ

Abbreviation for *equalization*. The process of modifying audio by amplifying or attenuating different frequencies (for example, high-pass filtering to eliminate low-frequency sounds).

FCC

Abbreviation for *Federal Communications Commission*. The U.S. government agency responsible for regulating electronic communication (for example, radio and television broadcasts). The FCC currently has no jurisdiction over podcasts transmitted via the Internet. For more information, see www.fcc.gov.

fill light

The second light in a three-point lighting setup, used to fill in the shadows created by the key light.

FTP client

Abbreviation for *File Transfer Protocol client*. A piece of software that allows you to open a connection with an FTP site and transfer data to and from it. This is an important means by which you can get your podcasts uploaded to the web for others to access.

high definition (HD)

A relatively new set of television standards, offering much higher resolution and much larger picture sizes. 720p is 1280×720 pixels, and 1080i/p is 1920×1080 pixels.

HTML

Abbreviation for *Hypertext Markup Language*. A markup language used to structure the vast majority of the content on the Internet. For more information, see www.w3.org/MarkUp and www.w3schools.com/html.

ID3 tag

A tag used to attach metadata to an MP3 file containing information such as album name, artist name, track name, track number, and so on. This information can be edited using an ID3 tag editor (such as the one provided by iTunes), and it can be very useful when searching for tracks.

interlaced video

A video image that is scanned from left to right and from top to bottom, but every other line is skipped. On the next pass, the remaining lines are scanned, completing the image. Each pass of every second line is called a *field*.

ISP

Abbreviation for *Internet service provider*. A company or service that provides Internet access via services such as dial-up, cable, and DSL.

J-cut

An audio/video transition in a film/video where the audio from the upcoming scene begins as the video from the current scene continues to play.

key light

The main (and brightest) light in a three-point lighting setup.

LAME

Acronym for *Lame Ain't an MP3 Encoder*. An open source MP3 encoder that is ideal for turning your podcast WAV or AIFF files into MP3s. For more information, see `http://lame.sourceforge.net` and `www.apple.com/downloads/macosx/ipod_itunes/ituneslameencoder.html`.

latency

The time it takes for audio signals to travel around your system. In audio terms, latency comes into play when a delay is caused in the audio because of processing or transmission. As an example, if you are recording on your computer and using a number of audio effects, the audio being monitored in the headphones may have a delay between when you speak and when you hear your voice in the headphones. Latency is also a big issue when using Skype and other Internet telephony programs.

lavaliere microphones

Also known as lapel mics, these tiny microphones are often attached directly to the talent by a small clip. In television and film shoots, they are often hidden under the talent's clothing.

L-cut

An audio transition in a film/video where the video from the upcoming scene begins as the audio from the current scene continues to play.

location

The actual physical space in which you plan to shoot some or all your video or film project. This is different from the "setting" of the story.

long shot

A camera angle that includes the entire subject or location of the shot in the frame, often used as an *establishing shot*, to orient the characters within the scene or reveal the location of the action.

mark

The specific place the talent must stand on a set to be in proper lighting and focus, often "marked" on the floor by a *T* made of colored tape.

mastering

The process of preparing audio into a final form (in terms of tone and levels of the different elements contained in the audio) on a wide range of audio playback devices by using software and hardware tools such as equalizers and compressors.

medium shot

Any shot that is tighter than a long shot but not tight enough to be a close-up, commonly starting around the actor's waist or so and including all of the top of the head.

monopod

A non-free-standing, one-legged camera support.

A

MP3

An audio file encoded using the MPEG-1 Audio Layer-3 (MP3) format.

over the shoulder

A camera setup where the camera is looking over the shoulder of one actor (from behind) at the face of the other.

NTSC

Abbreviation for *National Television System Committee.* The analog television system used in the United States, Canada, Japan, South Korea, the Philippines, Mexico, and several other countries.

PAL

Abbreviation for *Phase Alternating Line.* The color encoding system used in broadcast television throughout much of the world outside the United States, Canada, and Mexico.

PHP

Abbreviation for *PHP: Hypertext Preprocessor* and a dynamic web scripting language that allows you to write web pages that will display different information depending on variables such as user input, time of day, and so on. The pages are processed, and the results are then turned into HTML for display in a web browser. PHP is an ideal language to create blogs in. For more information, see www.php.net and www.w3schools.com/php/default.asp. See also **HTML**.

plosive

A consonant pronounced by completely closing the lips or air passage and then releasing air suddenly (for example, *p*, *b*, and so on).

podcast

An audio program available for download from the Internet via subscription by way of an RSS feed with MP3 audio enclosures.

podcast badge

A graphic (typically 80×15 pixels in size) used to promote a podcast.

podcatcher

Slang for *podcast aggregator.* Software used to manage podcast subscriptions and automatically download new episodes. See also **aggregator**.

podroll

A list of favorite podcasts. Listeners typically share their podrolls with others by posting them on their blogs or websites.

pop filter

A windscreen or foam filter that helps reduce the popping noises created by breath or speech when a person says a plosive such as *p* or *b*. See also **plosive**.

progressive scan video

A video image that is captured or displayed on a monitor from left to right and from top to bottom. When the image is complete, the next image is begun, again at the top left, scanning each line again to create the next image.

RIAA

Abbreviation for *Recording Industry Association of America*. A trade consortium that supports and represents the U.S. recording industry and strives toward a business and legal climate that protects its members' creativity and financial viability. For example, RIAA works to protect record companies' intellectual property rights, and it certifies gold, platinum, multiplatinum, and diamond sales awards. More than 900 companies are part of the RIAA, including BMG, EMI, and Sony Music. For more information, see www.riaa.com.

RMS

Abbreviation for *root-mean-square*. A way to accurately measure the overall magnitude (loudness) of a sound recording over time. To improve the mix of your audio, you should set the levels of the different tones that make up the audio in accordance with a recommended RMS value (we recommend −12dB RMS with a peak setting of 0.2dB). Various audio-editing applications have RMS normalization functions to help you do this (for example, Ozone 3, which you can find on this book's companion CD).

RSS

Abbreviation for *Really Simple Syndication* (or *Rich Site Summary*). An XML format for syndicating web content. An RSS feed describes content (such as a podcast) and allows it to be collected by an aggregator. RSS is said to be a precursor to Atom, but it is still far and away the most common protocol for podcasts. See also **aggregator**, **Atom**, **XML**.

sample rate

The frequency at which analog data (in the case of podcasts, sound) is recorded or "sampled" and converted to digital information (for example, 44,100kHz or 44,100 samples per second).

SESAC

Acronym for *Society of European Stage Authors and Composers*. A for-profit performing rights society. SESAC licenses public performing rights for musical compositions, so if you want to perform someone else's song on a record or television show, for example, and the original composer/artist's song is licensed under SESAC, you have to pay a fee to SESAC for legal permission to do so. For more information, see www.sesac.com.

shotgun microphone

A microphone whose long, slender barrel makes it incredibly focused in its pick-up pattern. Commonly used to record dialogue in television and film, it's mounted to a lightweight pole and hung over the talent.

standard definition (SDTV)

A term used to distinguish digital television signals that have roughly the same resolution as analog television signals from high definition. 480i/p is 720×480, which is the same resolution as your digital video (DV) camcorder.

A

storyboards

A shot-by-shot comic book–style telling of your planned video or film project. Storyboards are used to help plan shoots and shots and to foresee any potential complications in the production process.

three-point lighting

The common technique for lighting for video or film that uses a bright key (main) light, a fill light to fill in shadows, and a backlight to add depth and highlights to the figures on the screen.

treatment

The telling of a planned video or film project story in prose. A treatment is between an outline and a full script, because it involves more specific details than the first but not complete dialogue and action.

tripod

A free-standing, three-legged camera support.

URI

Abbreviation for *Uniform Resource Identifier*. A term for a classification of identifiers of resources on the Internet. For example, a URL is a type of URI. Other types include Uniform Resource Classification (URC), relative URL, and Uniform Resource Name (URN). See also **URL**.

URL

Abbreviation for *Uniform Resource Locator*. Also known as an Internet address, or link, a URL provides the location of a directory or file on the web (for example, http://www.friendsofed.com or http://www.podcastsolutions.com).

VST

Abbreviation for *Virtual Studio Technology*. A format for audio plug-ins used with audio processing software.

WAV

The de facto standard file format (especially on Windows, where it originated) for storing raw, uncompressed sound. You'll deal with WAV files often as you record your podcast. A WAV file recorded at 44.1kHz and 16-bit samples offers quality equivalent to that of a CD, but its large file size means it isn't practical for delivering audio over the web. This is why podcasts are always turned into MP3s before they are published.

waveform

A graphic representation of a sound recording.

WMA

Abbreviation for *Windows Media Audio*. A proprietary Microsoft audio format similar to MP3. For more information, see www.microsoft.com/windows/windowsmedia/9series/codecs/audio.aspx.

XML

Abbreviation for *Extensible Markup Language*. A markup language that can be extended, allowing you to create your own custom vocabularies for describing data. RSS and Atom are two examples of XML vocabularies. For more information, see www.w3.org/XML, www.w3schools.com/xml/default.asp, and www.xml.com. See also **Atom**, **RSS**.

Appendix B

PODCASTING RESOURCES AT A GLANCE

This appendix presents a short list of websites and podcasts to check out to get your feet wet. Please note that this is not even an attempt at a complete list of anything—it's just the tip of the iceberg.

Audio podcasts: entertainment

Reel Reviews—Films Worth Watching (www.reelreviewsradio.com)

The Bitterest Pill (www.thebitterestpill.com)

Grape Radio (www.graperadio.com)

Coverville (www.coverville.com)

Cush: Things I Say (www.cushrocks.com)

The Dawn and Drew Show! (www.dawnanddrew.com; adult content)

Evil Genius Chronicles (www.evilgeniuschronicles.org)

The Hollywood Podcast (www.hollywoodpodcast.com)

Illinoise! (www.illinoise.net)

Keith and the Girl (www.keithandthegirl.com; adult content)

Norm Augustinus (www.normaugustinus.com; adult content)

The Radio Adventures of Doctor Floyd (www.doctorfloyd.com)

The Rock and Roll Geek Show (http://rockandrollgeek.podshow.com)

Verge of the Fringe (www.vergeofthefringe.com)

Audio podcasts: music

Old Wave Radio: New 80s Music (www.new80smusic.com)

Accident Hash (www.accidenthash.podshow.com)

Coverville (www.coverville.com)

IndieFeed (www.indiefeed.com)

Insomnia Radio (www.insomniaradio.net)

Audio podcasts: podcasting

Podcast Solutions (www.podcastsolutions.com)

Podcast Academy (www.podcastacademy.com)

Behind the Scenes (www.godcast.org/categories/behindTheScenes)

Podcast Brothers (www.podcastbrothers.com)

Video podcasts: entertainment

Animal Rescue Force Friends! (www.arff.tv)

dotBoom (www.dotboom.ca)

Four Eyed Monsters (www.foureyedmonsters.com)

French Maid TV (www.frenchmaidtv.com)

Good Night, Burbank (www.goodnightburbank.com)

Mr. Deity (www.mrdeity.com)

RocketBoom (www.rocketboom.com)

Sam Has 7 Friends (www.samhas7friends.com)

TikiBar TV (www.tikibartv.com)

Video podcasts: podcasting

Izzy Video (www.izzyvideo.com)

Video Grunt (www.gruntmedia.com)

Pod Grunt (www.gruntmedia.com)

Video sites (nonpodcasting)

YouTube (www.youtube.com)

Vimeo (www.vimeo.com)

Blip.tv (www.blip.tv)

Directories

indiepodder.org (www.indiepodder.org; previously iPodder.org)

Podcast Alley (www.podcastalley.com)

PodcastPickle.com (www.podcastpickle.com)

Feed validators

Feed Validator (http://feedvalidator.org)

Podcast FeedCheck for iTunes compatibility (www.nobodylikesonions.com/feedcheck)

Podcatchers

Apple iTunes (www.apple.com/itunes)

Doppler (www.dopplerradio.net)

iPodder Lemon (http://ipodder.sourceforge.net)

Miro (www.miro.com, video)

Podcasting resources

iLounge (www.ilounge.com)

Podcast Alley (www.podcastalley.com)

PodcastPickle.com (www.podcastpickle.com)

The Podcast Academy Forum (www.podcastacademy.com/forum)

Podcast Expert (www.podcastexpert.com)

Podsafe music resources

IODA/Promonet (www.promonet.iodalliance.com/)

Internet Archive: Live Music Archive (www.archive.org/audio)

GarageBand.com (www.garageband.com)

B

Magnatune (www.magnatune.com)

Podsafe Music Network (http://music.podshow.com)

Podcasting events

New Media Expo (www.newmediaexpo.com)

Podcast Academy (www.podcastacademy.com)

PodCamp (www.podcast.org)

Podcasting magazines (print/PDF/online)

Blogger & Podcaster (www.bloggerandpodcaster.com)

Podcast User (www.podcastusermagazine.com)

Mailing list

Yahoo! Podcasters Group (http://groups.yahoo.com/group/podcasters)

Our production companies

Michael: Willnick Productions (www.willnick.com)

Dan: Jacket Media (www.jacketmedia.com)

INDEX

Special Characters

& (ampersands), 191

Numbers

1/4" phone jack, 55
1/8" mini plug, 56
$14 Steadycam, 126–127

A

AAC (Advanced Audio Coding), 233
ad insertions, 228
Adobe Audition, 70
Adobe Premiere Pro, 140
Advanced Audio Coding (AAC), 233
advertising and sponsorships
    ad rates, how set, 222–223
    advertisers vs. sponsors, 224–225
    advertising and promotion policies, 227
    audience, understanding, 225
    Google AdSense, 223
    overview, 222
    podcasting association, joining, 227
    policies, developing, 227
    sales kit, creating, 225–226
    selling categories, 225
affiliate programs, 219–221
aggregators, 233
AIFF (Audio Interchange File Format), 234
album art, 169–170
Alexis MultiMix 8 USB Mixer, 54, 62
Amazon.com associates program, 220
Ambrosia Software's WireTap Pro, 73
American Society of Composers, Authors, and
    Publishers (ASCAP), 36, 234

AMP (Association of Music Podcasting), 41,
    42, 234
ampersands (&), 191
amplifiers, headphone, 52
Apple Final Cut Pro, 140–141
Apple GarageBand, 71
Apple iPod, 2
Apple iPod AV cable, 120
Apple iTunes. *See* iTunes
Apple Soundtrack Pro, 71
Apple TV, 121
archived files, 185
ASCAP (American Society of Composers,
    Authors, and Publishers), 36, 234
aspect ratio, 121, 234
associates program, Amazon.com, 220
Association of Music Podcasting (AMP), 41,
    42, 234
associations for podcasting, 227
Atom feeds, 181, 234
attack, 81
Attribution-NonCommercial-NoDerivs
    license, 39
Audacity audio editor, 69–70, 86
Audacity with LAME, 158–159
Audible.com, 216
audience, learning about, 225
    overview, 213
    surveys, 213
    what willing to pay for, 214–215
audio, encoding and compressing MP3 to
    Audacity with LAME, 158–159
    encoding in iTunes, 154–155
    encoding software, 154
    encoding standards, 153–154
    enhanced podcasts, 152–153